open &
distance
learning
series

D0223556

FLEXIBLE LEARNING
in a digital world
experiences and expectations

betty collis   jef moonen

**KOGAN
PAGE**

First published in 2001

Kogan Page Limited
120 Pentonville Road
London N1 9JN
UK

Stylus Publishing Inc.
22883 Quicksilver Drive
Sterling VA 20166–2012
USA

British Library Cataloguing in Publication Data

A CIP record for this book is available from the British Library.

ISBN 0 7494 3372 8 (hardback)
ISBN 0 7494 3371 X (paperback)

Typeset by Jean Cussons Typesetting, Diss, Norfolk
Printed and bound in Great Britain by Biddles Ltd, Guildford and King's Lynn

Contents

About the authors

Betty Collis and Jef Moonen are currently both full professors in the Faculty of Educational Science and Technology in the University of Twente in The Netherlands but their backgrounds and reputations in the field of educational technology are broadly based.

Professor Dr Betty Collis (collis@edte.utwente.nl) was born in the United States and holds both US and Canadian citizenship. She began her professional exposure to the field of educational technology in the 1960s while a graduate student at Stanford University and has been a pioneer in two waves of technology applications – those relating to computers in education in the 1970s and 1980s and those relating to networked applications in education in the 1980s and 1990s. She remains at the forefront of pioneering work, at the current time with respect to WWW-based course-support systems in education through her leadership of the TeleTOP initiative in the Faculty of Educational Science and Technology at the University of Twente. This initiative involves institutional change towards more flexible learning supported by the TeleTOP WWW-based course-management system developed under her leadership (see http://teletop.edte.utwente.nl for more information). She is Professor of Tele-learning at her institution and also Senior Researcher, Advanced Learning Technologies for the interfaculty research institute, Centre for Telematics and Information Technology (http://www.ctit.utwente.nl) at the same institution (for more information, see http://users.edte.utwente.nl/collis/).

Professor Dr Jef Moonen (moonen@edte.utwente.nl) holds Belgian citizenship and was a pioneer in the design and development of computer-based teaching materials for statistics for use in higher education at the University of Leiden in The Netherlands using mainframe computers and including the PLATO authoring system in the 1970s. Since then he has served as founder and director of the National Centre for Computers in Education in The Netherlands (1981–89) as well as Professor of Educational Instrumentation (Educational Technology) at the University of Twente (1987 to the present). From 1991 to 1994 he was Dean of the Faculty of Educational Science and Technology at the

University of Twente and during the period 1987 to 1999 he was also chairman of the Department of Educational Instrumentation within this same faculty. His expertise is in the area of the design methodology for electronic learning resources, implementation of electronic learning environments in education and training, and in the cost-effectiveness of educational technology, in particular in higher education (see http://users.edte.utwente.nl/moonen/). He has managed many large projects relating to technology design, development and implementation. He regularly participates in national and international projects, panels, review boards and steering groups relating to technology in education.

While both authors have extensive professional and publishing experience, they are also practitioners themselves, and *practise what they preach* in their own courses. This balance of professional and practitioner is reflected throughout this book.

Series Editor's foreword

The world of teaching and training is changing – and changing dramatically. There is increasing pressure to admit more learners to higher and further education, to broaden access and to do so without a corresponding increase in funds. It is a pattern that can be recognised around the world. There is also increasing interest in the role of Communication and Information Technology (C&IT), the Knowledge Media and flexible/distributed learning as a panacea. Indeed, it would appear that wherever one looks, institutions are rushing headlong to embrace the Knowledge Media and to adopt open and distance learning practices. Unfortunately, closer inspection often reveals that many are diving in without an understanding of the strengths and limitations of C&IT, and with little awareness of the evidence that informs effective and efficient use of flexible learning.

The publication of *Flexible Learning in a Digital World* by Betty Collis and Jef Moonen is thus timely. It draws from almost thirty years of research and development in flexible learning and the use of computer-based learning. The 4–E model that Betty and Jef outline offers a framework that will be invaluable to all of us engaged in teaching and training – whether in conventional or flexible learning, using old or, more likely, new media.

Their skilled review of the research, coupled with insights into the process of creating flexible learning material, has resulted in 18 lessons they have learnt and which they share with us. No matter what role you play in the teaching or training of students, I am confident that both you and your students will benefit greatly from this book.

Fred Lockwood

Introduction

What this book is about

This is a book about changes in learning, teaching, and the support and enterprise of education, and the role of technology in those changes. The book considers those changes in a broad and integrated way via a study of four major perspectives: the institutional perspective, the implementation perspective, the pedagogy perspective and the technology perspective. These could be summarized as: making decisions at the institutional level about what is to happen, carrying out the decisions at the institutional level via an implementation strategy, translating the decisions into the learning setting for the individual instructor and course, and facilitating the decisions with technology. The learner perspective is closely woven into each of these perspectives. One function of the book is to present this integrated perspective based on current and emerging developments.

Although fresh waves of factors are pushing these changes, not the least the fact that the Internet and World Wide Web (WWW) technology is becoming a pervasive tool in the normal communication and information-handling strategies of people throughout the world, there is still much to be learnt from the last several decades of experience with technology and learning-related change. Thus the second major function of this book is to ground current and emerging experiences in a series of 18 major lessons learnt from previous cycles of educational change and technology potential.

About the lessons

We both have been involved in research and practice relating to technology and educational change since the 1970s and we are still deeply involved. Over the years we have reflected and written about many issues involving technology and learning-related change, based not only on our own experiences but on experiences accumulating throughout the world. In this book, we draw on this background as the basis for the *18 lessons learnt*. The lessons are presented in this book not in the style of results of a literature review, but in the style of practical guidelines. The purpose of the lessons is to crystallize past experience and make it useful in the present and future.

Each lesson can be supported by considerable research as well as experience: we supply many references to previous publications of ours that can supply this sort of scholarly basis and justify our guidelines. The book does include a substantial reference list but what is in it is only a small portion of what we could have cited. The lessons are introduced chapter by chapter, but we present them in their entirety in Table 0.1.

Table 0.1 *The lessons learnt*

Lesson 1 *Be specific.*	We need to define our terms and express our goals in a measurable form or else progress will be difficult to steer and success difficult to claim.
Lesson 2 *Move from student to professional.*	Learning in higher education is not only a knowledge-acquisition process but also a process of gradual participation in and contribution to a professional community. Pedagogy should reflect both acquisition and contribution-oriented models.
Lesson 3 *You can't not do it.*	The idea whose time has come is irresistible.
Lesson 4 *Don't forget the road map.*	Changes takes a long time and is an iterative process, evolving in ways that are often not anticipated.
Lesson 5 *Watch the 4 Es.*	An individual's likelihood of voluntarily making use of a particular type of technology for a learning-related purpose is a function of 4 Es: the environment context, the individual's perception of educational effectiveness, ease of use, and the individual's sense of personal engagement with the technology. The environmental context and the individual's sense of personal engagement are the most important.
Lesson 6 *Follow the leader.*	Key persons are critical.
Lesson 7 *Be just in time.*	Staff-engagement activities to stimulate instructors to make use of technology are generally not very effective. Focus on just-in-time support for necessary tasks.
Lesson 8 *Get out of the niche.*	Most technology products are not used in practice beyond developers. Keep implementation and the 4 Es central in choosing any technology product.
Lesson 9 *After the core, choose more.*	Technology selection involves a core and complementary technologies. The core is usually determined by history and circumstances; changing it usually requires pervasive

contextual pressure. The individual instructor can make choices about complementary technologies and should choose them with flexibility in mind.

Lesson 10 *Don't overload.*

More is not necessarily better.

Lesson 11 *Offer something for everyone.*

A well-designed WWW-based system should offer users a large variety of possibilities to support flexible and contribution-oriented learning not dominated by any one background orientation. If so, it is the most appropriate (core or complementary) technology for flexible learning.

Lesson 12 *Watch the speed limit.*

Don't try to change too much at the same time. Start where the instructor is at, and introduce flexibility via extending contact sessions to include before, during and after aspects, with each of these made more flexible. Move gradually into contribution.

Lesson 13 *Process yields product.*

Through the process of contribution-oriented learning activities, learners themselves help produce the learning materials for the course.

Lesson 14 *Aim for activity.*

The key roles of the instructor are becoming those of activity planning, monitoring and quality control.

Lesson 15 *Design for activity.*

Instructional design should concentrate more on activities and processes, and less on content and a predetermined product.

Lesson 16 *Get a new measuring stick.*

What we are most interested in regarding learning as a consequence of using technology often can't be measured in the short term or without different approaches to measurement. Measure what can be measured, such as short-term gains in efficiency or increases in flexibility.

Lesson 17 *Be aware of the price tag.*

It is not going to save time or money to use technology, at least not in the short term.

Less on 18 *Play the odds.*

A simplified approach to predicting return on investment (ROI) that looks at the perceived amount of relative change in the factors that matter most to different actors is a useful approach.

In our opinion, the lessons are valuable, not only in anchoring the present but in predicting and steering the future. We try to demonstrate this throughout the book.

Who this book is for

This book is intended for a broad audience. It can be read cover to cover, by those interested in an overall view of a complex phenomenon – technology and flexible learning. It is a cohesive and integrated book where each chapter builds upon those before, not a collection of chapters from a variety of authors.

However, the individual chapters can be read separately, by those with a particular interest in the perspective focused upon in the chapter. The chapters, and the book as a whole, can be used as a text in higher education but also are intended as a resource for those actually dealing with flexible learning and technology in practice.

Although the book is based in a higher-education (post-secondary) context, the lessons and the issues discussed are also applicable to other sectors. We are finding the lessons and the pedagogical ideas particularly useful in current work we are doing in the corporate-learning context, as well as in the school sector. The institutional perspective involves many issues also confronting schools and training settings. The implementation problems we discuss are also common in schools and training institutions. The technology perspective is relevant to all. In addition, we do not restrict our view of flexible learning or our use of technology to 'distance education', as we discuss in Chapter 1, but apply it to any type of learning setting, including traditional face-to-face meetings.

How this book is organized

Flexible learning is a complex phenomenon even when expressed in terms of only four key components: technology, pedagogy, implementation and institution. We can visualize the relationship among the four components via the diagram in Figure 0.1.

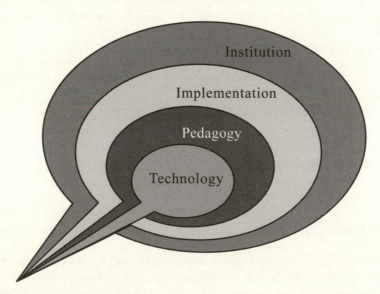

Figure 0.1   *The four key components of flexible learning in higher education*

The size of the various shapes indicates in a general way their complexity and the number of actors involved. The nesting of the shapes indicates their interrelationships. Using the components shown in this figure there are different sequences that could be used to describe how flexible-learning activities are steered and carried out in higher education. Common approaches are from top down or from bottom up. From a top-down perspective we should start with the institutional context, then implementation, then pedagogy, then technology; for a bottom-up approach we should begin with the technology and move through the increasingly complex levels. In this book we will choose the top-down level first (Chapter 2), because of the importance of the institution in any structural change involving flexible learning. From this, we will move to implementation (Chapter 3) and the 4-E Model. We will follow this with technology (Chapter 4) in order to show how pedagogy can work in practice for flexible learning (Chapter 5). All levels are, however, interrelated; thus in Chapters 6, 7, 8 and 9 we will focus on combinations of levels.

For a first glimpse at the contents, the following paragraphs outline the chapters to follow.

Chapter 1 focuses on the concept of flexible learning. Flexible learning can involve many dimensions, only one of which is related to location of participation. While flexible learning offers many opportunities, we show that trying to implement it brings with it many problems and challenges. We introduce four key components of flexible learning – technology, pedagogy, implementation strategies and institutional framework – whose interaction forms the focus of this book.

In Chapter 2 flexible learning is related to major changes facing higher-education institutions throughout the world. For flexible learning to be meaningful in an institution, it must be more than the effort of occasional pioneers; the institution must commit itself to a change. In this chapter we focus on the institutional perspective. What sorts of changes are occurring? What factors have influenced institutions that have already made a commitment to more flexible learning and technology use? What motivates policy in these areas? The main lesson framing this chapter is: *you can't not do it*.

For flexible learning to be implemented, instructors and learners will probably need to make use of technology. Chapter 3 deals with these implementation issues. Implementation involves acceptance as well as actual use in practice of the technology. What if instructors do not want to do this? In this chapter we look at what we have learnt with respect to the likelihood of an individual – instructor or learner - making use of a technological innovation in a learning-related setting, express this in terms of the *4-E Model* and apply the model to the flexible-learning situation. We also use the 4-E Model to help predict implementation success, particularly during the initiation phase, and to comment about the importance of leadership and staff engagement to any implementation effort.

We see in Chapters 1 and 2 that higher-education institutions have a collective desire to change towards more flexible learning mediated by technology. But it is the instructor who must ultimately make this happen, and many instructors do not yet make use of technology. The 4-E Model (Chapter 3) helps us understand this. In Chapter 4 we use the 4-E Model to steer a direction for proceeding in terms of the technology itself. After discussing technology selection in general, we discuss WWW-based course-management systems as the current key technology to implement flexible learning, and argue why, in terms of the 4 Es, they are more likely to succeed than other current forms of technological products. We also illustrate how an implementation perspective can be used to guide the selection of any technology product, and in particular a WWW-based system.

In Chapter 1 we characterize pedagogy around two dimensions: a dimension relating to flexibility and a dimension relating to an educational model about learning activities. We identify two basic types of activities: those relating to acquisition of content and those relating to contribution to a learning community. In Chapter 5, we focus more specifically on pedagogical combinations that involve more flexibility and relate them to the instructor's pedagogical decisions based on a new definition of an *active student*: one of co-contributor to the course study resources and co-member of the course as a learning community. We will introduce the *U Approach* as a pedagogical model for flexible learning and illustrate ways to realize this approach in different practical settings. The key to the U Approach is a focus on learner activities supported by a properly designed WWW-based system. Furthermore we will illustrate a range of activities and tools for the U Approach. Finally, we discuss the implications for the instructor and for the instructional designer of this new approach.

In Chapter 6 we take a different focus. Many times we are asked to advise on cost-effectiveness questions, particularly from decision makers in an institution considering a commitment to a new technology investment. Traditional cost-effectiveness approaches have not been useful. We suggest instead a *simplified return on investment strategy* based on the 4-E Model (Chapter 3) and involving the institutional, pedagogical and technological perspectives. In this chapter, we explain how this strategy works.

In Chapters 1–6 we develop a set of *18 lessons learnt*, which we predominately argue via literature references and general statements about our own experience. In Chapters 7 and 8, we make that experience explicit. In particular, we focus on our experiences since mid-1997 in leading our faculty to more flexible learning with technology. Do we practise what we preach? These illustrations will involve a case from our own institution, the University of Twente in The Netherlands, during the years 1997–2000. The purpose of Chapters 7 and 8 is not only to illustrate the lessons, but also to give practical examples that others hopefully can shape to their own situations. The chapter will be a success to the degree to which others can say, 'Yes, this is like our situation; I have an idea of how to apply the experiences in our own setting.'

Major changes are occurring in society: in the ways that we work, produce wealth, spend our money, interact, and amuse ourselves. Collectively, these changes are leading to a new system for human commerce and communication that is being called the *new economy*. Is there a new economy emerging for education? In Chapter 9 we argue that this is so, and use the lessons to suggest its characteristics and implications. We begin by taking some major characteristics of the new economy in the business and consumer world and speculate on the forms those might take as a new economy for education also emerges.

In writing this book, we are well aware of the speed of change in terms of technology applications in learning-related practice. For this reason, we have not included many screen dumps of current WWW pages, even in the case studies in Chapters 7 and 8. However, to complement the book a *Webliography* will be available at http://education1.edte.utwente.nl/00FlexibleLearning.nsf/FramesForm?ReadForm. It is intended that this dynamic reference list should extend this book beyond what is possible on the printed page, an example of the complementary technology idea in Chapter 4. Most of our internal documents (when written in English) mentioned in the reference list at the end of the book will be available through this Webliography.

Chapter 1

Flexible learning: it's not just about distance

Flexible learning is becoming somewhat of a buzzword: everyone is for it, but often people have not thought further about it, except perhaps that it means something about distance education. In this chapter we introduce the first of our lessons learnt: that such vagueness is not desirable and is even counter-productive. To put the lesson into practice we show that flexible learning can involve

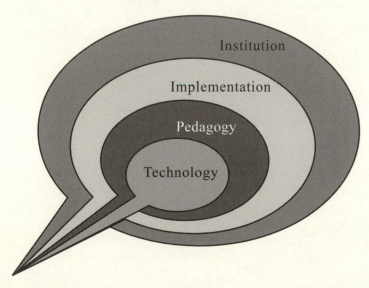

Figure 1.1   *Flexible learning in higher education – the four key components*

many dimensions, only one of which is related to location of participation. While flexible learning offers many opportunities, we also show that trying to implement it brings with it many problems and challenges. We introduce four key components of flexible learning – technology, pedagogy, implementation strategies and institutional framework – whose interaction forms the focus of this book. Although many combinations of these components have stimulated forms of flexible learning in the past, the new technologies of the Internet, particularly those of the World Wide Web (WWW), coupled with new pressures on higher-education institutions are bringing new possibilities for the realization of flexible learning, perhaps more than ever possible before. However, there is still much to be learnt from previous experiences with flexible learning and technology. We believe that lessons learnt from previous experiences with technology, pedagogy, implementation and institutional responses can shape and temper our expectations for the future.

What is flexible learning?

Flexible learning is not a new phenomenon. Students in higher education have for a long time chosen from a variety of courses, studied their textbooks in a variety of locations and times, and selected from a variety of resources in the library. Learning also takes place outside of explicit course settings, as students interact with others or take part in events such as guest lectures or debates or use built-in tutorials to help them learn how to use a software package. But the term flexible learning is the focus of a new wave of interest. 'There must be more flexibility to meet the needs of the learner, through adaptability to different learner needs, learning patterns and settings, and media combinations' (Van den Brande, 1993: xxi). In this section, we take the first steps in responding to this conclusion by asking: what is meant by flexible learning? What are major opportunities and challenges in realizing flexible learning in a higher-education institution? Who is it that really wants it?

Flexibility: more than distance

To begin, what is flexible learning? Flexible learning is often taken as synonymous with distance education. This is not necessarily so. As we will illustrate throughout this book, there are many ways to make education more flexible that can benefit students who are in full-time residence on a campus and even benefit those who are in the same room together. Flexibility can involve options in course resources, in types of learning activities, in media to support learning, and many other possibilities. There is more than distance that can vary.

In this book, we will use the term *flexible learning* in a broad way, with the key idea being *learner choice* in different aspects of the learning experience. (But as we will show later in the chapter, not everything can be flexible and still be scalable

Flexibility related to time:
Fixed time <===> Flexible
1. Times (for starting and finishing a course)
2. Times (for submitting assignments and interacting within the course)
3. Tempo/pace of studying
4. Moments of assessment

Flexibility related to content:
Fixed content <=======================================> Flexible
5. Topics of the course
6. Sequence of different parts of a course
7. Orientation of the course (theoretical, practical)
8. Key learning materials of the course
9. Assessment standards and completion requirements

Flexibility related to entry requirements:
Fixed requirements <==================================> Flexible
10. Conditions for participation

Flexibility related to instructional approach and resources:
Fixed pedagogy and resources <=========================> Flexible
11. Social organization of learning (face-to-face; group, individual)
12. Language to be used during the course
13. Learning resources: modality, origin (instructor, learners, library, WWW)
14. Instructional organization of learning (assignments, monitoring)

Flexibility related to delivery and logistics:
Fixed place and procedures <===========================> Flexible
15. Time and place where contact with instructor and other students occur
16. Methods, technology for obtaining support and making contact
17. Types of help, communication available, technology required
18. Location, technology for participating in various aspect of the course
19. Delivery channels for course information, content, communication

Figure 1.2   *Dimensions of learning flexibility: options available to the learner (revised from Collis, Vingerhoets and Moonen, 1997)*

beyond a small number of students.) Flexible learning is a movement away from a situation in which key decisions about learning dimensions are made in advance by the instructor or institution, towards a situation where the learner has a range of options from which to choose with respect to these key dimensions. What are some of these key dimensions? Figure 1.2 shows 19 flexibility dimensions identified as a result of a multinational study supported by the European Union.

And this is not an exhaustive list. Distance relates only to Item 15. Clearly there is much more that can be involved in moving from fixed, or less-flexible, to more-flexible learning. How can this work in practice? We need to move from abstractions to options.

Putting flexibility into practice: opportunities

Although a first step is being aware of different ways in which flexibility can occur, a next step is operationalizing it so that it is translated into opportunities for the student. Table 1.1 shows seven different aspects of flexibility from Figure 1.2 and indicates some of the sorts of options from which learners could choose for increased flexibility. Throughout this book we will illustrate these and others. In the table we use the term *course provider* to indicate the actors who make decisions about how a course will be offered to students. Usually this is some combination of institutional decision makers and, to a lesser extent, the instructor of the course.

Table 1.1 *Opportunities for more-flexible learning: options for the learner (revised from Collis, 1996a)*

CURRENT SITUATION (FIXED OR LESS FLEXIBLE):	DESIRED SITUATION (MORE FLEXIBLE):
Course provider decides in advance how the dimension will be offered in the course.	*Options are offered to the learner*
Social organization of learning: Course provider determines the approach to the social organization (face-to-face lectures or remote classroom), or individually oriented.	*Offer a choice:* (a) Does the learner prefer being part of a group that participates together throughout the course? (b) Does he or she prefer working individually, without a sense of having classmates? Or (c) does the learner prefer to make his or her own combination, selecting face-to-face for some course events, asynchronous group activities for others and individual work for the rest?
Content: Course provider determines the selection of content, content sequencing and content approach (theoretical or practical).	*Offer a choice:* (a) Does the learner wish the course provider to specify the content, content sequencing and content approach (theoretical or practical)? Or (b) would the learner prefer making his or her own choices, entirely or partially as to content, content sequencing and content approach (theoretical or practical)?
Learning materials: Course provider determines the learning materials of the course.	*Offer a choice* as supplements to the core resource (usually a textbook): options include educational software, distributed resources via the WWW (located by the course provider or the learners themselves), video resources, resources from multimedia databases, additional library resources.
Interactivity: Course provider determines the major way or ways in which learner interactivity is to occur in a course.	*Offer a choice:* (a) Does the learner prefer real-time, human-to-human interaction? (b) Does the learner prefer written human-to-human interaction, asynchronously, so that time is available to reflect on his or her comments and to answer when he or she wants? (c) Does the learner prefer to interact cognitively with an appropriately designed computer program or other learning materials instead of via communication with a person? (d) Does the learner prefer a combination of the above, chosen by him- or herself?

Technology: Course provider decides on the technical platform for the course.	*Offer* a choice among major platform variations (or their combination): (a) a low-end platform, with television, telephone, video recorder and player, and a stand-alone computer; (b) a computer-network platform, with access to e-mail and the WWW via the Internet or an intranet; (c) a high-end platform, via a fast network connection, allowing video access on demand and real-time application sharing.
Language: Course provider decides on the language(s) to be used in the course.	*Offer* a choice on the language to be used in (a) lesson materials, (b) asynchronous communication, (c) real-time two-way video or audio interaction, and (b) face-to-face contacts.
Location: Course provider decides if course is to be experienced entirely at a distance, or with fixed events on campus.	*Offer* a choice: (a) Does the learner wish to experience the entire course at a distance, or (b) does he or she want to combine distance and self-study aspects with some number of face-to-face sessions?

Figure 1.2 and Table 1.1 show that flexible learning is not a simple goal nor does it necessarily mean only distance flexibility. Also, within each flexibility dimension, there are many possible options. Even within traditional distance education, for example, many variations exist that can limit flexibility related to distance, and students may not be offered an option about participating. Learners may be occasionally required to attend residential sessions on specific days or go to local study or participate, via technologies, at a preset time in distributed group discussions or sessions. All of these requirements impinge on the learner's freedom in choosing where he or she will learn.

No flexibility option is simple to carry out in practice. If an institution wishes to commit itself to flexible learning, it needs to make explicit choices as to which flexibility dimensions it will focus upon and what range of options will be feasible to offer within these dimensions. Dimensions being frequently chosen by traditional institutions currently include (Collis, 1998b):

● Improving *flexibility in location* of where the learner can carry out different learning activities associated with a course. Many of the learning activities in a course can be carried out from a location outside of the physical campus, allowing learners the choice of maintaining their home and work situation. However, many institutions are not offering flexibility for every aspect of every course. Some learning experiences, such as the first meeting of a course, are felt to be best experienced in a face-to-face setting and thus all students are required, or at least urged, to forgo flexibility of distance for these occasions.

- Improving *flexibility in programme*. Assuming the learner has relevant previous experience, subgroups of courses can be chosen in terms of his or her needs and interests. This implies in turn that instructors must be more flexible, in terms of prior expectations of the students and in providing extra resources and opportunities to compensate for different backgrounds.
- Improving *flexibility in types of interactions* within a course, so that, for example, students who benefit from group interaction and group-based project work can choose these sorts of opportunities, while other students, perhaps with families and work commitments, who benefit more from the freedom to organize their own times and ways of studying, can also be accommodated within the same course. Not all students need to work in groups, and not all students prefer social interaction as part of a learning experience.
- Improving *flexibility in forms of communication* within a course, so that learners and instructors have a wider variety of ways for more targeted and responsive communication than is the case when communication is limited to what occurs during face-to-face sessions such as lectures, or incidentally in the hallways. Students should be able to ask a question of their instructor from their own location and at their own time, but in turn the instructor should also have flexibility in managing his or her own time in terms of handling communication.
- Improving *flexibility in study materials*, so that the students not only have a wider choice of resources and modalities of study materials from which to choose than only what the instructor has previously selected for them, but also come to share in the responsibility of identifying appropriate additional resources for the course and even contributing to the learning resources in a course.

Thus an important first step in a move towards more-flexible learning is to take the time to develop consensus within the institution as to what is meant by this term. Flexible learning needs to be made operational, expressed in terms that can be turned into manageable options to offer to students. This operationalization has several benefits: it helps to guide and steer a change process in a practical and coherent way, it is a necessary step toward implementation planning (see Chapter 3), it facilitates a return-on-investment estimation (see Chapter 6), and it is critical in the selection of the most appropriate technologies for the decided new situation (see Chapter 4).

Also important, a concrete operationalization helps make it clear that flexible learning involves many possibilities in addition to time and distance flexibility. Even if an institution does not want to move away from face-to-face lectures, for example, it should still consider the potential benefits of other forms of flexibility, such as offering options with respect to the way students carry out self-study activities (for example, in groups or individually?); flexibility in the types of learning activities; and flexibility in the amount of monitoring from the instructor.

While it seems sensible to take this sort of care in terms of moving from a goal stated in general terms (flexible learning) to goals stated in specific and operational terms, it has been our experience that this is often not done, particularly in change initiations involving technology. A typical phenomenon with earlier waves of interest in computer-related learning has been the statement of abstract goals ('revolutionize education', 'individualize learning', or even 'increase economic competitiveness'), expressed in vague and non-concrete terms. One of the consequences of such vagueness is a subsequent lack of evidence of success. Another consequence is that decision makers move on after the vague statement of goals and leave it to the subsequent implementation manager to make the vision concrete. This may not turn out to fit the unspoken ideas of the original decision makers, leading to problems with institutional support and funding (see Chapter 2). Thus, we would like to introduce the first of our *lessons learnt* here, and continue to apply it throughout the chapter, and book:

Lesson 1: *Be specific.* We need to define our terms and express our goals in a measurable form or else progress will be difficult to steer and success difficult to claim.

Putting flexibility into practice: challenges

Just as flexible learning is complex to describe and multidimensional, it is also complex to implement in practice. While there are new opportunities, there will be challenges of many different sorts to surmount relating to the extent to which options about learning dimensions can be offered to students and still be manageable for the instructor and institution. Some of the challenges as seen from the perspective of the instructor, the learner, the educational institution and those who validate the learner's learning experience in terms of accreditation and legitimacy are described in the next points.

From the perspective of the instructor

When the learner is given more choices, the instructor is increasingly required to respond and individualize rather than plan and deliver. In some ways this is liberating for the instructor: he or she can choose from a wider range of approaches, of material, of learning settings, in order to make these options available in response to the wishes of different learners. In addition, instructors can alter their own times of working, responding to students late in the evening, at their homes, with a cup of tea in hand, instead of at a fixed time in the day. Thus more-flexible learning for the learner brings more options to the instructor as well, although not always reflecting the instructor's choice but rather in reaction to the learner's choices.

Moving to more-flexible scenarios will also have an impact on the instructor's pedagogical patterns. This also means that the time burden on the instructor and support provider will become constraints on the goal of flexible support for the learner. More-tailored training is more time- and effort-consuming than standardized approaches for the instructor. The more choices the learner has, the more demands and thus challenges there are for the instructor. (See Chapters 5, 7 and 8 for more about the impact of flexible learning on the instructor.)

From the perspective of the learner

Flexibility for the learner brings him or her not only new choices but also new responsibilities. Instead of being told what to do by the chosen educational institution and instructor, he or she becomes more like a client in a supermarket. 'Modular structures, credit accumulation schemes, independent learning and so on, can create a supermarket system in which students wander freely, picking up this course or that, having as little contact with lecturers as supermarket shoppers have with anything resembling the friendly village grocer. These changes may empower learners' (Fleming, 1993: 321). However, such a cafeteria approach can confuse rather than empower the individual learner. Not all students want to make their own choices or be responsible for the quality of their choices. More flexibility brings with it more independence but also the need for more self-direction and more self-motivation. These traits are not automatic in many learners. Flexible study locations and time can mean solitary study, not comfortable for some. Giving learners their own choice of time, content, method, media, route and pace will mean less chance of group interaction and peer-to-peer communication. These are intrinsic problems in offering more learner-centred learning. Many learners will need or appreciate an expert making many of the choices for them. Thus, in flexible learning there still should be the option of selecting predetermined choices, as well as making one's own decisions. But again, this requires multiple versions of the same course or course components.

From the perspective of the educational institutions

Flexibility options for the learner and the instructor will have significant organizational impact on the course-delivery institution. The institution will have to take the key decisions in order for flexible learning to occur on a meaningful scale (see Chapters 2 and 9). There will be conflicts from the point of view of course delivery and organization. If students are to be promised time flexibility, for example, at what times is a lecture scheduled? How can timetabling of rooms occur? When are extra sittings of final examinations to be held, where and with whom supervising? Handling student registration, accrediting student progress, timetabling rooms for contact sessions and examinations: these and many other logistical aspects can quickly become unmanageable for the institution even with sophisticated database systems.

More than this, the institution will have to deal with complaints: from instructors who feel change is being forced upon them, or is coming too fast, or is not occurring as they feel it should; from students who may feel they are being forced to incur new expenditures for technology; from governing boards who may doubt the financial soundness of the planning or its implications in terms of other key strategies for the institution.

From challenges such as these, and others, Table 1.2 summarizes some of the major barriers confronting the desire to make learning more flexible.

But the situation is not static and we should not sound overly pessimistic; there are ways to offer at least some aspects of flexible learning within human, organizational and societal constraints. This book is based not only on lessons learnt about problems and constraints, but also on lessons learnt about successes.

Table 1.2 *Factors constraining learning flexibility (revised from Collis, 1996a)*

Key Constraints on Flexibility	Key Actors Related to the Constraints
Flexibility is unmanageable.	– Instructors cannot handle what can amount to individualized instruction because of time and also cognitive constraints if the number of learners increases. – Instructors do not have the time or resources to anticipate the permutations of options that a learner may choose and produce cohesive, good-quality variations of courses available to reflect those options.
Flexibility is not acceptable.	– The legitimizing agency related to a course cannot handle a wide variety of course permutations in terms of recognition for the course. – The culture of which the learner is a part is not oriented towards the idea of learner choice, but instead expects the course provider to be responsible for pre-specified decisions about the course offering.
Flexibility is not affordable.	– Each combination of options may require some *re-engineering* of the course; economy of scale is not likely to occur. Personal and technical implications of many learner choices are much more costly than any course provider could support.
Learning flexibility is not realistic.	– Learner flexibility may require an imaginative and creative approach to course redesign that is outside the scope of many instructors (relatively few persons are innovators). – Some combinations of options are not compatible with one another by their very nature (if a learner prefers to work at an individual pace, choosing his or her own content and sequence of content, that learner cannot be expected also to be having real-time interactivity via video-conferencing with classmates; if a learner chooses to work in his or her own language and it is a language that others in the course do not speak, the learner cannot insist on a stress on human-human interactivity, either real-time or asynchronous).

Who wants flexible learning?

Given all the complexities, why continue? Who is it that wants flexible learning? Throughout the book we will respond to this question. The answer in general is: educational institutions and their competitors, technology specialists and students.

The changing characteristics of students in post-secondary education are among the most important arguments for flexible learning. Students in the normal intake routes, directly from secondary school and resident at or near the physical campus, are being joined by increasingly diverse cohorts. These cohorts are diverse in age, educational backgrounds, experiences, distances in which they live from the campus and even cultures and native languages (Langlois, 1997). These diversifying demographics are in turn a reflection of the need in society for *lifelong learning* particularly in the international context of increasing career mobility (Krempl, 1997). This need has at least the following aspects:

- Students will increasingly require educational programmes and a way of experiencing them tailored to their own situations, rather than fitting a standard model, especially when this standard model is based on young, professionally inexperienced, full-time students, living on the campus and needing a full range of courses for a certain degree.
- For some learners, there would be less time needed and lower expenditures for a particular learning event if it could be experienced as a module, instead of the learner having to participate in an entire course and if he or she could participate in the event in a time period and location convenient to him or herself.
- For the working person, better quality of results could potentially be achieved, in that only the necessary content, in the most up-to-date versions of resources, would be chosen.
- Theories and experience with adult education show such education to be effective to the extent that it is relevant to adult learners, is closely related to their own learning history, has transfer value to their work and is efficient in terms of demands on their time and energy (Van Enckevort *et al*, 1986).

All of these require individualization of learning experiences, and thus call for increased flexibility in learning alternatives. If higher-education institutions do not respond to this changing demand from students, other service providers will (see Chapter 2).

Thus, we identified flexible learning as a complex domain and one that could be experienced in many different ways. We have also seen some of the opportunities as well as constraints that will confront translating abstractions into practice. The demand is here, the demand is real and we must proceed. The next step is to consider components of flexible learning in the higher-education setting that interact with one another to determine the success of the change process towards more-flexible learning.

Components of flexible learning in higher education

Although in Figure 1.2 we discussed possibilities for flexibilization in terms of five sets of dimensions (time, content, entry requirements, instructional approach and resources, and delivery and logistics) within which to offer learners choices, flexibility can also be expressed in terms of four main components necessary to make it possible in practice. These components are: technology, pedagogy, implementation strategy and institutional framework. They form the focus of the chapters in this book. We introduce them here.

Technology

When we speak of *technology* in this book, we are generally referring to the combination of information and communication technologies. Information technologies involve computers; communication technologies will be taken as involving network systems, and in particular data networks running under the Internet protocol (IP). Because network connectivity is becoming standard for computers in higher-education institutions, the use of the term technology in this book generally refers to some aspect of computers connected to an IP network. Video-conferencing may or may not be classified as a computer-related technology; it depends on whether the video-conferencing system is experienced by the user as being associated with a computer (ie desktop video-conferencing) or not. We include video-conferencing in our general use of the term technology, because in the future there will be more and more convergence of analogue video-conferencing of the room-type variety with digital, network-accessible video-conferencing.

Computers and networks do nothing without software tools and applications; thus the term *technology applications* will be used (see Chapters 4, 7 and 8) to refer to the various categories of software that can typically be used for the learning-support process in higher education. Table 1.3 gives an overview. When we speak of a particular example of a type of technology application, such as a particular WWW site or a particular computer-conferencing system, then we will call that particular example a *technology product*.

In this book, particularly Chapter 4, we will focus on technologies and technology applications, but never in isolation from their place as part of an integrated system of which pedagogy is another major component.

Pedagogy

Pedagogy is defined (at least in some countries) as '*the art and science of teaching...* the knowledge and skills that practitioners of the profession of teaching employ in performing their duties of facilitating desired learnings in others' (Dunkin, 1987: 319). Although there are other terms that could be used, for example *didactics* or *instructional approach*, we will use the term *pedagogy* in this book to

Table 1.3 *Types of technology applications related to categories of course support in higher education (Collis, 1999f: 38)*

Major Educational Use	Examples of Technology Applications
1. Publication, information dissemination	Word processing: HTML editors; WWW sites and the browsers to access them; WWW sites associated with database environments; software to facilitate file transfer and document attachments to e-mail; tools for cross-application format retention (ie pdf).
2. Communication	E-mail systems; computer-conferencing tools, including WWW boards and other forms of WWW-based conferencing; WWW sites offering communication options for the direct sending of e-mail and forms for structured communication; software for Internet telephony; software environments for audio-video desktop conferencing, for voice e-mail, for creating video attachments for e-mail; software systems for text-based chat.
3. Collaboration	Groupware, which includes application-sharing software, shared workspaces, WWW-based shared workspaces, WWW-based application sharing, workflow tools; WWW sites designed for collaboration support; tools to allow collaborative writing on documents that are then commonly available to a group.
4. Information and resource handling	CD ROMs with resource collections, which may or may not be linked with a WWW site; WWW-based search engines; distributed database systems (WWW-based and proprietary); WWW sites designed for information organization, access and sometimes creation; tools to retrieve and display distributed multimedia resources stored as digitized audio and video (including streaming audio and video).
5. Specific for teaching and learning purposes	Stand-alone software for tutorials, simulations, electronic workbenches, demonstrations of processes, collections of resources; interactive software (such as tutorials, quizzes, simulations) stand-alone or accessible via WWW sites; computer-based testing systems; video-capture tools for lecture or presentation capture; video-conferencing (point-to-point and multicasting) for lecture participation; WWW-based pages or environments.
6. For course integration	WWW-based course support (or management) systems.

indicate the manner in which the teaching and learning processes and settings in a course are organized and implemented by an instructor. Teaching in higher education most generally takes place in a course context with an individual faculty member responsible for an entire course, but many variations occur. For convenience in this book, and because it is the majority situation in traditional higher-education institutions, we focus on pedagogy within the course context, and use the term instructor in the singular.

Pedagogical approach

There are many approaches that can be used to define the pedagogical approach used in a course. One approach is to analyse a course in terms of components, each related to categories of pedagogical activities involved, and within these components identify ways to meet goals such as more flexibility. One such set of categories is:

- *general course organization*, including administration and record keeping of student marks and absences, as well as general planning for the course;
- *lectures* and other forms of instructor-led class sessions;
- *self-study*: readings, activities and assignments, (perhaps) practical exercises;
- *major assignment* (essay, report, product, case study, etc) intended to synthesize various aspects of the course and usually expected to occupy a substantial portion of the student's time for the course – the assignment can be individually done, or done by a group;
- *testing*, (partially) to determine a mark in a course;
- *communication*, in addition to what occurs as part of the above categories.

We use this set of categories in Chapters 5 and 7. If the amount of time that the instructor spends on each category is roughly estimated and expressed as a percentage of the whole, a *pedagogical profile* of the course can be obtained (Collis, 1996d). Courses will vary in the amount of time and attention the instructor gives to each of these categories. The pedagogical profile of a course oriented around a lecture-textbook-essay-examination model will differ quantitatively and qualitatively from that of one oriented around students participating in a group-based project or one organized around a series of predefined practical activities. Each category can be analysed in terms of its flexibility and made more flexible for the students involved (Chapters 5, 7 and 8). Table 1.4 gives several examples of how WWW-based tools, environments and systems are being used to increase the flexibility of courses within each of these categories. Chapters 4 and 5 discuss this in more detail.

Pedagogical models

In contrast to a pedagogical *approach*, which is a way of doing things such as illustrated in Table 1.4, a pedagogical *model* relates to the abstract concepts about the learning and teaching process that underlie the approach. Sfard (1998), for example, identifies two basic types of educational models, the *Acquisition Model* and the *Participation Model*. With the Acquisition Model, the focus of learning activities is on the acquisition of pre-specified knowledge and the development of predetermined concepts. With the Participation Model, the focus of learning activities is on becoming a member of a community of practice, learning from the community but also contributing to it. With the Acquisition Model, what is to be learnt is generally predetermined. Frequently the extent to which the learner has learnt is measured by a written test. Often there are predetermined

Table 1.4   *WWW-based applications; extending flexibility within pedagogical categories (Collis, 199b: 55)*

Pedagogical Category	WWW-based Applications
1. Course organization	– A course calendar is available on the course WWW site via which relevant dates and times for different aspects of the course are highlighted. The calendar and updates are always available.
2. Lectures, contact sessions	– Highlights of lectures are captured as digitized video and made available as video-on-demand via the course WWW environment, synchronized with lectures notes, for students not physically present. – Follow-up reflections or questions can be posted and responded to via various WWW-based forms and communication tools in the course WWW site, at a time and location convenient to the student.
3. Self-study, assignments	– Study materials are expanded and updated by using links to additional resources via the WWW; course assignments involve students contributing new resources to the WWW site, along with written comments as to why the resources are appropriate.
4. Major assignment	– Tools to support group activities such as shared workspace are available; group members can have their own private communication areas within shared workspaces.
5. Testing	– Password-protected (practice) test sessions are available, with automatic feedback when approriate to the test questions.
6. Mentoring, communication not specific to nos 1–5	– Convenient communication through an e-mail centre in the course WWW site can occur, where not only individuals can be messaged but also groups within the course, including instructor groups.

right answers. In contrast, with the Participation Model, the interactions that the learner contributes to may serve to change the knowledge base of the community even as he or she participates. There are no right answers, but rather degrees of insight, belonging and participating. Table 1.5 summarizes Sfard's interpretation of these two fundamental educational models.

Sfard emphasizes that both models are needed in higher education. The Participation Model needs to make use of the Acquisition Model. Learners cannot communicate in a professional community if they do not share basic vocabulary and concepts; learners cannot participate in an apprenticeship without acquiring many basic skills of the domain in which the apprenticeship occurs. Thus the Participation Model is not enough in itself. But what is powerful about Sfard's analysis is her claim that the Acquisition Model is also not enough in itself. She makes her arguments for these claims in philosophical

Table 1.5 *Comparing the Acquisition and Participation Models (summarized from Sfard, 1998: 5–7)*

	Acquisition	Participation
Key definition of learning	Learning as knowledge acquisition and concept development; having obtained knowledge and made it one's own; individualized.	Learning as participation, the process of becoming a member of a community, 'the ability to communicate in the language of this community and act according to its norms' (p 6); 'the permanence of *having* gives way to the constant flux of *doing*' (p 6).
Key words	Knowledge, concept, misconception, meaning, fact, contents, acquisition, construction, internalization, transmission, attainment, accumulation.	Apprenticeship, situatedness, contextuality, cultural embeddedness, discourse, communication, social constructivism, co-operative learning.
Stress on	'The individual mind and what goes into it' (p 6); the 'inward' movement of knowledge' (p 6).	'The evolving bonds between the individual and others' (p 6); 'the dialectic nature of the learning interaction: The whole and the parts affect and inform each other' (p 6).
Ideal	Individualized learning.	Mutuality; community building.
Role of instructor	Delivering, conveying, facilitating, clarifying.	Facilitator, mentor, 'expert participant, preserver of practice/discourse' (p 7).
Nature of knowing	Having, possessing.	Belonging, participating, communicating.

terms; we think however that support of the need for both Acquisition and Participation Models can be more directly seen in emerging conditions in society.

Contribution-oriented activities

The need for participation is a reflection of current developments in society. Internationalization, the world being a global community, the fact that individuals can expect to work in different settings and as members of multifaceted teams, the need for social skills and the capacity to function effectively as a member of a team: all are commonly being described as characteristics of living and working that are rapidly gaining in importance. The Internet is stimulating the development of professional communities in which the individual interacts, not just once a year at a conference but regularly via WWW portals and mailing lists.

Even participation is not enough: the participant must also contribute in order to make a difference. Reigeluth (1996) itemizes major differences between the industrial age and the information age that affect education and notes the bipolar pairs: adversarial vs co-operative relationships, bureaucratic vs team organization, autocratic vs shared leadership, one-way communications vs networking, and division of labour vs integration of tasks. These pairings can map on to Sfard's acquisition–participation dimension but also extend the participation dimension to include a contribution orientation.

Acquisition and participation are not new ideas, but contribution is less discussed. The tendency in education has been the overemphasis of acquisition. 'Unfortunately, most courses are structured to transmit knowledge... Putting disciplines into bite-sized units that are to be taught through lectures across a series of weeks has a long tradition' (Nicaise and Crane, 1999: 29). Sfard calls for the restoration of a balance. We too have seen the need for this balance in our own experiences. When participation/contribution-type experiences are graded in a course content, they are typically field experiences, such as practice teaching or residencies in a professional setting.

We agree with Sfard that it is a balance that should be found, not a choice between one model and the other. For some courses and learners, the balance will favour activities with acquisition goals, such as might be the case in an introductory course in a mathematics programme. But even in these, students could have the opportunity to contribute to the learning experience for themselves and other learners, for example via submitting an answer to a 'frequently asked question'. For other courses, the balance could shift towards contribution, while still including acquisition aspects. Because activities are the instructional experiences that learners participate in beyond getting input through reading or listening (Brophy and Alleman, 1991), we will speak of educational models with activity goals related primarily to acquisition or primarily to participation and contribution, and argue that a movement towards the latter in higher education is desirable. Because contribution cannot occur without participation (although the converse is not necessarily so) we will refer in particular to a distinction between an acquisition model and a contribution-oriented model. In Chapter 5 we will develop these ideas further and explain why we feel contribution is so important, and has new possibilities because of technology support. Because the educational models relating to activity goals are fundamental to our discussions of pedagogy throughout this book we summarize them here as a lesson:

Lesson 2: *Move from student to professional.* Learning in higher education is not only a knowledge-acquisition process but also a process of gradual participation in and contribution to a professional community. Pedagogy should reflect both acquisition and contribution-oriented models.

Flexibility–Activity Framework

By using the activity-goal dimension, we have a way to relate pedagogy to flex-

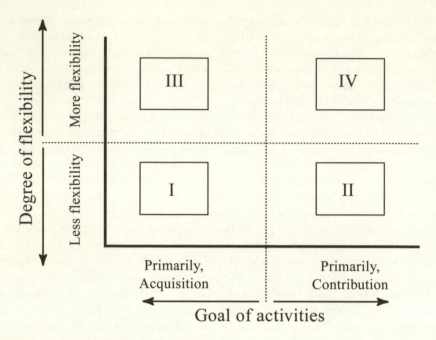

Figure 1.3 *Flexibility–Activity Framework*

ible learning. By combining an educational-model dimension with activity goals focused on acquisition or contribution with a flexibility dimension with categories relating to less and more flexibility, we can define a *Flexibility–Activity Framework* as shown in Figure 1.3. We will be referring to this framework throughout the book.

Extending Sfard's analysis to include a movement towards more flexibility as well as toward more contribution, we believe that courses in higher education should become identified with Quadrants III and IV, with a tendency towards Quadrant IV. We believe they are now predominately in Quadrant I. We will illustrate opportunities for this migration throughout the book.

Implementation strategies

Next to technology and pedagogy, the third component of flexible learning relates to its *implementation* in practice. A pedagogical theory means little if instructors do not apply it, and technological resources have no value if not used. A fact that has long been seen with computer-related products is that they are not used by the majority of instructors. In Chapters 3 and 4 we analyse why. Implementation is a critical component of a move towards more-flexible learning in an institution, because without implementation efforts stimulated at the institutional level it is likely that only pioneers will move forward. The number of instructors who choose to be innovators with technology and pedagogy is limited. An implementation strategy, with incentives, a methodology for gaining instructor involvement, and an effective manager are necessary. We discuss these aspects frequently in the book, particularly in Chapters 3 and 7.

Factors that influence the implementation of a technology innovation in an educational setting have been well studied and are reported in Chapter 3. We see these factors as having a relationship with one another, which we describe by the 4-E Model (Collis, Peters and Pals, 2000). This model says that an individual's likelihood of making use of a technological innovation for a learning-related purpose is a function of four groups of factors: *Environment* (the institutional context), *Educational effectiveness* (perceived or expected), *Ease of use* and *Engagement* (the person's personal response to technology and to change), each expressed as a vector. In the 4-E Model, the Environmental factor determines the level of the success threshold; a stronger environmental climate pushes the threshold lower so that the vector sum of the other three vectors does not have to be as high as when the threshold is associated with a weaker environmental vector. Figure 1.4 shows a 4-E Model profile of an individual with a weak Ease

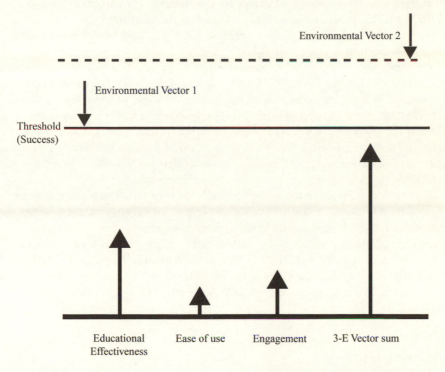

Figure 1.4   *The 4-E Model, showing how educational Effectiveness, Ease of use, personal Engagement and Environment factors are interrelated in predicting an individual's likelihood of use of a telematics application for a learning-related purpose (Collis, Peters and Pals, 2000, in press)*

of use vector, a weak Engagement vector and a moderately positive Educational effectiveness vector. The individual's vector sum is (almost) high enough in Environment Condition 1 probably to make use of a telematics innovation in his or her teaching. In Environmental Condition 2, the push from the Environmental vector is too weak and thus the threshold is too far away; the individual is not likely to make use of the innovation.

We will use the 4-E Model throughout the book as an intuitive guide to predicting implementation success and shaping implementation strategies.

Institutional framework

The manner in which pedagogy is carried out in a course and technology is used is influenced by many factors outside of the particular course itself. Courses are offered as part of a programme by an educational institution, and therefore must relate to that programme in terms of content and expectations for the students. Also, courses must occur within the operational processes of the institution, in terms of length, time-related aspects, admission criteria, examination procedures and in terms of the resources available to the students for carrying out course requirements. Thus, the pedagogical decisions of the instructor are constrained by many factors outside his or her control. They are part of the institutional framework affecting flexible learning.

Institutions also differ in the amount of support that is offered to the instructor relative to his or her teaching. This support can include direct support during the course itself, in terms of persons available to assist in some of the course-execution tasks; can relate to support during the preparation of the course; and can be offered more generally, in terms of helping instructors gain new skills and insights relating to their pedagogical practices. Support also relates to the library services and technological infrastructure available to the instructor for use in the teaching process. These are also part of the institutional framework.

There are other institutional aspects as well, some of which are more difficult to quantify. The social and professional climate in an institution, the management style of its leaders, the institution's previous experiences with technology-related change, and the vision of the leaders and of key persons with an influence in the institution all affect the movement toward flexible learning. In the 4-E Model, we visualized the importance of the institutional context on implementation success. We will discuss the institutional framework more, in Chapters 2, 3, 7, 8 and 9.

Summing up

Flexible learning is a complex phenomenon even when expressed in terms of only four key components. We can visualize the relationship among the four components discussed in this chapter via the diagram in Figure 1.5.

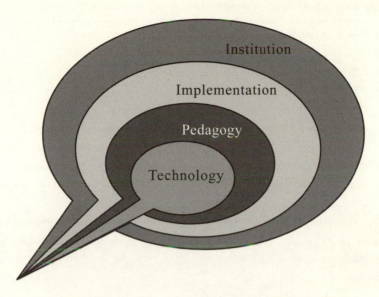

Figure 1.5   *Flexible learning in higher education – the four key components*

Using the components shown in Figure 1.5 there are different sequences that could be used to describe how flexible-learning activities are steered and carried out in higher education. Common approaches are from top down or from bottom up. From a top-down perspective we should start with the institutional context, then implementation, then pedagogy, then technology; for a bottom–up approach we should begin with technology and move through the increasingly complex levels. In this book we will choose the top-down level first (Chapter 2), because of the importance of the institution in any structural change involving flexible learning. From this, we will move to implementation (Chapter 3) and the 4-E Model. We will follow this with technology (Chapter 4) in order to show how pedagogy can work in practice for flexible learning (Chapter 5). All levels are however interrelated; thus we will focus in Chapters 6, 7, 8 and 9 on combinations of levels as well. The structure of the remainder of the book relates to Figure 1.5 as is given in Table 1.6.

In conclusion, a major portion of this chapter has been the attempt to define the term *flexible learning* in a way that can be made concrete within of the institutional framework that will shape and steer it, implementation strategies that will make it happen, pedagogical approaches that will give it learning value and technology that serves as its tool. The lessons we discussed in this chapter relate particularly to two important aspects of this relationship: the need to have a clear view of what is intended by flexible learning for a local context and the need for an underlying educational model for any change process involving technology. Repeating the lessons:

Table 1.6 *Components of flexible learning and chapters of this book*

Ch 2	You can't not do it	Institutional framework
Ch 3	Will they use it?	Implementation
Ch 4	Something for everyone	Technology
Ch 5	The U turn	Pedagogy
Ch 6	Getting our money's worth?	Institutional, pedagogy, technology
Ch 7	Getting started	Implementation, institution, pedagogy, technology
Ch 8	Keeping going	Pedagogy, technology, implementation, institution
Ch 9	A new economy?	Institution, technology, pedagogy, implementation

Lesson 1: *Be specific.* We need to define our terms and express our goals in a measurable form or else progress will be difficult to steer and success difficult to claim.

Lesson 2: *Move from student to professional.* Learning in higher education is not only a knowledge-acquisition process but also a process of gradual participation in and contribution to a professional community. Pedagogy should reflect both acquisition and contribution-oriented models.

With this analysis, we are ready to go more deeply into the components of flexible learning shown in Figure 1.5. We begin, top down, with the institutional framework, in Chapter 2.

Chapter 2

You can't not do it

Flexible learning is related to major changes facing higher-education institutions throughout the world. For flexible learning to be meaningful in an institution, it must be more than the effort of occasional pioneers; the institution must commit itself to a change. In this chapter we focus on the institutional perspective. What sorts of changes are occurring? What factors have influenced institutions that have already made a commitment to more flexible learning and technology use? What motivates policy in these areas? The main lesson framing this chapter is: *you can't not do it.*

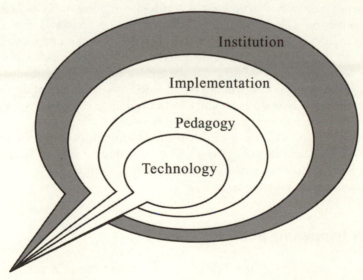

Figure 2.1   *Flexible learning in higher education – institutional perspective*

The context for change in higher education

Although the institutional level is the outmost of our circles in the figure at the start of the chapter, institutions themselves are situated within a number of broader contexts that shape and constrain their own developments, which are not shown on this figure. This broader context includes government, the business community, accreditation boards, agencies determining the national technological infrastructure, and the market itself: potential clients and those who influence them. Many trends can be identified in developments in this broader context relating to flexible learning and higher education. These include (Collis and Gommer, 2000; Encarnação, Leidhold and Reuter, 2000):

● *Virtualization*. People are becoming more comfortable with Internet technology as an everyday tool. Thus, using the Internet for learning will become a normal extension.
● *Lifelong learning*. New forms of learning experiences are being seen as necessary in order to keep up with continuing changes in work and the context of work (see Chapter 1).
● *Personalization for the individual client*. As individual tailoring, via the computer, becomes part of e-commerce and society more generally, its application to education, particularly lifelong learning, will be strong.
● *Globalization and internationalization*. Throughout the world, business is more and more taking place as a combination of local and international. Businesses are forming alliances to take advantage of one another's local markets and to have the combined resources to operate internationally.

These trends suggest two main lines of development. One is the line relating to *quality control*: on one extreme, the Internet can be seen as a free channel, allowing anyone to access and contact anyone else. On the other extreme, the Internet can be seen as needing to be ordered; made secure; made a place to do business with consumer confidence; made a place to go for entertainment, with confidence that one's norms will not be offended. A second line of development relates to the *local vs global* aspect: will customers shop at the corner store or via a virtual portal whose server may be continents away?

Given the unstoppable surge of use of the Internet throughout society, these trends and questions are affecting all sectors, including higher education. In Chapter 9 we discuss the implications of this for the future. In this chapter, we focus on current developments.

What's happening in universities?

Higher-education institutions throughout the world are in a period of rapid change. Changes occurring in the primary processes of higher education –

courses and degree granting – are closely related to the contextual trends of virtu-alization, internationalization, lifelong learning and customer orientation that are part of society in general. In this context, there is a strong message appearing in the popular media as well as in professional circles: 'Traditional universities and colleges face a bleak future unless they significantly alter their instructional methods to keep pace with developments spurred by the Internet. In order to survive, these institutions must… understand their own strengths and reputation among the public, and customise their teaching methods to the different age groups of students' (*Financial Times*, 2000). As institutions are more and more trying to reach students who do not fit the standard residential degree programme, individual courses or even entire degree programmes are being offered via the Internet, which is perceived as saving both universities and students money and time.

Flexibility is seen as the key idea, and flexibility requires technology. Thus, new developments in technology feature in much of the change in higher educa-tion. In this section, we look at this change from an anecdotal perspective via an overview of ways in which universities are responding to the perceived social demand for flexible services. These can be clustered in terms of new characteris-tics of the university ('being wired'), new models for flexible delivery, and new partners and competition.

Being wired

Throughout the world technology expenditures have become a major item at higher-education institutions, moving from support for certain technical faculties to required infrastructure for all staff and students. In a recent survey in the USA, the degree of *wiredness* of a university was seen as an important part of its profile to potential students. 'Undergraduates are as interested in a college's Net resources as in its curriculum or social life. Schools are as boastful of network infrastructures as of celebrity professors… The Net is transforming the college experience and at a breakneck pace' (Bernstein, 2000: 114, 116).

What are some of the manifestations of being wired? What is it that the public, at least in the countries that can be grouped with the US, is coming to expect of universities? Bernstein's survey identifies criteria such as:

- Incoming students receive or are required to purchase a computer.
- Lecture halls and an increasing number of classrooms are wired for high-speed network (local area network and Internet) access.
- Student residences offer computer equipment including printers and network connectivity for student use.
- Prospective students can contact appropriate persons for information via the WWW, through which they may also apply.
- Students can register for classes, drop classes, access their grades and access their course schedules via the WWW.

- Space on a WWW server is available for instructors and students.
- Students have institution-hosted e-mail and network accounts; Internet access is unrestricted in terms of time, cost and what can be accessed.
- Library resources can be perused and reserved via the network.
- Technical support is generously available.

Usually, justifications for all this wiredness are not given in terms of specific learning-related needs. Rather, the expectation of students and society is that the institution must do it, because everyone else is doing it. The move towards making this technology push concrete is occurring through a variety of institutional models. In this section we look at the general trend toward being *virtual* as well as new sorts of initiatives taking place within higher-education institutions themselves as examples of these models.

Models for flexibility delivery

Higher-education environments of the future are being envisioned to include many aspects of flexibility, such as in the student's choice of modules to combine together to meet course and degree requirements (Ben-Jacob, Levin and Ben-Jacob, 2000). There are many ways in which this flexibility increase is being realized. The individual institution can become more flexible in its own practices, can join with other universities in a variety of models, or can join with other non-university partners in a variety of models. Also, new players, both related to traditional universities and not, are becoming providers. Often these new approaches are collectively and metaphorically called *being virtual*. We discuss these in terms of the idea of being virtual in itself, and of how this is being expressed in the form of new initiatives within institutions.

Being virtual

The term *virtual university* and its companions *virtual classrooms*, *virtual reality* and *virtual libraries* (no one yet seems to offer a virtual degree) are typically used as metaphors. Usually what they refer to is less radical than the terminology might suggest. The business of the *real* university continues, often with little or no contact with the fringe services or courses offered via the *virtual* approach. Many different uses of the term virtual appear not only in the popular media but also in professional and academic journals. Among the many different meanings are:

- virtual as a vision or metaphor for the idea that anyone, anywhere, can experience the benefits he or she needs from a university, while remaining at home and at work;
- virtual as a way of describing how the traditional university can gradually move to be more flexible in the options it offers to students in terms of how, when and where they complete certain course requirements;
- virtual as a way of describing how the resources and experiences available

within the traditional university are being broadened for those within the university (ie the services of the university library are no longer bounded by its own physical collection);

- virtual as a way to describe specific organizations and consortia, sometimes comprised of traditional universities but often not, which now offer alternative experiences in competition with the traditional university;
- virtual in terms of mobility, where a student can stay at home (or home university) and still participate in a course at another university;
- virtual in reference to specific technical environments (typically WWW-based) that serve as the realization of these ideas in terms of providing the interface by which the individual interacts with the *virtual* situation;
- virtual in reference to some sort of informational service such as a portal site via which links to information and contact persons about courses and programmes are provided.

Combining these perspectives, at least 11 pay-offs can be suggested for the *virtual university* relating to virtual mobility and internationalism. All are being facilitated at the present with WWW-based environments. Table 2.1 shows these pay-offs.

Table 2.1 *Implications of becoming virtual*

Perspective	Pay-offs
Student perspective	1. Improved preparation for actual mobility; improved contact with home university while away; improved contact between supervisors at home and external universities. 2. Improved chances to participate in learning activities, ranging from short interactions to full courses, with students at external universities but while staying (completely or partially) at home.
Faculty perspective	3. Improved opportunities for collaboration with external colleages in learning activities for students from involved universities (see 2 above). 4. Improved opportunities for research and professional interactions with external colleagues in conjunction with physical mobility or in place of it.
Institutional perspective	5. Increased opportunities for new student intake. 6. Increased opportunities for consortia patnerships and other collaborative initiatives. 7. Reduced costs and time demands relating to external travel. 8. Increased efficiency in information dissemination, in information access about programmes elsewhere.
Strategic perspective	9. Increased multicultural and international awareness, and sense of European identity. 10. (Possibility of) increased exposure to other languages, relative to their economic value (ie better business opportunities).
Technologists' perspective	11. New markets, new research questions and new creative opportunities.

The most likely benefits to trigger real development of virtual ideas are those that relate directly to the market: for the increasingly competitive lifelong learning market, for institutional decision makers who seek new streams of intake and income (Collis, 1998a). As another observation, those who use the term *virtual* are not so often those who actually are carrying out the *virtual* activities, but instead politicians or marketers or social prophets who fuel the mass media with images of the changing world. While social prophets may not be of direct impact to traditional higher education, the fact that they often articulate the public mood is. The *more-flexible, more-international, more-virtual university* is a metaphor whose time has come.

New initiatives within the institution

Individual universities are also engaged in many other forms of new initiatives relating to flexible learning. Many traditional universities are paralleling traditional distance-education universities in making courses available to students at a distance (Collis, 1999f). Even if this does not occur, WWW environments are becoming the portal through which course registration occurs, course materials are obtained, course interactions and communication occur, and course examinations or final projects are managed. There are many different types of approaches within the traditional institution:

- An individual department can offer a *special course or programme* to a non-typical cohort of learners, such as professionals from a certain company. These are on a contract basis, and usually have no overlap with the regular programme.
- An individual faculty can offer a *variant of a department's Masters' programme* via a distance model. In contrast to traditional distance-teaching institutions, in a traditional campus-based institution this usually means that the instructors involved are expected to handle both a face-to-face cohort and a distance cohort, usually without extra support or training (see Chapter 5).
- An institution can be systematically organized for *dual-mode delivery*. Dual mode generally involves two separate but equal versions of a course, such as an on-campus and distance version. It is an extension of the above *variant approach* in that there is usually institutional support in place for the distance students.
- An institution can maintain a service for *continuing education* or *professional development*. Typically such a unit is outside the faculties, negotiating with them for the availability of certain courses and instructors for particular courses to be brokered by the unit.

The variation that is occurring with these sorts of courses is increased flexibility in terms of time and place. Learners in these different variations increasingly have the possibilities of taking some variations of courses via the WWW or on the Internet. Most often, courses offered via use of a WWW environment and not having any face-to-face contact sessions are not yet a common feature of the entire institution, but are more frequently on a small-scale or experimental basis. There still seems to be a general belief in many cases that in the regular programme learners expect face-to-face time with the instructor and will somehow feel cheated with less of this.

Another way that the individual university is responding is in not necessarily offering courses at a distance, but in making the course-participation process more flexible in other ways. The University of Twente is the site of many examples of on-campus use of network technology to diversify instruction (see Chapters 7 and 8). Many other institutions now are developing such ideas, hoping to draw students to the home campus and programme. *The Pew Learning and Technology Program Newsletter* (http://www.center.rpi.edu/PewHome.html) reports monthly on examples of 'redesigned learning environments' using technology for more-flexible learning within traditional institutions.

In summary, there are many models via which an individual higher-education institution is experimenting with more-flexible delivery. But perhaps more than 'doing it alone', institutions are looking into new collaborations.

New collaborations

While individual universities are investing heavily in technology, the trend toward more-flexible learning is frequently being carried out via the university joining in a partnership with other universities or other partners. A major development is the emergence of new groupings of institutions, coming together apparently to find a more potent way of market penetration than if they continued to operate only on their own. These can be seen in different forms: international education consortia that may or may not involve commercialization, corporate universities where a major player is a multinational company, university networks of various sorts and start-up ventures with technology companies (Brockhaus, Emrich and Mei-Pochtler, 2000; Cunningham *et al*, 2000). Partnerships can also take place between a group of universities and new partners such as telecommunications vendors, software companies and the media industry, or companies whose primary business is not education, but which control facilities and resources (Latchem, 1998). Such new partners often serve as *brokers*, in collaboration with organizations that can deliver content, such as universities.

The main trends that compel universities to seek collaboration in the area of technology and flexible learning are twofold. 'First, the huge investments and complex multi-sided expertise that are necessary to develop and implement comprehensive ICT strategies require sharing of costs and joining of forces. The second reason is related to ICT itself: the use of these new technologies is resulting in more and global competition among universities' (Van der Wende and Beerkens, 1999).

There are a number of models that can be identified in which the traditional university may be included as a partner (or excluded):

- new alliances with other educational institutions such as *university networks or consortia and international educational consortia* (and variations of these with non-university partners);
- *corporate universities* (companies now offering on-site training programmes for their employees are moving to online variations);
- partnerships between private *online enablers* (Anderson and Downes, 2000) and public institutions;
- *virtual universities* that operate entirely online, are not extensions of an existing university and may offer an entirely Internet-based degree.

From several of these a model is emerging in which actual courses are chosen from expert instructors around the world, with the local institution providing the personalized support, social and technical infrastructure, and application settings.

Other partnerships are taking place among universities themselves, without broker services or non-traditional partners. These can include partnerships where smaller universities identify courses offered by some that are not available at the others, and then arrange for students to participate, via the Internet, in courses that are not available at the home institution. Other times a partnership occurs among several universities that have some pragmatic connection with one another. Or the partners may share a common professional base, such as the arrangement whereby MBA students at three US universities will be able to take classes at one another's institutions using technologies such as chat and video-conferencing as well as the WWW. At a less-integrated level, there are examples of universities teaming up around a common portal site. Yet another model is the formation, usually at the governmental level, of a new entity, which integrates in some way the course offerings of some number of institutions in its jurisdiction, and often offers some extra added services.

Thus, there is a great deal going on with regard to flexible learning and technology in higher education. We indicated that social trends such as virtualization, lifelong learning, customization and internationalization are stimulating these changes. But how does this stimulation process work in practice in terms of the influences on policy in an organization? We move from the descriptive overview to an analysis of factors underlying this description. What factors influence change towards flexible learning in higher education?

Factors influencing change in higher education

Change occurs in an educational institution in a number of ways. Sometimes change is a bottom-up affair, where a few individuals or events stimulate a multiplier effect. Change can also occur in a top-down manner, where a decision or policy is announced or phased in from those above and outside those who will have to implement it. Those involved with top-down decisions may be department heads or institutional administrators or government policy makers.

In the case of a change towards new technologies and more-flexible learning, an institution can typically be categorized in one of three phases with respect to the bottom-up/top-down nature of change. The use of technology in higher education can take place at the level of the individual instructor – the *pioneer*; it can be supported by decisions that convince and help instructors to use technology – *encouraged use*, or by decisions that require all instructors to make use of technology – *systemic use* (Collis and Van der Wende, 1999). The first case, where the initiative is limited to the individual instructor and no decisions are taken at the unit, faculty or institutional level, is that of *no policy*, whereas the second and third reflect some levels of policy development and top-down stimulation. The third, systemic use requires policy and top-down involvement. In this section we look at factors influencing change, including one particular factor – the sense of inevitability.

Why change?

There have been many analyses of why institutions feel the need to incorporate more technology into instructional practice, at either the encouraged-use or systemic-use level. Fisser (2000), from a literature review as well as a review of reports from 35 institutions already having policy with regard to technology use for flexible learning, identified 38 factors that are stimulating the use of technology for flexible learning in higher education. She grouped these factors into seven categories as shown in Table 2.2. The number of times each factor was mentioned in the 35 institutional reports is also shown.

Fisser's was not a full-scale study in the sense that the institutions were not each asked specifically about the influence of the 38 factors. Only a secondary analysis of the text of internal reports and conference papers was used, and thus authors may not have intended to be exhaustive in their comments. However, the results that were obtained are still interesting. The factors mentioned most often related to the need for more flexibility as a stimulus for technology use (n=24); for technology as a medium for new teaching models and for new conceptions of learning (n=29 and n=23); and for technology just because it is there (emerging technology, n=20; new technology, push/hype, n=30; available technology, n=27; and available technology-support facilities, n=26). Many of these suggest a technology orientation. In her further analysis, Fisser found a nearly even split between economic reasons (ie getting more students or new sources of funding) and reasons relating to social concerns (ie reaching the disadvantaged, offering re-entry possibilities, supporting lifelong learning) as motivating top-down policy for increased technology use.

You can't not do it

These results have a close similarity to our own experiences from interviews with decision makers at a number of universities in 13 countries during 1998, 1999

Table 2.2   *Factors stimulating change involving technology in higher education, and number of institutions (n=35) reporting the factors*

Grouping of Factors	Factors from the Literature	Number of Institutions Surveyed (n=35) Reporting the Factor to be Important
Environmental pressures	New market	11
	Business education	1
	Part-time students	7
	Lifelong learning	14
	On-demand training	2
	Funding	15
	Partnerships	13
	Tailor-made products	2
	Dynamic environment	0
	Competition	7
	Response to threats and opportunities	2
	Flexibility	24
	Knowledge management	0
	Changing student demographics	15
	Fiscal constraints	0
	Demands from employers	5
	Demands from learners	11
Technology developments	Emerging technology	11
	Dependence on IT	2
	New technology (push, hype)	30
Institutional conditions	New organization structure	7
	Broad participation	13
	Shared vision	4
	Concrete plans	12
	Improved access to education	10
	Leadership	10
Educational developments	New conceptions of learning	23
	New teaching models	29
	Focus on learner/learning	19
	Individual differences	3
	Active learning	11
Cost reduction/ cost-effectiveness	Reducing costs	10
	Cost-effectiveness	11
	Benefits	2
Support facilities	Administrative support	9
	Technical support	18
	Availability of technology	27
	Availability of facilities	26

and 2000 (Collis, 1999d, in press a; Moonen, 2000d). In each case we asked the policy makers why their institutions were considering policy or had already made policy about network technologies (the WWW and Internet). While Fisser found a nearly even split between economic reasons and reasons relating to social concerns (ie reaching the disadvantaged, offering re-entry possibilities, supporting lifelong learning) in her analysis, we came to the conclusion that the social concerns in turn relate to economic incentives: more students, more subsidies, more funds. We also analysed many different strategic plans involving technology for traditional universities and found they all included statements about offering high-quality education (as has always been the case) as well as about the importance of information and communication technology in the learning process. However, few operationalized their goals beyond general statements such as 'attention to individual students' or 'preparing the students for the future'. Operationalizations are typically left to internal committees and working groups. Our first lesson learnt, 'Be specific' (see Chapter 1), is not usually being followed.

Despite the source of information, however, we found a common theme emerging, either explicitly or implicitly, a theme related to a sense of inevitability. We call this the 'you can't not do it' persuasion.

The most consistent response in the interviews that we conducted was that the decision makers felt that 'you can't not do it'. There was a shared sense of inevitability, of urgency: if a university does not keep up, does not strive for new cohorts or to maintain existing cohorts, then it will face even more substantial difficulties than it is now encountering. Network technologies, particularly use of the WWW, are seen as necessary strategic tools in this task of keeping up, and of maintaining or gaining new students or new sources of funding. In terms of their stated aims for policy relating to the use of the WWW, university leaders, of course, do not make statements as direct as 'you can't not do it'. However, the sense of this inevitability came out of every interview.

There was also considerable interest at the decision-making level for the cost-effectiveness aspects and the effects of technology-mediated learning, but neither a specific nor even a general calculation of cost-effectiveness seems to be contributing to decision making. Again, the main argument is 'you can't not do it': everyone else is doing it, and if you don't want to lose students, then you have to do it, too. Economic reasons are agreed to be important, but estimated based on intuition (Moonen, 2000d; see also Chapter 6).

There is also another aspect of 'you can't not do it'. Universities are sensitive to their public images; having an image of making use of technology adds to their modern cachet. In contrast, not making use of the Internet and the WWW suggests not keeping up with the times, not being a leader in the information society. Such image aspects are nebulous but important, not only in the competition for students but also in the positioning of a university in its own circles, regionally and nationally.

These observations lead to our third lesson, a lesson relating to the power of the idea whose time has come:

Lesson 3: *You can't not do it*. The idea whose time has come is irresistible.

This is a lesson, as well as a current trend, in that we have experienced this irresistibility before.

Déjà vu and the pendulum effect

We perceive the 'you can't not do it' feeling as an iteration of a similar wave of 'you can't not do it' rationales occurring in the early 1980s with respect to computers in education. Beginning in the early 1980s, countries and regions around the world began to pursue various initiatives to stimulate and support the use of computers in their educational systems. These initiatives took many different forms in different countries, some focusing on strategic support for hardware- and software-related programmes, some on strategies more directly focused on curricular and instructional aspects of computers, some (fewer) on strategies for the school manager and others (many) on different approaches to teacher education and support. Different general patterns of motivations were identified, such as preparing students for future careers or strengthening the human-capital base in society (Hawkridge, 1991). Typically these motivations were stated in vague and non-measurable terms (see Lesson 1) but none the less fuelled large expenditures and high expectations.

The wave of social and technological developments that stimulated interest in computers in schools in the late 1970s and early 1980s appears now to be paralleled by a similar surge of interest in educational aspects of information and communication technologies in higher education. Throughout the world, the use of wide-area network capabilities for communication and access to new forms of information engagement is stimulating a wave of initiatives with respect to technologies related to the Internet such as e-mail and the WWW. This wave can be seen as an iteration of the 'computers in education' wave of 10 to 15 years earlier. What is most significant in this comparison is that the sense of inevitability, of 'you can't not do it', that appeared in the early 1980s is appearing again. Table 2.3 shows this comparison.

Knowing that this is the current climate can help the decision maker: he or she must respond, and responding at the present time means supporting technology for some aspect of more-flexible learning. The *why* is therefore not so important as the *how*. 'How' involves implementation, the focus of the next chapter. But a pendulum effect can also be expected. If there are only vaguely stated goals and a sense of irresistibility with regard to the motivation of decisions, then the experiences of 20 years of efforts relating to computers in education are likely to reap-

Table 2.3   *Push factors related to technology in education (updated from Collis, 1996c)*

Push Factors	Computers in Education, 1980	The Internet and Education, 2000
Technological breakthrough	The microcomputer.	Public access to the Internet and WWW.
Social response	We must have a computer, in our homes, in our schools.	We must be able to get on the Internet, in our homes, in our schools.
Social vision	Personal computers will revolutionize society and will create powerful new opportunities for those who can handle them.	The information highway will revolutionize society and will create powerful new opportunities for those who can handle it.
Commercial push	A vast new market for goods and services.	A vast new market for goods and services.
Social expectation	Schools must not be left behind; all students must make use of computers.	Universities must not be left behind; all students must make use of the Internet.
Vagueness	Metaphors and predictions are strong; results are anecdotal.	Metaphors and predictions are strong; results are anecdotal.
Pioneers show the promise	Both in theory and practice, there are impressive ideas and examples of how the computer can enrich and re-engineer education.	Both in theory and practice, there are impressive ideas and examples of how the WWW and other network environments can enrich and re-engineer education.
Educational decision makers must and do respond	Every school must get computers; funding must be found; new initiatives are needed; policy and strategy are needed.	Every course must make use of the WWW; funding must be found; new initiatives are needed; policy and strategy are needed.
The overall movement is unstoppable	Computers are pervasive throughout society; you can't not do it.	Interconnectivity via the Internet is pervasive throughout society; you can't not do it.
The rich will get richer	An incentive, and a fear.	An incentive, and a fear.

pear with the WWW in education. Those (often disappointing) experiences will be discussed in Chapter 3 as well as Chapter 4.

While Table 2.3 supports the impression that the current feelings of inevitability about network and Internet use are similar to those of two decades ago with respect to computers in education, we note one major difference. This new aspect is convergence. There is a convergence of technologies but also of pedagogies and institutional approaches (we discuss this later in this chapter) that suggests a more comprehensive response now than was the case with stand-alone educational software in the 1980s.

Convergence

Thus, there are pressures on the institution to expand its technology services and also pressures on it to experiment with new variants of courses and course-delivery methods. While there are many models and variations, and much hype, relating to the new role of the university, one trend is indisputable. This is the trend towards *convergence*. The traditional differences between distance-teaching universities and traditional universities are fading. There is a rapid, recent and substantial change in numbers of traditional campus-based universities providing distance education. In Canada, for instance, this resulted in an increase of 50 per cent in eight years. The proportion of universities offering distance education in some other countries are: France – 40 per cent; Sweden – almost all; USA – almost all; and for the UK – around 75 per cent (Daniel, 1996). In Australia, at least 23 (out of 39) universities are offering distance education (European Association of Distance Teaching Universities, 1998).

The division between traditional universities and universities organized around distance and open delivery is itself fading, not only because more and more traditional universities are offering courses to distance students. The concept of *distance* is rapidly losing meaningfulness (Collis, 1999f). Given the fact that many distance-teaching universities require their students to come occasionally to face-to-face sessions (perhaps with a local tutor or at a study centre) and are continually augmenting their own educational delivery to add more communication and interaction possibilities, the actual difference between their offerings and those of traditional universities seems to be getting less and less. The strengths of traditional distance-education institutions have been their carefully developed study materials and the flexibility they offer in terms of at least some aspects of time and place of participation. These strengths are now being picked up by traditional universities. This is widely understood in Australia, where student statistics no longer include the term 'distance education', but mode of study is classified as full time and part time. Karmel, of the Australian Department of Employment, Education, Training and Youth Affairs, in noting the trends in universities says: 'The way in which a student studies will be a matter of personal preference and will not depend to any important extent on where the student lives, which institution the student attends or whether the student is on campus, off campus, full-time or part-time. Distance education is becoming an anachronism' (1998: 617).

Given this convergence with relation to distance and other flexibility aspects, we believe there is one fundamental difference between the traditional distance-teaching universities in Europe and the traditional universities, which is less likely to change. This is the distinction that relates to the role of the instructor in a course. In the traditional university, the instructor is typically the author, developer, manager, teacher, administrator and evaluator of his or her courses. While this can and does have its weaknesses, it also has some important strengths. These strengths are often intangible: the opportunity for university students gradually to become 'initiated into the profession' of being an academic, of being formed as an intellectual (see Lesson 2, with respect to contribution as well as acquisition). This is a modelling process that overlaps but extends further than the experience of being in a course. The opportunity to have an *intellectual apprenticeship* with an experienced senior academic, the same person whose external scientific and professional work and research should be permeating his or her course-handling approaches, the same person who is expert enough to have written the course, is an important benefit of the traditional university. It has roots as far back as the master–apprentice relationships of the Middle Ages. (Perhaps 'mentor' and 'junior researcher' are more acceptable words in current times; see Chapter 5.)

Being part of an academic community is more than having e-mail discussions with fellow students and a tutor; it is the chance to learn the norms and absorb the energy and professional style of those who have leadership roles in the broader scientific world. Through the personal involvement of the experienced faculty member in his or her course, the pre-structured subject matter can be related to the new developments in the field and in the instructor's own research, something more difficult to do in mass-produced study materials. While clearly not every course in the traditional university brings such serendipitous benefits to its students, enough do, so that the experience of scaffolded development as a member of a professional community occurs over time for many students. It is important that this strength of the traditional university is not weakened in the attempt to become more flexible (Collis, 1999f). While there is a sense of 'you can't not do it' at the present, there can also be a pendulum shift towards the 'basics' and away from virtualism – unless an institution grounds its vision about technology and flexible learning in pedagogy and sound implementation strategies.

Summing up

In this chapter we have surveyed some of the current developments in traditional higher-education institutions and related these not only to social trends but also to a sense of inevitability about technology and flexible learning. Thus the lesson for this chapter was:

Lesson 3: *You can't not do it.* The idea whose time has come is irresistible.

But we also saw the risk of a pendulum swing unless changes relating to technology and flexible learning stabilize in the institution. In Chapter 9 we return to this institutional-change perspective, looking at scenarios for the future. In the following chapter we continue in the current time: once an institution decides it 'can't not do it' and chooses a flexible approach, how does it proceed? Will those on the workfloor – instructors, students, support persons – be able and willing to translate the vision into practice? This is an implementation problem.

Chapter 3

Will they use it?

For flexible learning to occur, instructors and learners will probably need to make use of technology. This involves acceptance as well as actual use in practice of the technology. What if they do not want to do this? There is a long line of experience that relates to instructors' and learners' responses to the use of technology in learning-related situations. In this chapter we look at what we have learnt with respect to the likelihood of an individual – instructor or learner – making use of a technical innovation in a learning-related setting, in terms of the 4-E Model, in order to be able to apply this to the flexible-learning situation. We

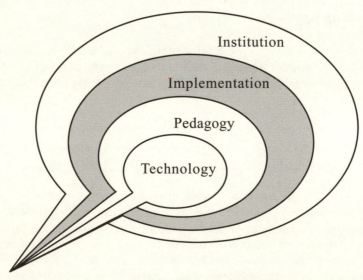

Figure 3.1   *Flexible learning in higher education – implementation perspective*

also use the 4-Model to help predict implementation success, particularly during the initiation phase, and to comment about the importance of leadership and staff engagement to any implementation effort.

Initiation, implementation, institutionalization: change phases in the institution

In Chapter 2 we looked at the big ideas and expectations relating to flexible learning and change in higher education. But we did not look at how to make these ideas concrete. In this chapter we turn to the 'how'. The 'how' is more difficult than the vision.

Moving from vision to practice

Despite all the possibilities for increased flexibility and the institution's perception that you can't not do it, the actual voluntary use of technology applications as a purposeful part of the instructional delivery of a course or related to a classroom lesson is still far from widespread. In Finland, for example, where network access is possibly the best in the world in terms of the proportion of the population with access to the Internet, 'teaching and learning in universities and polytechnics has not changed that much with respect to the use of telematics' (Kauppi and Vainio, 1998). In the USA, 'teachers have by and large not embraced new technology tools' (Inge, 1998: 5) and 'teachers are often apathetic toward technology, often viewing its use as taking too much time for what needs to be accomplished in a day' (Inge, 1998: 5, citing Darling-Hammond, 1996). In the UK, a formal study by the National Committee of Inquiry into Higher Education (called the Dearing Report, after its chairman) concluded that 'there is as yet little widespread use of computer-based learning materials' (1997: 119).

The gap between potential and use in practice is an implementation problem. For almost 30 years, the implementation problem relating to technology-related resources in educational settings has been a subject of concern for researchers studying the teacher's or learner's response. There are a number of conceptual models in the literature that try to elaborate the implementation process. Well known among these is the Concerns–Based Adoption Model (CBAM). This was developed, in the 1970, by researchers at the University of North Texas to predict and explain the relatively slow uptake by teachers of a technological innovation in their instructional practice (Hall, George and Rutherford, 1979). In their model, an individual goes through a series of seven predictable 'stages of concern' about the innovation, starting with the concern of not having enough information and moving through several levels of concern relating to his or her own personal competency in adapting the innovation before concerns related to more than routine use of the technology can be expected. The CBAM model has been extensively used to help understand the differential response of teachers to the possibility of being able to make use of a technological innovation in their instructional practice (see, for example, Wells and Anderson, 1997).

Another well-known conceptual model with respect to innovation was developed by Rogers in 1983 and is still routinely cited (see, for example, Northrup, 1997 and Siegel, 1998). Rogers' Innovation-Decision Model suggests that an innovation is likely to be accepted by an individual if it has the aspects (among others): relative advantage compared to the current practices; compatibility or fit to the previous experiences, values and needs of the individual; trialability, the degree to which the innovation can be tried out in non-threatening and experimental circumstances; and observability, the degree to which the efforts made will be observed and valued by others. A negative influence is complexity, the degree to which the innovation is perceived to be difficult to use. Rogers also emphasizes the impact of the individual's social network and its norms on the decision to make use of an innovation. He claims that 'the heart of the diffusion process is the modelling and imitation by potential adopters of the near-peers' experiences who have previously adopted a new idea' (1995: 304).

There are many other studies, primarily from the USA, that explore the factors that influence an instructor's decision to make use of a technology application in his or her pedagogical practice. However, despite being well studied over several decades with respect to computers in education (see, for example, Cuban, 1985), and during the last decade with respect to applications involving network technologies in education (see Collis, 1992a, 1992b, and Riel and Levine, 1990, for early summaries), a solution to the implementation problem has not yet been found. Thus, it is important to discuss the 'how' in some detail. We do this in terms of three phases, first in a general sense and then with more attention to each of the phases in itself.

Change as a three-step process

Although there is widespread agreement that the role of technology is critical to the future success of higher-education institutions, there is less agreement about how to move from vision to realization (Yetton, 1997). To use a metaphor, the line between vision and institutionalization of a technology-supported innovation in an educational institution is not a line but a meandering path, with gaps, traversed by a changeable group of travellers often with little or no collective memory of the beginning of the journey nor an up-to-date road map. Despite this vagueness, the change process can be seen as generally having three phases. The first is the initiation of the change. The second is the scalability of change beyond those most directly involved in the initiation as realized via an implementation process. The third is the institutionalization of change, its sustainability within the normal procedures of the institution after the special start-up initiatives are withdrawn. Although the implementation phase is only one of the three phases in the change process related to time, the entire process is often called an implementation cycle.

Based on experience in the change process (Collis, 1996d; Fullan, 1991; Moonen, 2000b) the 'ideal' life cycle of a technology innovation in an educational institution should probably include the following:

Pre-initiation and initiation

1. Bottom-up experience grows in the institution.
2. Building on the bottom-up experiences as well as experiences elsewhere (see Lesson 3), decision makers strategically choose for an institutional direction and make this choice clear and operational (Lesson 1), as well as based on an educational principle (Lesson 2).
3. A strategic plan is produced, based on implementation principles for how to move from the current position of the institution to a position in which the targets can be met.
4. An implementation leader and team are assembled, appropriate technology provision is determined and an implementation methodology is developed and carried out with an initial group.

Implementation

5. Ongoing formative evaluation, using as criteria the goals and targets that operationalized the initial vision, occurs for revision and fine-tuning of the implementation methodology, as well as its underlying strategic plan.
6. The change scales beyond the volunteers.

Institutionalization

7. The change becomes institutionalized, a sustainable part of the ordinary operating procedures of the institution.

It has been estimated that this movement from initiation through implementation to institutionalization with respect to a technological innovation in an educational institution can be expected to be something like a five-year process (Plomp, 1992) and thus overall success cannot quickly be expected. Within this life cycle the following observations can be made:

- Vision statements are often not translated into operational terms or into measurable goals.
- The linearity of the process is not as direct as these three phases would indicate. Within any innovation, there will be many subinnovations, some of which will only be at the initiation phase while others may be in the institutionalization phase. Steps can be bypassed or go astray, or evolve in a convoluted way.
- The collective memory of those involved in any of the steps often fails in terms of remembering previous steps.
- New players step in and previous leaders exit or lose interest, further straining the collective-memory aspect and often diluting the momentum of the process.
- Most often, the whole process never completes Step 6. The university does a

variety of things with technology, but the linkage to Steps 1–3 of the 'ideal' life cycle is hard to trace.

Much can occur, or not occur, in the change process. To use the traveller metaphor again, the journey can start without having a specific destination, can proceed without a road map, can involve many changes of drivers and can proceed without any of them keeping a log to compare their own stretches of the journey to the stretches of those who have gone before. This metaphor relates to our next lesson learnt:

Lesson 4: *Don't forget the road map.* Change takes a long time and is an iterative process, evolving in ways that are often not anticipated.

Factors that influence initiation

In Chapter 2 we have already analysed factors that influence the initiation of technology-related change in higher education. The initiation phase can also be studied at other moments. We discuss the moments relating to creating the strategic plan, setting up the responsibility for managing and carrying out the implementation phase, and moving from initiation into implementation.

Creating the strategic plan

An important period is that of strategic planning. Typically, institutions set up task forces or working groups who in a certain amount of time have to present a plan and budget (and increasingly a business plan) for the implementation phase. What should be in an institutional strategic plan? The Centre for Research in Education (CRE) in Geneva suggests planning for at least the aspects shown in Table 3.1.

Many institutional strategic plans are far less comprehensive. A common weakness is the premature handover by the central decision maker of the vision and mission statement to an implementation manager before specific and measurable targets are made part of the assignment. The central decision maker gives his or her vision, supports a mission statement and then pays little more attention to what is going on, moving instead to the next new issue. We will discuss the implications of this for the implementation phase later in this chapter, in reference to the responsibilities of leadership.

Assigning responsibility for the implementation phase

A major step in the planning for Step 6, scalable implementation, is the decision

Table 3.1 *Elements for an institutional strategy (CRE, 1998)*

1. *Pedagogical goals*
   Enunciated at university level
   Enunciated at faculty/programme level
   Developed in response to new initiatives
      and strategic positioning of the
      university

2. *Infrastructural requirements*
   Level of access and service
   Capital and recurrent costs
   Off-campus network access
   Reliability/robustness

3. *Evaluation, dissemination and debate*
   Monitoring practice internally
   Monitoring practice elsewhere

4. *Quality issues*

5. *Expertise for development, production distribution*
   Staff development
   Resourcing for support
   Links to similar groups outside
   Potential for strategic alliances with
      other institutions

6. *Funding developments*
   Negotiation and allocating funding to
      support technology initiatives
      (internal budgets)
   Support for drafting of funding proposals
   to external agencies

7. *Resourcing of planning*
   Resources for the development of a
   technology strategy and its implementation
   Mechanism for review and updating of plan

about responsibility for the implementation process. This will vary per institution, based on the organizational entities and practices within it. Yetton (1997) observes that there are three main organizational possibilities for this responsibility:

- the integrated approach, with a central unit managing the implementation of teaching and learning with ICT as well as other staff-development programmes;
- the parallel approach, creating an ICT-based teaching and learning unit that operates separately and in parallel with the existing staff-development unit(s);
- the distributed approach, which is bottom up and devolves responsibility for ICT-based teaching and learning developments to local innovators across a range of faculties and units.

The choice that is made here is critical for the leadership and acceptance of the initiative. The choice is often constrained by the operating procedures in the institution: existing teaching and learning support centres may not agree to be overlapped by new units and the local politics will require that they be given the leadership of the initiative, even if they are not particularly in tune with its ideas of the initiative or in contact with its pioneers. This relationship between existing support groups and special groups set up for an implementation process is delicate and often goes wrong. If the special group initiates new practices and brings in new people and perspectives different from those in the existing support groups, professional annoyance or infighting can occur.

Even if the relationship is harmonious, the transition later to the existing support groups, which must occur if sustainable institutionalization is to be reached, can be difficult.

Moving from initiation to implementation

In a recent literature review, 12 factors or change entities affecting the life-cycle process at the transition between the initiation and implementation phases were identified as most frequently mentioned (De Boer and Collis, in press; see also Chapter 8). For each of these entities, different situations or values were also found. Table 3.2 summarizes these 12 entities and their different values.

To check to see if the list of entities in Table 3.2 corresponded to actual experience, persons involved in leadership positions in implementation initiatives involving WWW-based course-management systems in 10 different universities were asked to indicate if the change entities applied to their own experiences, if important entities were missing and in which of the categories for each entity they would place their institutions. In each of these cases, there had been at least a transition from initiation to implementation, although the eventual success of the implementation could not be determined. (To read reports on the 10 institutions and their implementation experiences, see Collis and Ring, 1999.) Some of the major conclusions were:

- Most cases indicated that the university board or the dean rather than an experienced pioneer was concerned in the decision making about, and enabling of, the innovation.
- All cases already had a quality technical infrastructure in-house. Most added a technical support person to their implementation team. Educational support was less frequently represented on the implementation team.
- In only three cases was the success of the implementation seen to be related to finding a fit with the instructional practices familiar in the institution.

In addition, the change managers of the 10 institutions indicated that two other entities needed to be added to the set shown in Table 3.2: an entity relating to the commitment and involvement of the instructor, and an entity relating to the features of the WWW-based system itself (not only its origin). In their weighting of the importance of the entities to the implementation process, the two that change managers felt to be most important were the functioning of the implementation team and the reliability and quality of the technical infrastructure. Entities that were not seen as important by the managers were finding a fit with the existing practices in the institution, and eventually becoming supported by the existing support units (technical and educational) in the institution. These results are worrying, in that they signal eventual difficulties in the institutionalization of the initiative. Special project teams will only go on so long, and then, for a change to be sustainable and scalable, it must become part of the ordinary operations of the institution. There is a risk that project teams and their leaders

Table 3.2 *Change entities influencing the implementation process (De Boer and Collis, in press). Numbers based on experiences of 10 institutions*

Change Entities	Values
1. Institutional culture	Innovative culture (5) Conservative culture (2) In between (2)
2. Strategic initiation target	Flexibility for students (5) New or growing number of students (5) Effective use of resources (1) Strategic choice, to be ahead of others (4) New learning methods (3)
3. Key figures involved in initiation	University board or dean (6) Small group of innovators or pioneers (4) No particular key figure (2)
4. Budget sources	Grant or special funding (5) Own resources (4) No extra budget (1)
5. Strategy: top down or bottom up	Top down (4) Bottom up (3) Combination (3)
6. Project team characteristics	Project management background (5) Technical background (8) Educational background (6)
7. Pedagogical emphasis	Group-based learning (3) Active learning (3) Project work (1) Problem solving (2) Flexibility in learning (2) Other (2)
8. Fit of initiative with existing institutional practices	Fit (3) No fit (3) Partial fit (4)
9. Quality of hardware/network	Quality hardware and network (9) Deficiencies (1)
10. Source of technology product	Build the product oneself (4) Acquire the product from others (4) Build some, acquire some (2)
11. Embedding of technology use in institutional practices	Embedding of use (5) No embedding of use (3) Not yet but expected embedding of use (2)
12. Relationship with structural support group (as opposed to special project team)	Structural support available (2) No structural support available (8)

become too absorbed in their own functioning and futures to lead the transition to institutionalization. We discuss this more in the section on leadership.

Factors that influence implementation: the 4-E Model

There have been many studies that have focused on the implementation phase of a technical innovation in an educational context. In a recent analysis of over 200 studies in the literature (Collis and Pals, 1999), we found many different orientations and sets of guidelines for predicting and improving the likelihood of technology use in learning settings. The main questions underlying all of these studies are 'Will they use it?' and 'What happens in practice, when an individual has a choice about using a technological innovation or not?'. Our answer to these is expressed in the 4-E Model.

We have been studying this question of 'Will they use it?' for nearly a decade (Collis and De Vries, 1993; Collis, Veen and De Vries, 1994; Collis and Pals, 1999; Collis, Peters and Pals, 2000, in press; Moonen and Kommers, 1995), particularly focused on the implementation and institutionalization phases. In this chapter we will not go into the empirical validation of the model, but will apply it directly to practice. First, we will introduce the four factors, each beginning with the letter 'E' in the model, and show their relationship. Then we will apply the model to the initiation phase and the implementation phase, and in particular use the model to understand better the pioneer and his or her relationship to the implementation process in the institution. Finally, we conclude with a lesson based on the model.

The 4 Es and their relationship

The factors we have found to be most influential in an individual's likelihood of making use of a new technology product in a learning-related context are summarized in Table 3.3. The four clusters in the first column are what we call the '4 Es'. The Es also have subfactors. For example, for the 'E' Environment, we have found that the institutional-conditions subfactor is important, but there are also subfactors relating to technology push ('you can't not do it') and to social and cultural issues. The second column of Table 3.3 shows the most important subfactors for the 4 Es.

To express the relationship among the factors shown in Table 3.3, we have developed the 4-E Model. The 4-E Model hypothesizes that an individual's likelihood of using a network-related application in his or her teaching or learning (assuming a voluntary choice is involved) can be expressed in terms of four main features: (perceived) educational *Effectiveness*, *Ease of use*, (personal) *Engagement* and (institutional) *Environment* factors. According to the model, educational effectiveness, ease of use and engagement are expressed as vectors, and their vector sum can be interpreted as the likelihood-of-use vector. The variables relating to environmental factors can be expressed as a vector that determines the

Table 3.3 *Factors influencing an individual's use of a technology innovation in learning-related practice (Collis and Pals, 1999; Collis, Peters and Pals, in press)*

Cluster	Key Subfactors and Indicators
Environment: the institution's profile with respect to technology use	*Organizational-context subfactor* The vision, support and actual level of use within the institution for technology use for learning-related purposes. The readiness to change among the people in the institution when it comes to the use of technology in education.
Education effectivness: gain from the technology use	*Long-term pay-off subfactor* Likelihood of long-term tangible benefit for the institution or individual. *Short-term pay-off subfactor* Pay-off such as efficiency gains, doing routine tasks associated with learning more quickly. *Learning effectiveness subfactor* New forms of valuable learning experiences, improved communication, improved capacity to individualize aspects of the learning experience, valuable support to the existing curriculum.
Ease of use: ease or difficulty in making use of technology	*Hardware/network subfactor* The network is convenient to access, adequate in terms of speed and bandwidth, and reliable. Computer and printer access are convenient. *Software subfactor* Software associated wth the technology is user-friendly, does what the user wishes and is easy to learn.
Engagement: personal engagement about technology use for learning-related purposes	*Self-confidence subfactor* Personal orientation towards trying out new ways to carry out learning-related tasks, being interested in new technological developments and sharing these interests with others. *Pleasure with the WWW subfactor* Particular interest in new technologies, currently the WWW.

height of the 'likelihood-of-use' threshold line. Figure 3.2 shows an example of a 4-E relationship.

When the hypothetical vector sum of effectiveness, ease of use and engagement results in a vector of a high enough value to approach the likelihood-of-use threshold, then we say that the individual is likely to make use of the network application in his or her own situation. The height of the threshold is critical: environmental conditions can lower it, so that a less-strong vector sum of effectiveness, ease of use and engagement is needed to result in likelihood of use. Figure 3.2 (repeated from Figure 1.4) shows two situations where the same hypothetical vector sum of effectiveness, ease of use and engagement result in the first case in probable likelihood of use, and in the second case in non-likelihood. One way of looking at an implementation situation is to see if the threshold line

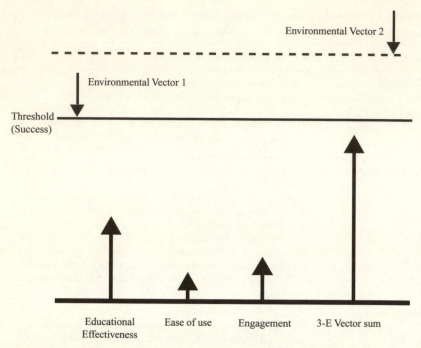

Figure 3.2 *The 4-E Model, showing how educational Effectiveness, Ease of use, personal Engagement and Environment factors are interrelated in predicting an individual's likelihood of use of a telematics application for a learning-related purpose (Collis, Peters and Pals, 2000, in press)*

could become so low that everyone is 'bumped in the head' by the innovation and makes use of it regardless of their own engagement, level of ease of use, or perception of its effectiveness. Better, however, is that there is the combination of a reasonably strong vector sum of effectiveness, ease of use and engagement, and a reasonably strong environmental vector, enough so that the vector sum and the likelihood-of-use threshold come to the same level.

We have found from our experience that in different situations certain of the Es are more dominant than others. We discuss this next, in terms of the initiation and implementation phases of the life cycle of a technology-related change process in an institution.

The 4-E Model and the initiation phase

In terms of the 4 Es, it has been our experience that the main issues at the initiation phase relate to the vectors environment and (perception of) effectiveness (De Boer and Collis, in press). For environment, the institutional subfactor plays a major role. For effectiveness, it is the (expectation of) learning effectiveness and long-term pay-off.

Institutional aspects

The key aspects of the institutional component for the initiation phase include:

- vision about technology within the institution;
- actual level of technology use in the institution;
- readiness to change in the institution;
- funding and incentives available;
- experiences in the past with technology in the institution;
- adequacy of the technical infrastructure in the institution.

Effectiveness

With regard to effectiveness, the following aspects are particularly important in the initiation phase:

Learning effectiveness
- The innovation can solve personally relevant educational problems.
- The innovation provides new forms of learning experiences.
- The innovation provides support for the existing curriculum.

Long-term pay-off
- The innovation is likely to result in eventual financial gain for the institution.

The idea of grounding an innovation in personally relevant educational problems is particularly important, and also difficult to accomplish. Much of the motivation for more-flexible learning is coming from pressures on the institution to respond to new conditions in the market, rather than from the personal motivation of individual instructors. Thus, it is important that the decision maker finds a way to link this long-range issue for the institution to a personal problem felt by individuals.

The emphasis on new forms of learning experiences is another good choice for the initiation period. Many instructors and students are content with what they now have and are sceptical of technology-related changes, either seeing them as fads (instructor's perception) or disguised attempts to provide less 'good teaching' or to save or make money at the student's expense (student's perception). Thus, articulating some positive, and likely to be valued, new form of learning experience in the initial strategic planning is a wise idea.

Finally, reassuring instructors and students that not all is changing, that valuable continuity will still pertain in terms of the core aspects of the study programmes in which they have invested time and effort is important. Not everything should change; the technology initiative should emphasize that things that are popular and work well are not the (initial) candidates for change, unless it is to extend their benefits even further. This can help to reduce much of the predictable resistance to technology-mediated learning that has been seen so often in the past.

The 4-E Model and the implementation phase

Once a change project associated with technology has been initiated, the gradual move into the implementation phase begins to occur. From our experience (De Boer and Collis, in press; Moonen and Kommers, 1995), the 4-E factors that are of most importance in the implementation phase are related to ease of use and engagement. There is a shift from abstract concerns about effectiveness to fingertip concerns about ease of use. Parallel to this is a shift from environmental conditions to personal engagement. Some guidelines relating to the 4 Es for the implementation phase include:

Ease of use
- Ensure that the instructors have up-to-date computers and good network connections.
- Arrange for network connections to be subsidized for home use, for both instructors and students.
- Choose a software environment that does not require training in order to use and does not require special client software that is unfamiliar to the user.
Engagement
- Take care that the first experiences of working with the technology 'fit' with the instructor's experience and beliefs about the learning process.
- Build the instructor's self-confidence by starting with a successful experience.

In Chapter 4 we focus on the technology requirements for the implementation phase, requirements that have these 4-E aspects as their basis. In Chapters 7 and 8, we show how we carried out the initiation and implementation phases in our own institution, using the 4 Es as a guide.

Moving from the pioneer

For every technology initiative that makes it through the initiation and implementation phases, there are many that go no further than the individual who started them. An instructor can be called a pioneer if he or she is a self-initiator of some form of technology use in courses. Another form of pioneer is the instructor who participates in a special project of some sort, supported within its framework to experiment with a new form of technology use. Such projects are typically outside of the ongoing activities and infrastructure for pedagogic technology use in the individual's own faculty or university. When the project is over, the technology use tends to stop (Alexander and McKenzie, 1998; see also Chapter 4). It is interesting to interpret the pioneer in terms of the 4 Es.

Pioneers and the 4 Es

In the case of pioneers developing a product for their own setting, we can predict that their expectation of educational gain will be high (we have found that pioneers expect positive results that non-pioneers do not expect: Collis and De Vries, 1991). Also, the fit of the product to the pioneers' own setting will be high (after all, they designed or adapted it). Most importantly, pioneers' engagement level is sufficiently high so that its strength can override the negative 'ease of use' vector that they inevitably face. Thus, they push on and perceive that success has occurred.

Pioneers are not like the majority of their colleagues (or classmates). The majority, compared to the pioneers, do not have the high personal engagement level; (possibly because of this) do not have the high expectation of educational learning effect; and do not have a reasonable fit between their preferred working situation and the technology use. They are not likely to push on despite a weak or negative ease-of-use situation. At some point, however, a shift has to occur away from the pioneer towards the mainstream.

The pioneer and the mainstream

Not only is it the case that a shift must occur away from the pioneer and to the mainstream for any application of flexible learning to occur that can benefit the institution, but it is often the case that the pioneer is excluded from new initiatives when the central decision makers decide to launch a new encouraged-change or systematic-change process. Pioneers are frequently not high on the influence ladder in an institution, and even if they are, they are perceived as more of a liability than a benefit in the scaling-up process. Their enthusiasm may be interpreted as indiscriminate by the non-pioneers, and their experience related to a level of technology fondness that is not shared by their colleagues. In general, it is not the pioneers who are involved in the scaling-up process in institutions, but instead a central group for teaching and learning is usually given the task. New stakeholders representing different university groups have to be included in the process, generally without themselves having previous experience. Thus, the process generally begins with a pilot study involving some new faculty groups, on a volunteer basis, rather than extending support to the pioneers. This discontinuity between individual experience and mainstream processes results in considerable time delays and 'rediscovery of the wheel', but appears to be a necessary component of mainstream acceptance. It can also frustrate the pioneer, whose experience is overlooked or even discredited. One of the special tasks of the leadership of an implementation project is to find the balance between all the new players in the situation and the pioneers with their extra experience.

More about the 4-E Model

Although the different Es vary in dominance in different situations, we have found that two of the subfactors shown in Table 3.3 seem to be regularly important. These are the subfactors related to institutional context and personal engagement with the technology. The latter relates to a number of variables, such as an individual's personal interest in technology and in innovations.

Some people are just more attracted to technology than others. Thus we think of these two subfactors first in planning or interpreting a usage situation. In Chapter 7 we illustrate how we focused upon them in our own implementation context. More information about the 4-E Model can be found at http://projects.edte. utwente.nl/4emodel/new/. The 4-E Model forms the conceptual framework for much of our thinking, in our work (see Chapters 7 and 8) as well as the rest of this book. We conclude here by stating the 4 Es as a lesson learnt:

Lesson 5: *Watch the 4 Es*. An individual's likelihood of voluntarily making use of a particular type of technology for a learning-related purpose is a function of the 4 Es: the environmental context, the individual's perception of educational effectiveness, ease of use, and sense of personal engagement with the technology. The environmental context and the individual's sense of personal engagement are the most important.

Follow the leader: initiation and implementation phases

There are several important groups of persons who critically influence the initiation and implementation processes for any technology-related innovation. These are:

● the decision makers in an institution who commit the institution to a direction and steer the political and financial aspects of initiating a change process;
● the implementation team, particularly its leader;
● other persons with influence in an institution, whose opinions through either formal or informal channels have a strong bearing on the climate towards the change.

The first two groups are relatively well defined, while the third varies from situation to situation. The 4-E Model can provide guidance for these leaders. The key lesson learnt about these persons from our past experiences with initiation and implementation cycles (Collis and Moonen, 1994) is:

Lesson 6: *Follow the leader*. Key persons are critical.

Decision makers

While it is obvious that decision makers are key players in the initiation phase of an innovation (Fullan, 1991, for one, discusses this at length), the initiative is critically affected by the actual engagement of the decision maker in different events of the subsequent implementation and in giving active and consistent support throughout the implementation (and into institutionalization). For example, some ways that this can occur are:

- meeting regularly with the implementation team and others involved in the change;
- attending public meetings to show interest and identification in the initiative;
- making use him- or herself of the technology being implemented by the initiative;
- making regular reference to the initiative, and a wide variety of persons associated with the initiative, during public and official occasions;
- finding a way to reward commitment to the initiative, both financially and through whatever mechanisms are available in the institution for commendation;
- being knowledgeable about the innovation, the status of the implementation and some comparable initiatives at other institutions, so that public comments are well informed;
- staying in contact and support of the initiative until it is mature enough to approach institutionalization;
- remembering (see the earlier metaphor about the traveller and the road map) the goals of the project; remembering promises that were made or implied; not forgetting about the project (remember, change takes time) with the next wave of impulses for strategic change;
- being consistent, particularly about level of funding and support; not reassigning team members midway in the project or unexpectedly reducing the amount of funding or other aspects of the working conditions of the team;
- not committing the institution or the implementation team to extra initiatives that they cannot handle or that in some way compete with the original project.

These guidelines seem to make good sense. However, many times they are not followed. Central decision makers are sometimes like politicians, responding to an opportunity ('you can't not do it'), making sure the announcement of the response is well broadcast, but bending to the comments and complaints of parties that appear to have influence. Decision makers are busy indeed, and caught up in each new wave of opportunities and circumstances. While it is not realistic to expect the decision maker to maintain extensive contact with a technology project, some regular contact is important. Some of the special ways in which key decision makers in our faculty supported the early days of our TeleTOP Project will be described in Chapter 7.

A key step for the central decision maker is who to appoint to be involved in the leadership and management of the project when it does start. A condition of the nationally funded Teaching and Learning Technology Programme (TLTP) projects in the UK (Stern, 1997) was that the projects were expected to involve main teaching departments and to have the active support of the participating institutions' senior management. Ownership by senior academics and management given the decision-making processes of higher-education institutions was seen as vital and a critical component in the legitimization of the innovation.

Despite all this, a conclusion of an evaluation of the TLTP project was that 'senior management support is still very weak, and awareness is restricted to enthusiastic individuals' (Stern, 1997). Furthermore, it was found that the institutions were still struggling with the general problems of balancing bottom-up and top-down tactics, whatever their implementation strategies, such as intervening when central steering might be desirable, for example for staff development support, reward and promotion systems, and infrastructure. Finally, the implementation of network technology was in many cases associated with the need to change the institutional culture, the need to pursue fundamental and systemic change in higher-education institutions (Stern, 1997; Van der Wende and Beerkens, 1999). The senior decision maker must follow up on this cultural and institutional change if necessary, and must intervene in the bottom-up/top-down balance when appropriate.

Implementation team

The members of the implementation team and particularly their leader are obviously also key figures. It is desirable that the team members have a blend of both technical and educational skill, not usually easy to find. In addition to didactic and technical literacy, the implementation-team leader must also have social-engineering skills.

There is another point of importance. The implementation leader should have practical and personal experience of what he or she is asking others to do, and should speak from his or her own experience and skill base. This is a serious problem with many implementation initiatives. The pioneers with personal experience are not the managers or central-support unit directors who are typically given project responsibility. The pioneer has the experience, but not the central-unit position (and probably not the managerial skills) to be the leader of the implementation team.

Staff engagement: the big challenge

A major task of the leadership during an implementation project involving technology innovations in an educational institution is staff engagement. (We prefer the term staff engagement to the more familiar term staff development in that the latter may be too narrowly translated into setting up a course or workshop, while the former also makes clear that there is an important level of commitment and buy-in involved.) In this section, we note some predictable difficulties with gaining staff engagement, indicate how the 4 Es can guide efforts aimed at the increase of this engagement and suggest a just-in-time approach.

Difficulties

Hammond and Karran in the UK identify 'lessons learnt' about staff engagement, and indicate that 'the crucial ingredient is the participation of staff at all levels in proposed development' (1998: 232). Such full-scale participation is hard to secure unless staff are sufficiently stimulated, usually by the central administration. But top-down change is notoriously difficult to carry out in university contexts, so the balance between sufficient administrative stimulation and too much for academic acceptance is a delicate one. Staff engagement, even when willingly occurring, takes time that many faculty feel to be excessive, given their research-related responsibilities (Holtham and Tiwari, 1998). Also, many academics feel strongly that the ways they have always taught are in fact the appropriate ways to teach their own discipline; change for abstract reasons such as the future of the university does not weigh heavily enough to convince them to teach in what they feel will be an 'inappropriate way' for their course and habits. Many different initiatives are occurring in traditional universities to deal with these issues involving staff engagement, most typically through centrally situated 'teaching and learning centres'. These centres, however, generally only deal with those who volunteer for their services, thus missing the hard core of resistance that is confronted when an entire faculty must change.

How to proceed? We can apply the 4 Es to look for clues as to how to enhance the engagement.

The 4 Es as a guide

Clearly, the instructor is more likely to proceed if he or she is convinced of the effectiveness and pay-off of the change. Thus, in some way, arguments about this effectiveness need to be convincingly communicated. One method is via staff-development activities. Environmental factors are also important; if the instructor perceives that a critical mass of associates is in fact moving with the innovation, then he or she is more likely to move as well. Staff-development activities can serve to provide a forum for exchange of experiences that can in turn allow this modelling to occur. With respect to personal engagement, the element of self-confidence with technology is generally a major focus of staff-development activities. It seems reasonable enough to assume that instructors need to learn a number of new skills before they will be self-confident, and an efficient way to do so is via staff-development activities.

Looking more broadly, how can the 4 Es help steer implementation strategies that aim at increased instructor engagement and participation? Some recommendations, addressed to the implementation leader, are:

Effectiveness
- With respect to educational effectiveness, find an argument for the technology-related change that is concrete and meaningful to the instructor, and set concrete targets for its realization. Set a target such as: 'Prepare for all Masters' programme courses by 2001 to be open to both students at a distance and students attending the local campus; use WWW technology so that both groups of students can be served by the same WWW course sites and participate together in class discussions and projects.' Success in terms of this kind of concrete target can be measured. Also, this kind of concrete target provides a mechanism to force progress; those students are coming in September 2001 and have to be provided for.
- With regard to institutional benefits of educational effectiveness, be explicit with staff what the perceived benefits will be to the institution, and why those benefits are important. An argument such as 'Improving our competitive position' is not good enough; 'Doubling our number of students within two years because only then will we be able to maintain our current staffing load for the Masters' programme' is better in terms of winning (reluctant) acceptance from resistant staff members.
- Also with respect to educational effectiveness, be prepared to reward participation. Reward mechanisms include: provision of extra financial support, released time, incorporation of participation in the staff evaluation procedures that relate to promotion, and other forms of pay-off such as funding for conference attendance if reporting on one's innovative work with the new technology. Interestingly, these mechanisms are well within the control of institutional administrators, but not often utilized, leaving the situation that instructors are not rewarded in terms of meaningful pay-out for their efforts.

Ease of use
- With regard to ease of use, fund adequate staffing for those who support the technical infrastructure needed for technology use: a Webmaster and a network manager as well as help-desk personnel. Invest in continual upgrades of the internal network and the WWW server.
- Also, make sure all faculty have computers on their desktops that are adequate for handling the technologies that will be used in their teaching. Install new versions of key software tools, such as plug-ins and regular updates of browsers.
- Subsidize at-home connectivity, so that instructors can prepare, give feedback and otherwise communicate with students from both office and home.

Environment
- Key figures in the institution should provide leadership not only in public recognition and funding, but also in personal engagement: they should use the technology themselves in any teaching that they might do, or at least be familiar with it so that they can handle it themselves in demonstrations.
- Choose an implementation strategy that (a) respects the instructor's concerns and current ways of teaching, and builds upon them, (b) is as easy as possible

for initial engagement and success, and (c) acknowledges the instructor's limited time (and perhaps interest) and thus is as efficient and well organized as possible.

● Appoint a strong figure to lead the implementation, someone with internal credibility who also has experience in the use of technology in teaching; provide funding for this figure to appoint his or her own team to support the implementation.

In Chapter 7 we will illustrate how we have applied these principles in our own institution.

A just-in-time approach for staff engagement

There are several typical models for staff development, as part of the broader concept of staff engagement. The most familiar is the short course or workshop, which can last from a brief hour to several consecutive sessions. Most universities have some sort of teaching and learning centre that regularly offers these sorts of brief courses for instructors. Many times the focus is directly on the technology itself rather than on the pedagogy and strategy of managing the technology in instruction. Almost always these courses are voluntary, with no particular pay-off for the instructor, other than increased knowledge.

There are many problems with short courses or workshop sessions. The sessions are voluntary, so most instructors will not have the time or incentive to come, or to come to all in a series. Sessions run for a group are difficult to tailor to the particular situation of the individual; thus the session may be partly too elementary or too complex or too technical. The instructor may feel uncomfortable if he or she is obviously clumsy with handling the technology that is the object of the session, particularly in the presence of peers or centre staff, or senior students. With initial experiences with new technology, many instructors become overly focused on handling it, and cannot at the same time also think about instructional management.

Most serious are the following two aspects. First, staff development is effective when carried out in a context meaningful to the instructor, and for the instructor in higher education, this is his or her class, with its own culture, and the instructor's own, often deep-seated, views on what is appropriate pedagogy for the discipline. Hardly anyone else will have this same context. This observation about professional development has been made for a long time (Moonen, 1989b). Secondly, what is learnt in the session often cannot be directly tried out in practice, and thus is forgotten.

What is needed is some sort of method whereby, just in time, before instructors have to work with the technology in practice, they have support for doing precisely what they are going to be doing with their own class. They practise with the technology no more and no less than what they will need for their own teaching, thus making their time expenditure as economic as possible, and maximizing the transfer from the support to their own practice.

Given all these components, one of the lessons that we have learnt over the years is the following:

Lesson 7: *Be just in time.* Staff-engagement activities to stimulate instructors to make use of technology are generally not very effective. Focus on just-in-time support for necessary tasks.

An important aspect of staff engagement is that it must be sustainable, after the impulse of the implementation project has passed. Support tools and sets of examples preferably from the instructor's colleagues, easily available via his or her computer just in time as he or she prepares for a new course or through being able to pick up the telephone and get personal help, may be better for sustainable support when the implementation project evolves into mainstream institutionalization.

From implementation to institutionalization: new leaders, new focuses

There is still one major set of problems that needs to be confronted in the happy event that an institution makes it far enough in an implementation process to move toward institutionalization. This is the business of transferring leadership from the special project to the mainstream support agencies in the institution. Many of the same difficulties that confronted the scalability of special projects or of the work of pioneers are encountered here. If the implementation leader is already a member of a mainstream support agency, then problems have been confronted earlier rather than later, but problems still can be expected. Some of the differences between the implementation project and institutionalization are given in Table 3.4.

It is not usual that the same person is responsible for both implementation and institutionalization of a technology-related innovation. They involve different skills, and different perspectives, including feelings of annoyance when those in the mainstream units are overshadowed or overlooked by project personnel during the course of the project. Conversely, the implementation team leader may be overlooked when the mainstream units take over. These are not new problems in the context of the Internet and the WWW; we analysed the different requirements for special-project leaders and mainstream leaders in 1994 and found problems such as those illustrated in Table 3.4 in many different educational-software projects (Collis and Moonen, 1994). A particular new wrinkle with WWW-based course-management systems compared to older-style educational software relates to the responsibility for network services in an institution. Usually, the WWW-based project will involve new servers and demands

Table 3.4 *From special project to institutionalization: potential problems*

Aspect	During the Initiation and/or Implementation Phase	During the Institutionalization Phase
Ownership	Position as leader established by decision maker; temporary basis of personal identification for the leader.	Must be taken over by units that might have been excluded from special project activities; the sense of ownership by these units may be limited or even rejected.
Skills and situation	To introduce, stimulate, using special resources and team	To integrate with other activities, some of which may be threatened by the new initiative.
Conditions	Special funding, special team, usually no other tasks besides the project.	Must integrate with other ongoing tasks, possibly little or no extra funding, possibly no new staff.
Focus	Being a change agent.	Maintaining a stable, smoothly running service; change is disruptive.
New developments	Innovation is welcomed.	Innovation is disruptive.

on the network, a network maintained by members of the ongoing network service in the institution. Issues such as giving passwords for access to the network are small irritants that can occur; the project personnel wish to stimulate access and use of the new WWW services, for example to new cohorts of students. But this involves new network accounts, and when this is handled by the traditional network service group, slowdowns can occur.

More important than the technology, however, are the human feelings involved. When someone who was the leader of an initiative, and very much identified with it, has to pass this leadership over, human frustrations can occur. Also, for those being served – the instructors and students – the transition can involve new ways of doing things, less immediate and personalized support, and the risk of a lapse of momentum – unless someone steps in to take a leadership interest in the initiative. Many good, innovative ideas involving technology in teaching simply fade away after time because the new leader may not feel a sense of ownership.

Summing up

The 4–E Model provides a handy way to think of four clusters of variables that have a major effect on an individual's likelihood of making use of a technology innovation in his or her learning-related setting. The 4–E Model can also be used to steer implementation strategies. Using the 4–E Model as a frame of reference, implementation success can be improved by increasing the height of any or all of the vectors representing perceived educational effectiveness, ease of use, personal engagement and environmental factors.

These comments are but one example of the application of the lessons learnt from the 4–E Model. How these lessons can help with respect to the use of technologies to support more-flexible learning will be the focus of Chapter 4. Incentives relating to the teaching and learning process will be discussed more fully in Chapter 5. We conclude this chapter with a review of the lessons introduced in the chapter.

Lesson 4: *Don't forget the road map.* Change takes a long time and is an iterative process, evolving in ways that are often not anticipated.

Lesson 5: *Watch the 4 Es.* An individual's likelihood of voluntarily making use of a particular type of technology for a learning-related purpose is a function of the 4 Es: the environmental context, the individual's perception of educational effectiveness, ease of use and sense of personal engagement with the technology. The environmental context and the individual's sense of personal engagement are the most important.

Lesson 6: *Follow the leader.* Key persons are critical.

Lesson 7: *Be just in time.* Staff-engagement activities to stimulate instructors to make use of technology are generally not very effective. Focus on just-in-time support for necessary tasks.

Chapter 4

Something for everyone

We have seen in Chapters 1 and 2 that higher-education institutions have a collective desire to change towards more flexible learning mediated by technology. But it is the instructor who must ultimately make this happen, and many instructors do not yet make use of technology. The 4-E Model (Chapter 3) helps us understand this. In this chapter we use the model to steer a direction for proceeding in terms of the technology itself. First we introduce four more lessons learnt about technology (non-)adoption, and relate these to the 4 Es. Then after discussing technology selection in general, we discuss WWW-based course-

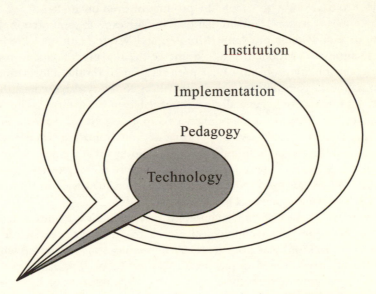

Figure 4.1   *Flexible learning in higher education – technology perspective*

management systems as the current key technology to implement flexible learning, and argue why, in terms of the 4 Es, they are more likely to succeed than other current forms of technology products. We also illustrate how an implementation perspective can be used to guide the selection of any technology product, and in particular a WWW-based system.

So much available, so little used

Ever since the presence of the microcomputer made it feasible to have a market for information-technology products for education (historically, called educational software), there has been a frustration with the fact that many good products don't get used. In this section, we offer a brief historical overview about software (non-)use, talk about the idea of niche products as products that function well in a certain local context but are not used outside of this context, and apply the 4-E Model to explain these phenomena.

Why aren't more instructors making use of technology products?

In the early 1980s, the first layer of reasons why educational software was little used in practice related directly to technology limitations (Collis and De Diana, 1990; Collis, 1996b). Software made for one brand of computer did not run on other brands. There were also other frustrating barriers, for example barriers related to awareness and distribution. It was very difficult for information about a certain product to come to the attention of potential users, and even if it did, for the user to have a way to sample the product or even obtain it.

A number of national and international initiatives were sponsored in the 1980s to try to address these problems (Moonen and Wuite-Harmsma, 1984; Plomp, Van Deursen and Moonen, 1987). Some of the initiatives focused on the platform-compatibility problem. Other projects focused on the information aspect. Clearinghouses were set up with information about available educational software. Information was generally made available in print form, although some initiatives also worked on providing access to an electronic database of reviews and descriptions. Even with information dissemination, bottlenecks still remained. If the instructor found out about a product that seemed to have potential for his or her own purposes, there was usually no way to try it out before purchase. Issues got even more complicated when the dissemination of educational software across national borders was considered.

The initial problems with technology incompatibility gradually faded with changes in the broader technological world, but then it became clear that the problems of lack of uptake of someone else's educational software went deeper than the first level related to technical incompatibility, lack of information and lack of opportunity to try software out. Even when these problems were solved, software made in one setting was generally not being used by anyone else outside that setting, and 'setting' could be as small a domain as one person's computer. The reasons were deep-seated and fundamental: there was a 'not invented here' reaction, because instructors were never quite satisfied with products made by others. The products didn't fit the instructor's preferred tone and style, or the curriculum, or the language wasn't quite appropriate for the students involved, or the use of the software just didn't fit in one way or another with the local instructional setting and climate (Collis, 1996b).

One response to this problem was to present instructors with partial products, or with authoring systems of various sorts, hoping that then he or she could make the final tailoring of the product and thus satisfy his or her objections to completed products (Barker, in press; Moonen, in press b; Moonen and Schoenmaker, 1992). Even with this turn towards authoring systems, we concluded in 1989: 'This "authoring" approach... did not bring a solution. Partly this is due to the limited scope of the didactical framework of the authoring systems offered, partly to lack of time and imagination of teachers in the creation of new materials' (Moonen, 1989a: 108).

Niche products

Time passed, but the educational-software uptake problem continued. In the 1990s several major national projects were established to create educational software for higher education, with the eventual use of it beyond those who had developed it as a major objective. Notable among these was the *Teaching and Learning Technology Programme* (TLTP) in the UK, involving hundreds of instructors working in 76 special projects between 1992 and 1996 (www.tltp.ac.uk/tltp/). The government, through the TLTP, spent £32 million on this initiative, with participating institutions spending at least as much. Despite this, most of the (predominately stand-alone) products had relatively little uptake or impact. Those few that did had *niche-based success*: finding a niche in a local setting, usually associated with the developer of the software product. The advice from the evaluation of the TLTP was that 'courseware developers should concentrate on developing materials and systems that can be used by large numbers of persons' (Draper, 1998: 119).

Similarly, in a national review of more than 100 ICT projects in higher education in Australia, Alexander and McKenzie found that that 'only a small number of the products developed in the projects were reported as being used in other institutions' (1998: 250). If a technology product did develop into sustainable and scalable use, it was most likely to be related to a common subject (for example chemistry, medical resources) and make use of a common technical platform (now, the WWW).

These experiences echo results elsewhere. Stand-alone products developed in project settings are generally not used by others and fade from use even by those in project teams after project funding ends. There are relatively few examples of successful commercial educational software products for higher education compared to all the products being created as parts of research projects, within the framework of multi-partner collaborations, or with support of in-house teaching and learning centres. Products that stay in use are typically niche products, serving a particular local situation (Collis, 1999b).

Why? The 4 Es offer a framework for analysis.

The 4 Es and technology choices

The 4 Es can suggest a number of guidelines relating to the niche problem or to other reasons for the non-use of potentially useful technology:

Effectiveness
- *Educational effectiveness*. Search for a learning-related problem that instructors in a discipline or institution agree is frustrating them in their work. Then look for a technology application or product that can be consulted or a tool that can be used, as students and instructors wish, which allows flexible demonstrations and investigations of the problem.
- *Short-term pay-off*. Relate use of a new tool or system to the institutional reward system for instructors. Use of the technology counts, and can be weighted similarly to other criteria such as writing articles and serving on committees. Stimulate instructors to present papers at conferences relating to use of technology in higher education, and thus earn publication credits for their technology experiences.

Environment
- *Fit with the institution*. Identify a technology product that fits with the culture and style of the institution.
- *Start where the instructor is comfortable*. Identify a technology product that builds on the strengths of the instructor, rather than attempts to replace or alter his or her strengths (at the start of using the product, at least).

Ease of use
- *Access and management*. Before launching any initiative involving a technology product, the change manager should try to use the product him- or herself, in a realistic context if possible (ie in a teaching situation) and see what practical issues need to be addressed and solved.

Each one of the above guidelines can have a practical realization. As one example, the guideline 'Start where the instructor is comfortable' could be translated as:

For an instructor who enjoys lecturing, offer tools that can be used to make the lecture more convenient (for example, having handouts and supplementary notes in a WWW site rather than being photocopied and distributed during the lecture) or even more effective (for example, having links to demonstration materials or audio-visual resources available through a

WWW site, easy for students to find and use during the lecture and available for them to review after the lecture, and even for them to follow up on with reflections or additional examples). Don't start by advocating that the instructor begin technology use by replacing his or her lectures with tutorial-type educational software.

Thus, there is a way for the persons making decisions about technology choice to move from the institutional vision and general decision about technology (hopefully expressed in measurable terms: see Lesson 1) to the identification of the type of technology product that is likely to have uptake acceptance among staff and students. This way involves considering implementation from the first. The 4 Es help steer the analysis process. We conclude this analysis with a summary of the lesson learnt:

Lesson 8: *Get out of the niche.* Most technology products are not used in practice beyond their developers. Keep implementation and the 4 Es central in choosing any technology product.

How can this lesson be put into practice? In addition to the 4 Es, there are classic approaches to technology choice at which it is also appropriate to look.

Technology selection, theories and research

There is a long history of interest and research in the topic of technology (media) selection for learning (Bates, 1984; Clark, 1983; Collis, 1996d; Pohjonen, 1994; Reisner and Gagné, 1982; Romiszowski, 1993; Sorenson, 1991). This research has traditionally been oriented around media-based technologies such as books, videotapes, non-WWW computer software (usually stored on CD ROMs or floppy disks), and a large variety of types of printed materials. In many higher-education settings in the USA, Japan, Brazil, Mexico and China among other countries, there is also the use of television or compressed-video broadcasts, with or without direct interactivity opportunities. Interaction and communication can take place via telephone, fax, e-mail, or via local discussion groups led by a local tutor. In this chapter we briefly look at main messages from this technology-selection research in order to see how they can apply to the current context of technology-supported flexible learning in higher education. We introduce the ideas of core and complementary technology as a guide for the selection process.

Technology selection: from the research

Technology choice in the research literature has been typically seen as (a) a selection based on logical analysis from an overall palette of technology choices, or (b) a selection based on explicit empirical comparisons between specific technology alternatives, or (c) both. When flexibility in terms of distance is the focus, there have been many studies relating to technology choice. Print has been and remains the core medium for distance flexibility (with print replacing most or all face-to-face contact with the instructor or other learners) but many other types of technologies have been also studied. A general result has been that the more modern or complex the technology, the more the potential advantages but also the more the implementation complexities, particularly costs. Also, (assuming the technology is feasible to use) it is not the technology itself, but how it is used that determines the outcome.

Which is better, X or Y?

While researchers such as Bates (1995) attempt to survey the overall range of possibilities for technology selection in distance learning, there are many studies that look more specifically at one technology compared to another, to answer the (apparently) straightforward question: is it better to deliver this course using technology X or technology Y? While such a question seems reasonable to ask, particularly for institutional decision makers (see Chapter 2), such comparison studies are always limited in how much of a direct answer they can provide.

There are serious methodological problems in such research, primarily because of interrelating and confounding variables (see Chapter 6). The overall reason is that there are too many local, contextual variables, and in particular 'effective learning from technology still depends on how teachers characterize and use them for instruction' (Saga, 1993: 158). A researcher called Russell maintains a database related to what he calls *the no significant difference phenomenon* (see http://nova.teleeducation.nb.ca/nosignificantdifference/). In this database there is information about more than 350 studies relating to technology in distance education or to a comparison of education with network technology compared to classroom teaching with or without technology. The main trend that he has identified is that there is no significant difference (usually in terms of learning outcomes in the course) in many of these comparisons (Russell, 2000). The site 'Distance Learning' (http://distancelearn.about.com/education/distancelearn/mbody.htm) offers links to a wide variety of studies and sites, including Russell's, related to this type of research.

Decision making about technology selection thus cannot turn to a literature base of studies that will give a definitive answer. And yet decisions about technology are still being made every day, for every course. How does this occur, if not based on guidelines from research?

Core and complementary technology

The answer that we see most often in practice with respect to technology selection relates to the idea of *core* and *complementary technologies* (Heeren, Verwijs and Moonen, 1998; Verwijs, 1998). By core technologies, we mean the major artefacts around which the course is planned and carried out: if these technologies are not available, there would be a serious problem for going forward with the course. In traditional campus-based higher education (Quadrant I in the Flexibility-Activity Framework, Figure 1.3 in Chapter 1), the core technologies are often the textbook and the lecture. Sometimes the core technology is the textbook alone (Quadrant III, with respect to traditional distance education). In television-type distance education, the core technology is the one- or two-way video-conferencing equipment. In a chemistry course the core technologies may be the textbook and the laboratory.

All the other technologies used in a course (handouts, videotapes, WWW sites, PowerPoint presentations, etc) can be seen as complementary to this core technology or technologies (usually there are not more than two). Perhaps the complementary technologies extend or enrich the core technologies in some way. Perhaps they compensate for something that is not well handled in the core technology. But generally they are expendable: if the video the instructor has chosen to demonstrate a certain concept during the lecture doesn't work, he or she can just explain to the group what they have missed, and at most remove a test question based on the video from the final examination.

It is generally the case that the core technology for a course is largely predetermined for the instructor, mostly by the tradition in the institution and the culture or expectation that students, peers and the institution in general have for course delivery (Heeren, Verwijs and Moonen, 1998). The institution will be organized around this core technology. Lecture halls and times for lectures will be standard information about a course in a setting where the lecture is expected to be a core technology. Instructors gain experience with the core technology; students and instructors alike think of the course in terms of the core technology as providing the basic structure or reference point. Other technologies are add-ons, complements, or compensations.

In our observations, decisions about core technologies occur slowly, and when they do they often involve a culture change as well as institutional change. They happen when there is enough push in the broader context of the institution to make the time right for the change of the core technology. The change requires institutional commitment, often in the context of the 'you can't not do it' feelings (Lesson 3). For many institutions now, the shift to a WWW-based course-management system is such a change in core technology.

Where instructors do have more personal choice is with complementary technologies. A decision approach towards technology based on both an acknowledgement of the core technology expected in the culture of the institution and a rational analysis of how this core technology can be extended or complemented or compensated for is, we believe, a more realistic recommendation for technology selection than the theoretical models found in instructional design textbooks (for example, see Sorensen, 1991, for a collection) and never used in practice (Heeren, Verwijs and Moonen, 1998). These observations are summarized in the following lesson:

Lesson 9: *After the core, choose more.* Technology selection involves a core and complementary technologies. The core is usually determined by history and circumstances; changing it usually requires pervasive contextual pressure. The individual instructor can make choices about complementary technologies and should choose them with flexibility in mind.

The 'you can't not do it' stimulus associated with WWW technology and more-flexible learning that we discussed in Chapter 2 is such a pervasive contextual pressure.

A caution: watch out for too much

Because a system can support a large amount of features does not necessarily mean that all those features should be used, particularly by instructors new to the system. There can be an urge to have more and more available on a CD ROM, for example, or in a WWW site, because it is so easy to link and add more resources. Multimedia allows audio, video, animations, so why not add them? Communication possibilities are easy, so more communication can occur. But... so can overload.

One aspect of overload is that of cognitive load. Clark (1999) is one of many researchers who urge caution with respect to avoiding extremes of cognitive load in learning, either too little, which leads to overconfidence and insufficient mental effort, or too much, which leads to frustration and lack of persistence in the learning task. These recommendations parallel those of Heeren when she talks about media richness and task complexity (1996). By richness she means the increased density of features (for example, more interactivity) or the idea that video is richer than audio, which in turn is richer in stimuli than text. In her research she found that a simple technology is enough for a simple task while for a complex task, a richer environment is often better. However, there is also evidence that for better learning results, a simpler environment can force the learner to a higher *amount of invested mental effort* (Salomon, 1984). Thus, with technology, more is not necessarily better (Moonen, 1994).

These considerations lead to another lesson:

Lesson 10: *Don't overload.* More is not necessarily better.

The idea of core and complementary technology ideas in these lessons can also apply to the Flexibility–Activity Framework (Chapters 1 and 5). We discuss this in the next section.

Technology choice: a new approach

The Flexibility–Activity Framework combined with ideas about core and complementary technologies gives us a systematic way to approach and predict technology choice that differs from the traditional technology-choice models in a number of ways. In this section we illustrate the approach and also comment about trends in technology that will provide the candidates for core and complementary technologies in the future.

Relating core and complementary technologies to the Flexibility–Activity Framework

Table 4.1 shows the Flexibility–Activity Framework with comments made about the most typical core and complementary technologies for each of the quadrants. We summarize the current situation and also predict the now-emerging future.

Core and complementary technologies: future trends

Our predictions about the future in Table 4.1 are based on current trends (Collis, 1999b, 1999e; Collis and Van der Wende, 1999) and our reviews of trends and future directions (Collis, in press b; Collis and Gommer, 2000). These trends can be broken down into categories relating to networks and access, products and tools, and convergence.

Networks and access

Many trends can be identified in the technology of learning environments. Network developments such as ADSL and Internet2 will make access to the Internet much faster and give more possibilities for its use, for example for more use of video on demand and multicasting in education. Where video-related applications have been often avoided because of low speed or quality, in the near future this will no longer be a problem for a wide audience. Also, new access possibilities via TVs will simplify access.

Another major development (that is also related to developments in Internet connectivity) is *wireless* or mobile computing. Wireless Internet connections, handhelds and Internet telephones are getting more and more popular and the first experiments on using this technology in traditional education institutions have already started.

Table 4.1 *Flexibility–Activity Framework showing typical core and complementary technologies, now and in the future*

Flexibility	Acquisition Model	Contribution Model
More flexible	***Quadrant III*** *Current:* Core (traditional distance education): print, or print and television (one- or two-way) Complementary: e-mail, computer conferencing, WWW sites, face-to-face sessions *Future:* Core: WWW-based systems including information, communication, dissemination, collaboration and learning-specific resources (applets, small tutorial segments, quizzes, etc), integrated with enterprise-wide information systems Complementary: print, real-time sessions (in the same room, or distributed)	***Quadrant IV*** *Current:* Core: WWW-based systems including information, communication, dissemination and collaboration tools Complementary: other WWW-based tools and resources (search engines, streaming video players, etc), print face-to-face sessions *Future:* Core: WWW-based systems including information, communication, dissemination, collaboration and learning-specific resources (applets, small tutorial segments, quizzes, etc), integrated with enterprise-wide information systems Complementary: print
Less flexible	***Quadrant I*** *Current:* Core: book and lectures Complementary: e-mail, application software (word processing), videotapes, handouts, WWW browser and search tools, WWW sites, sometimes a local niche sofware product *Future:* Core: book and contact sessions Complementary: same as Current	***Quadrant II*** *Current:* Core: field experiences Complementary: face-to-face seminars and discussions, reporting forms (log book, etc) *Future:* Core: field experiences Complementary: e-mail, WWW site for reporting, resources, communication and collaboration, face-to-face seminars and discussions

Products and tools

Laptops are becoming increasingly lightweight and increasingly powerful. Handheld devices are also a new type of interface. Thus, mobility is increasing. E-books are becoming available and some educational institutions have made contracts with publishers in order to make electronic access to journals and databases available for all of their students. Also, educational materials are increasingly being offered in digital form: via a WWW site, on DVD, etc. Students no longer have to carry around physical stacks of books. One problem that is emerging is how to store and reuse these digital educational materials. Standards and metadata are major topics of discussion as competing consortia strive to capture the market. An educational variant of XML is being developed to address this reuse problem.

Pervasive (or ubiquitous) computing is possibly the next breakthrough technology area (as was WWW technology in the early 1990s). By these terms are meant environments where people interact with various portable, wearable, or invisible computers. New forms of collaboration and eclectic networking are being studied.

Convergence

A major current characteristic of information and communication technologies is convergence. One aspect of convergence is the fact that digital data involving a variety of signal types, such as text, audio and video, are now handled within the same application. Technically, the convergence of mass-media communication technologies (radio and television) with telephone technologies and data-network technologies is well under way. In Table 1.3 of Chapter 1 we saw another major aspect of convergence: that of the convergence of different sorts of computer use in the same (WWW-based) environment. Another convergence is that of learning resources. The increased use of the WWW does not necessarily mean that books will disappear but rather that the book will be extended via its associated WWW site. This will occur through the addition of examples, of links to contact key persons and of links to the instructor's own resources via a course WWW environment. The textbook will be soon no longer the core medium for a course, which will be the course WWW environment. The convergence of real-time communication and video on demand is another technical convergence of high significance to education. Students and instructors can capture moments of valuable communication as they occur and make these available for expansion and reuse as asynchronous video via an integrated WWW environment.

Predictions based on the 4 Es

Given these technology trends, why have we made the predictions that we have in Table 4.1 with respect to future core and complementary technologies? In our opinion, WWW-based course-management systems, integrating information handling, communication, and collaboration tools, with learning-specific resources and tools and authoring capabilities are the core technology of the future, when more-flexible learning is the target. Such systems, when well designed, can fit with different teaching situations and approaches; can support new types of assignments and activities that would not be feasible or as likely to be carried out in practice without them; can make use of a variety of tools and resources easy in that they are integrated in one system via one interface; and when adopted by an institution in a way that includes recognition of the importance of implementation and pedagogy, can be associated with a strong environmental component.

If WWW-based course-management systems are the emerging core technology for flexible and participative learning, what do we know about their current manifestations?

WWW-based course-management systems

In this section, we define WWW-based course-management systems and show some of their possible features. We also relate these features to the background orientation of the systems and to their eventual fit for flexible learning in an institution. The 4 Es again form a guide.

What is a WWW-based course-management system?

A WWW-based course-management system is a comprehensive software package that supports some or all aspects of course preparation, delivery and interaction and allows these aspects to be accessible via a network. Such systems in broad terms offer tools for computer-mediated communication; tools for navigation within course content and around the various features and tools available for learning support; tools for course management, most generally for keeping track of students and their records and to manage security and access; tools for assessment of learning; and authoring tools (Robson, 1999). All of these tools, at least for student use, are made available via a uniform WWW-based user interface. The 'back-office' aspects of the system now most commonly involve a combination of a database, database technology, an HTTP server (the type of computer software that allows a computer to perform as a WWW server) and some variety of integrated tools and templates. The templates, when used with database-driven systems, allow the user to upload or enter information into the system via form-like entries, and then view what is in the database.

The term 'WWW-based course-management system' is not yet fixed: many different terms are also used, some of these metaphoric, such as 'course in a box' or 'virtual university', some slightly more informative, such as 'learning environment' or 'course support systems' (Robson, 1999). Barron and Rickelman (in press) make a distinction between course-management systems and learning-management systems by saying that the former deal only with courses while the latter involve the integration of the course-management system with other information systems in the institution, so that the learner has 'one-stop shopping' for all his or her learning- and communication-related needs. Landon (2000), who maintains a popular WWW site with information about more than 60 commercially available systems, calls them 'online educational delivery applications'. Just as the name is not yet fixed, neither are the possible components and different combinations of features. These different combinations reflect the backgrounds from which a particular system has emerged. Landon compares available systems on the basis of the components shown in Table 4.2.

Table 4.2 *Features for WWW-based course-management systems (from Landon, 2000, http://www.c2t2.ca/landline/option2.html)*

Learner Tools	Support Tools
Web browsing:	*Course tools:*
accessibility	course planning
bookmarks	course managing
multimedia	course customizing
Asynchronous sharing:	*Lesson tools:*
e-mail	instructional designing
BBS file exchange	presenting information
newsgroups	testing
Synchronous sharing:	data
chat	marking online
voice chat	managing records
whiteboard	analysing and tracking
application sharing	*Resource tools:*
virtual space	curriculum managing
group browsing	building knowledge
tele-conferencing	team building
video-conferencing	building motivation
Student tools:	*Administration tools:*
self-assessing	installation
progress tracking	authorization
searching	registering
motivation building	online fees handling
study-skill building	server security
	resource monitoring
	remote access
	crash recovery
	Help desk tools:
	student support
	instructor support

Backgrounds and features of the systems

Table 4.2 shows not only the large variety of resources that can be found in WWW-based course-management systems, in various combinations, but also suggests the different backgrounds from which those resources have come:

- *Information systems background*
  Systems that emphasize resource management (access, handling and dissemination) come from a mixture of information systems and database management, where the emphasis is on efficient location and labelling of information, and desktop publishing, where the emphasis is on effective and efficient layout and content presentation. There is some experience of these sorts of systems in education. To access resources in libraries, users have long made use of database systems, although almost never have they had the opportunity to enter their own selections into such systems. Educational databases on CD ROMs and distributed over networks also have a long history although not much broadscale use, with the exception of encyclopaedia- and atlas-type collections on CD ROM comprising a major resource for both formal and informal learning. Coming from another direction is the use of word processing and presentation software for personal expression. In WWW-based course-management systems it is revolutionary that users can both access powerful and extensive libraries of information, form their own interface for a personally collected and organized set of information (via bookmark tools and forms), and contribute their own resources seamlessly to their own collections as well as to public distribution. WWW-based systems that emphasize information handling, management and dissemination range from portal-like collections of external links to systems emphasizing user uploading of various types of files into the system.
- *Communication background*
  Communication tools and systems are well established in all manner of institutions, including education, and also for individual use. WWW-based course-management systems that emphasize communication place particular emphasis on message organization and handling, threading and sorting of messages and tools for both asynchronous and real-time communication. Such systems may be more of the nature of managed and password-controlled mail systems, but the dominant metaphor is that of community forming and social interaction.
- *Collaboration background*
  Collaboration or groupware tools allow a group of participants to have common access to shared information, usually in the form of files organized in nested directories, to add files to those common directories, to edit or revise common resources and to communicate while doing these activities or before or after. Important to collaboration tools are tools to help remind group members of tasks and roles and agreements. With real-time collaboration, tools for taking turns and taking control are also important. Security is an issue; members of the group have access while others may not, or may only have access to certain elements of the shared resources. WWW-based systems emphasizing collaboration and groupware place priority on the support of the group, on the ease of uploading, downloading, editing different versions of documents and managing the 'group memory'.

● *Educational authoring-systems background*

The fourth category has evolved from the long experience in the field of computer-based learning and authoring systems (Barker, in press). Instructional-design paradigms starting with content and learner analysis and moving through content sequencing and chunking, through interactivity in terms of questions or learning activities and answers and feedback, are all reflected. Computer-based test systems, and types of learning tools such as simulations, tutorials, workbenches for educational purposes, can all be included in this background. Following the line from authoring systems, tools for the instructor or system manager to maintain data on student performance, to manage the sequence and nature of student activity, and to scaffold and support student learning in various ways can be present. Systems that emphasize this line of development require professional and lengthy pre-development of content and interactivity planning (questions, answer-evaluation, feedback, branching, etc).

Regardless of the background emphasized in the system, WWW-based course-management systems make tools available for the users and provide an environment for them to use in an integrated way. The background orientation and the design of the system make a difference in its flexibility for its users. Systems based on the authoring background and assuming a pre-structured learning approach will suffer the same constraints in terms of lack of flexibility as confronted and daunted users of the previous generation of authoring systems. Such systems also tend to put the focus of the course on pre-prepared learning content, more appropriate for an acquisition approach than an approach emphasizing communication or student contributions. Systems oriented about an information-management approach will be less likely to stimulate student contribution to the underlying system database than ones oriented around a groupware approach.

According to the 4 Es the need for personal engagement and a personal conviction about the effectiveness of a technology product are essential. A WWW-based course-management system in itself is not enough to be a prime candidate for uptake unless it allows the user to choose what he or she wants to use, and how, and why. Systems that constrain the user to a preset educational paradigm or force one of the background orientations on the user (information management, communication, collaboration, or lesson-material authoring) even if the user does not wish it, will not be flexible enough to meet the requirement of 'Fit with the user's situation'. A well-designed WWW-based course-management system needs to offer this choice and flexibility. For this reason, we offer the following lesson:

Lesson 11: *Offer something for everyone.* A well-designed WWW-based system should offer users a large variety of possibilities for flexible and participative learning not dominated by any one background orientation. If so, it is the most appropriate (core or complementary) technology for flexible learning.

There is a major 'if' in the previous paragraph. Not every system offers the same flexibility. In the following section, we look more specifically at criteria for evaluating and choosing a WWW-based course-management system in terms of eventual implementation and the 4 Es.

Choosing a WWW system

The question of how to choose a particular course-management system is of considerable interest and thus many sets of evaluation criteria and checklists are being developed (Collis, 1999c; Hazari, 1998). The majority of these evaluation schemes involve a long list of possible functionalities, against which checks can indicate if the functionality is present in a system or not (see Landon, 2000, and Van der Veen and De Boer, 1999). But knowing if a sort of tool is present or not is not the same thing as making a decision about what to acquire.

Key questions

What are key questions for choosing such a decision? For us, it is not so much knowing how many possibilities are available through a system, but instead being able to make a choice based on the answers to a few key questions. In Chapter 7 we give the specific key questions we asked for our own institution. In general, we believe these key questions should relate to the 4 Es:

1. How much will use of the system cost at initiation, implementation and institutionalization phases, and is this cost acceptable? (Environment – organizational).
2. Is there a social and political climate in the institution to justify investment in such a system? Is there a key person, with influence in the institution, committed to the system (or to using a system at all)? (Environment – organizational).
3. What will be the general emphasis for the system (information management, communication, collaboration, authored lesson materials)? The extent to which the background orientation of the system fits the culture of the institution will determine 'fit' with the environment. (Environment – organizational; engagement; educational effectiveness – learning).
4. Is the system flexible enough to anticipate local adaptation and new developments with WWW technologies? (Environment – technologies).
5. Is the learning curve for use such that beginning users (instructors and those responsible for the system) can move quickly into a first level of usage and experience? Is the starting-point easy and intuitive for the instructor? (Ease of use; engagement).

If the above considerations cannot be confidently answered 'yes', it is likely that only a few persons will invest considerable time for one or two years in the system and, while several but not all instructors will make use of it, no sustainable and institutionalized use will develop. There will not be enough impact on the institution to notice the difference. Within a few years, a new search for a new system will begin.

Key possibilities

Another approach, complementary to the key-question approach, is to focus on certain strategic goals for the use of the system, and then see what sorts of activities and thus system functionalities relate to those goals. For example, for goals associated with the third and fourth quadrants of the Flexibility–Activity Framework (Quadrant III: more flexible, and Quadrant IV: more flexible plus more contribution-oriented), an analysis can be made of what sorts of activities and system supported can be relevant. Table 4.3 shows an example of the results of such an analysis.

Table 4.3 *Increasing the flexibility and contribution-oriented aspects of a course: some examples involving WWW support (Collis, 1998b)*

Component	To Increase Flexibility: (Quadrant III of the Flexibility Activity Framework)	To Increase Flexibility and Support a Contribution-oriented Pedagogy (Quadrant IV)
1. General course organization	– Post all announcements about course procedures on a course WWW site. – Make a calendar available on the WWW site via which relevant dates and times hightlighted.	– Have students add links to resources related to the course, and to the work and homepages of experts related to the course.
2. Lectures/ contact sessions	– Have fewer traditional lectures and introduce new forms of contact sessions whose results can be studied by those who were not participating in it directly. Extend the lectures and contact sessions so that: (a) the most relevant points are expressed in notes available via the WWW site; (b) particularly important comments by the instructor are captured as digital audio and/or video and linked to the course WWW site for later study; (c) students who were not at the session can review the instructor's notes, listen to or see the instructor explaining particular points (via streamlining audio and video synchronized to the text	– Extend the lecture in terms of participation by having the students who are present at the same time (not necessarily at the same place) interact with one another in a way that engages them in discussing the lecture material and articulating their ideas in a summary. Segments of the instructor's lecture can be chosen, and expanded upon. These new materials are immediately posted on the course site. – Extend the lecture after the contact time by having all students reflect on some aspect and communicate via some form of structured comment via the WWW page; or students can add to the lecture materials themselves, or take responsibility for some of the lecture resources. – The instructor uses the students' input as a basis for the next session or activity. – Capture student debates and

	notes) and can review the materials created and posted by the students who were present.	discussions, make available as video-on-demand and use as a basis for asynchronous reflection and further discussion.
3. Self-study and exercises; practical sessions	– See the above; exercises and guided self-study are now integrated with the contact sessions; all can be engaged in from wherever the instructor and student have network connections. – For some sorts of practical or laboratory sessions, provide students with licensed versions of the software used in the sessions for their own use at home or work. – For activities not possible to handle away from the campus, use some time during the common periods when all students do come together for these.	– Facilitate students using one another's submissions as learning resources once these are available as part of the WWW environment. – Structure communications and interaction via the WWW site so that students are guided as how to respond productively to one another's work and questions. – Address personal questions via e-mail and other methods of capturing communication; guide students to take responsibility for answering one another's questions (with monitoring by the instructor).
4. Multi-session projects or activities	– Make available shared workspace tools along with other communiction and reporting tools in the WWW site to allow group members to work collaboratively on projects without needing to be physically together. – Use real-time communication tools via the Internet for students in different locations who wish to meet and discuss. – Stimulate reporting of ongoing planning, work in progress, etc to increase the feedback and effectiveness of project work.	– Make shared workspace tools along with other communication and reporting tools available in the WWW site to allow group members to work collaboratively on complex projects without needing to be physically together. – Use real-time communication tools via the Internet for students in different locations who wish to meet and discuss. – Guide students to provide constructive ongoing feedback to one another, through the use of structured communictaion forms and by having their partial products accessible via the course WWW site.
5. Testing	– Present test items at a certain time, under secure conditions, so that students can write a test if not in the physical testing location. – Provide feedback in a quick and targeted manner, without the student needing to wait to see the instructor face to face. – Post feedback on the WWW about aspects on the test where difficulties were encountered. – Send feedback to different groups of students, based on their needs as shown by the test.	– Integrate new forms of assessment, such as all students maintaining their own portfolios, with the course WWW environment.

6. General communica- tion	– Add a communication centre to the course WWW site so that groups of students, or individuals, can be easily contacted via e-mail Use real-time collaborative. – tools so that students can see and hear the instructor or other students during a fixed time appointment, but without being face to face.	– Add a WWW board for discussion about course topics as a major activity in the course; have students take responsibility for moderating the discussions, adding links to external resources to justify their comments when appropriate. – Involves experts from outside the course in the discussions.

With such goals, requirements for the choice of a WWW-based course-management system should be based on the extent to which the system can support these kinds of flexibilities and activities.

Summing up

In this chapter we have focused on the technology for flexible and contribution-oriented learning. We considered various ways to make a technology choice, and identified the idea of core and complementary technologies as representative of how technology decisions are being made in educational institutions. We related core and complementary technologies to our Flexibility–Activity Framework and came to the conclusion that a (well-designed) WWW-based course-management system is a major candidate for both core and complementary technology choice in the near future. But we also developed a number of lessons, all of which will be important when we focus on pedagogy in the next chapter.

In review, the lessons of this chapter are:

Lesson 8: *Get out of the niche*. Most technology products are not used in practice beyond their developers. Keep implementation and the 4 Es central in choosing any technology product.

Lesson 9: *After the core, choose more*. Technology selection involves a core and complementary technologies. The core is usually determined by history and circumstances; changing it usually requires pervasive contextual pressure. The individual instructor can make choices about complementary technologies and should choose them with flexibility in mind.

Lesson 10: *Don't overload*. More is not necessarily better.

Lesson 11: *Offer something for everyone*. A well-designed WWW-based system should offer users a large variety of possibilities for flexible and participative learning not dominated by any one background orientation. If so, it is the most appropriate (core or complementary) technology for flexible learning.

Chapter 5

Pedagogy: making the U turn

In Chapter 1 we characterized pedagogy around two dimensions: a dimension relating to flexibility and a dimension relating to an educational model about learning activities. We identified two basic types of activities: those relating to acquisition of content and those relating to contribution to a learning community. Using the *Flexibility–Activity Framework* (Figure 1.3) four different combinations of flexibility and activity were shown. In this chapter, we focus more

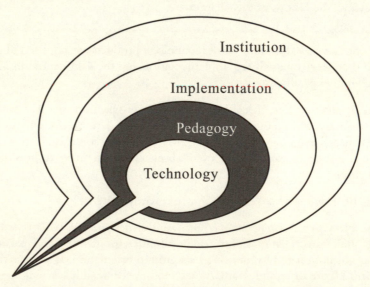

Figure 5.1   *Flexible learning in higher education – pedagogy applications*

specifically on the combinations of the framework that involve more flexibility and relate them to the instructor's pedagogical decisions based on a new definition of an *active student*: one of co-contributor to the course study resources and co-member of the course as a learning community. We will introduce the *U Approach* as a pedagogical model for flexible learning and illustrate ways to realize it in different practical settings. The key to the U Approach is a focus on learner activities supported by a properly designed WWW-based system. Furthermore we will illustrate a range of activities and tools for the U Approach. Finally, we discuss the implications for the instructor and for the instructional designer of this new approach.

What are the keys aspects of our pedagogical model?

In Chapter 1 we introduced the conceptual framework that we use for pedagogical decisions: one based on more flexibility but also a mix of acquisition and contribution-type activities. We put our stress on the activities of the learner, not the content in the sense of pre-prepared learning materials. While the idea of the learner being active is certainly not new, the idea of the learner as an active contributor to the learning experiences and resources of both him- or herself and others gets a stronger emphasis in our pedagogical model than is often the case. The choice of a theoretical basis for our pedagogical model is made around two key principles that we believe are central to our focus of flexible learning in today's participation-oriented society. These two key principles are: 1) learning situations should be designed for flexibility and adaptability (Chapter 1); and 2) learning situations should involve not only acquisition of skills and concepts but also opportunities to participate in and contribute to a learning community (Chapter 1, Lesson 2).

These principles are similar to those expressed by Jonassen, Peck and Wilson (1999) who assert that the primary goal of education at all levels should be to engage students in meaningful learning – which they define as active, constructive, intentional, authentic and co-operative. Interaction with learning materials and with others is also important to Laurillard's interaction-oriented approach (Laurillard, 1993). However, in both these approaches, it is possible that all the activities and interactions that take place are based on predetermined and pre-structured learning materials. In our approach to pedagogy, pre-structured learning materials are not the main focus. Instead, the activities themselves are central in our pedagogical vision, combined with an appropriate WWW-based system. Our model is an approach whereby students can contribute to the learning material based upon their own experiences, experiences from others, material available in the WWW-based system, in reality or in the literature. This approach is similar to the participation aspects of Sfard's two metaphors for learning (Chapter 1); Kearsley and Shneiderman's (1998) *Engagement Theory*; and *Action Learning* (Dopper and Dijkman, 1997; Simons, 1999). Table 5.1 contrasts these approaches with the key ideas of our pedagogical model.

Table 5.1 *Learning characteristics relating to active students*

'Participation-oriented' (Sfard, 1998: see Table 1.5, Chapter 1	'Action Learning' (Dopper and Dijkman, 1997; Simons, 1999)	'Engagement Theory' (Kearsley and Shneiderman, 1998)	'The Contributing Student' (this Chapter)
Key definition of learning: Learning as participation, the process of becoming a member of a community, 'the ability to communicate in the language of this community and act according to its norms' (p 6); 'the permanence of *having* gives way to the constant flux of *doing*' (p 6). *Key words:* Apprenticeship, situatedness, contextuality, communication, social constructivism, co-operative learning, belonging, participating, communicating. *Stress on:* 'The evolving bonds between the individual and others' (p 6); 'the whole and the parts affect and inform each other'. (p 6). *Role of the instructor:* Facilitator, mentor, expert participant.	*Key characteristics:* (a) Practical problems are central; learning is based on working on problems from one's own work situation. (b) When there are contacts among learners, these are focused on stimulating self-reflection and learning from others. (c) Instead of 'lectures' learners use contact time for activities. *Role of the instructor:* Leader, motivator and guide of the learning processes, giving feedback on evolving phases of the problem-oriented project, and evaluator of the final submission. Must ensure that learner contact is more than the sharing of experiences but also that experiences are related to theory. *Stress on:* Learning to learn, to collaborate to self-regulate.	*Key idea:* 'Students must be meaningfully engaged in learning activities through interaction with others and worthwhile tasks' (p 20). *Key characteristics:* Learning activities that (a) 'occur in a group context (ie collaborative teams) (b) are project-based, and (c) have an outside (authentic) focus' (ie are meaningful to someone outside the classroom). *Role of the instructor:* Supporting and screening the initial definition of projects and formulation of teams, provision of criteria to evaluate projects. *Role of technology:* 'To facilitate all aspects of the engagement' (p 23).	*Key ideas:* Learners contribute to the learning materials via contributions available to others in a WWW-based system. The others may be in the same group at diffferent group. *Key characteristics:* (a) The WWW site is largely empty at the start of the learning experience; the learners and the instructor will fill it via the process of many activities during the course. (b) Learners learn from realistic materials as well as peer-created materials as much or more than from professionally developed materials. (c) Learning materials contributed by students are reused in other learning settings. *Role of the instructor:* Designer of activities and of feedback and monitoring strategies for activities. *Role of technology:* To facilitate all aspects of the activities.

Our 'Contributing Student' conception differs from the others shown in Table 5.1 in that it is more flexible. It can be used also with acquisition-type learning (where the stress becomes activities such as contribution to a collection of model answers, of frequently asked questions, a databank of test items, etc), and thus can relate to both Sfard's Acquisition and Participation modes. It does not assume a particular activity approach, such as the projects for external audiences in Engagement Theory, as that may not be feasible in various learning contexts. Also, it does not assume learners can base their learning on their own work experiences as is at the base of Action Learning; again this depends on the nature of the course and the learner. It is a pedagogical basis that we have found to be applicable to students of many types and in many types of courses (see Chapters 7 and 8) and that provides optimal flexibility. And it provides a direct tool to operationalize the pedagogical model that we call the U Approach. A key idea in the U Approach is that of organizing learning activities around some number of three-step learning cycles.

Cycles of learning activities

We still see the organization of learning activities within the context of a 'course'. How do we organize a course in order to optimize our pedagogical model as well as flexibility for its users?

Three cycles of activities

To steer the course (re)design process, we need more than a conceptual model of learning. We need a general strategy that instructors can easily operationalize. This strategy that we use begins with the idea of thinking of a course as a series of cycles of *before, during and after* activities. The 'during' part of the cycle is some sort of focal activity, such as a lecture, a group meeting, or other form of contact. The focal event does not have to be face to face, although that is a familiar model for both educational institutions and company training. It is something that is prepared for. When participants happen to be at the same location, there is some special interaction between them, and this is something that is followed up. If participants are not at the same location, contacts can be made using technological means, such as audio- or video-conferencing. If participants are not available at the same time, asynchronous contacts focusing on the activities of the focal event can be organized. In terms of pedagogy, we do not make a distinction between a student physically attending a course on campus, a student only attending occasionally (a part-time student) or a student at a distance. The pedagogical approach takes care of all of them, in an appropriate way.

In order to make such an approach feasible, we assume a WWW course-management system is available. Such a course-management system provides technological facilities through which users (instructors and students) can retrieve resources, add resources or comments, and communicate with one another, and also whereby the instructor can monitor or even assess the contributions of students.

'Before' activities

Students should prepare themselves before a focal event so that they come to it ready to act upon what they have been learning about. This is no new idea in education, but in practice students often come to lectures unprepared. To stimulate their preparation, we believe that they need to do some sort of assigned activity (and thus an activity that counts toward their assessment in the course). These activities will usually include some reading, but can also involve other sorts of preparation, such as identifying examples that illustrate the study materials from the WWW and submitting them into the course WWW environment, or submitting questions or doing practice exercises and comparing their work to a model answer. The course WWW environment provides the tool for this submission process, and facilitates the reuse of submitted materials in the focal setting. The *before* phase of each *before, during and after cycle* also serves the purpose of stimulating students to stay on tempo and be prepared for active participation in the subsequent focal event. Conversely, it can point the instructor's attention towards students who do not prepare (as shown by no submission) so that personal intervention can occur, or to problems that the students are having, so that the focal session can be tailored appropriately.

In a professional context, the *before* activities can be built around a collection of key resources from the company or from the professional field instead of specially prepared study materials. Participants can be asked to preview these resources, follow up ones about which they would like to get more information or insight, perhaps contribute some relevant resources that they themselves are familiar with and indicate via the WWW site which topics or resources they would like to elaborate on in the upcoming focal session. Also, they can submit a resource to the collection from their own work or experience, along with a brief note as to its relevance.

'During' activities

During the focal event, the instructor can make use of materials and comments submitted by the students/participants during the *before* periods. For example, results of a preliminary quiz can alert the instructor to concepts that need more or less attention during the focal event, and examples submitted by the students can be used as demonstration and discussion materials at the focal setting. By copying various exemplars of student/participant *before* submissions into the portion of the course environment that will support the focal-event session, the materials can easily be used as points of reference for discussions or further activities.

During the focal event, there will usually be some period of instructor-led explanation, but we believe that an important step towards increasing the flexibility as well as the learning quality of the focal event is that students are active during it. Listening to a lecture may involve cognitive activity, but we mean activity that involves interaction and communication with other students and the instructor. For this to occur, a '*sandwich model*' can be used for the structure of a focal event. By a sandwich model we mean:

1. The instructor starts the event with a certain amount of explanation, building upon materials submitted in the *before* phase. In preparation for this explanation, the instructor has notes and demonstration materials such as PowerPoint slides already uploaded into the course WWW environment. While this start-off period can have some of the attributes of a traditional lecture, it differs in two important ways:
   - It is relatively short, and all demonstration materials are available via the course WWW site so that students who are not present can catch up on what was communicated.
   - It is aimed at launching a subsequent discussion or practice activity during the focal event itself, in which students who are present are engaged during the focal session and students who are not present are engaged either at a later time or from a different location at the same time. We think of these preparatory activities metaphorically: the first of the slices of bread of a sandwich.

     If appropriate, this start-off period can be captured on video and made available via the course WWW site as video-on-demand, synchronized with any visual aids such as PowerPoint slides that were being shown at the same time as the short presentation (Collis and Peters, 2000).
2. For the *filling* of the sandwich, the students are active, doing something besides listening. The instructor is available to monitor and interact, but is no longer lecturing. The course WWW site needs to make the instructions for this activity available for all students, including those not present at the focal session. The course WWW site can also serve as the tool via which submissions from this activity are obtained and organized, perhaps directly during the session or afterwards. Many times the focus of the activity will be to prepare for subsequent follow-up activities.
3. For the concluding part of the sandwich model during the focal-event session (the bottom piece of bread, to carry on with the metaphor), the instructor brings the students back together and makes culminating comments on what has occurred as students were being busy. Perhaps the instructor has noticed some reoccurring misconceptions or conceptual problems? These can be immediately commented upon. Or perhaps the instructor can make use of some of the results of the student activity as example material, to help extend and explain the key concepts that were at the heart of the focal session. He or she can also use this period of time to motivate the third part of the before, during and after cycle: the follow-up activities.

'After' activities

After the focal session, students remain active. The instructor devises some sort of follow-up activity that builds upon and extends what happened in the focal session. Students have a certain period of time to do this activity, individually or in groups, and submit their results via the course WWW site. The instructor gives feedback, but in a limited manner, usually not detailed comments to each student's submission. Often peer feedback is used, and evaluated, as part of the follow-up process. Misconceptions that show up in the *after* activities can be addressed in the next round of *before* activities or the next focal session.

Examples

Figure 5.2 shows an overview of an example of the before, during and after approach, for students in a regular course in higher education. Some of these students may be at the face-to-face session, others not. If they are not present, they participate in the activities that went on during the session at another time, via the WWW site. As this example is related to students in higher education, it is conceivable that their contribution potential could be limited, given their lack of real experiences. Therefore in the 'after' activity a combination of acquisition and contribution activities is mentioned.

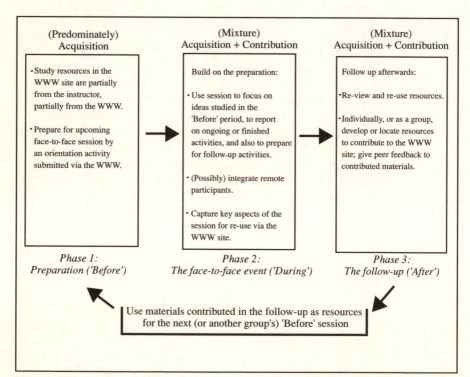

Figure 5.2   *Before, during and after cycle for students in a course in higher education*

The focus of this book is on higher education, but it is interesting to note how the before, during, after idea can also fit well with professional development in a corporate setting. Figure 5.3 shows the same before, during and after approach, in this case for a course for professionals based on some new or topical developments in their company or discipline, and including the idea of a planned one- or two-day seminar as the focal event. In contrast to students, professionals will use the follow-up phase predominately to build professional contacts with one another and for just-in-time learning in the workplace.

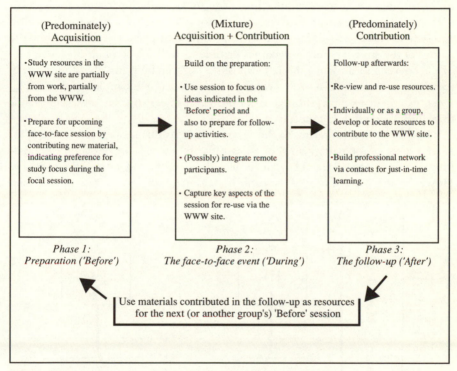

Figure 5.3   *Before, during and after cycle for professional learners*

Making the U turn

We now can put all of these ideas together to describe the pedagogical model that we call the 'U Approach' or 'U turn' in which the before activities are represented by the left arm of the 'U', the during activities by the base of the 'U' and the after activities by the right arm of the 'U'.

The 'U' as a pedagogical approach

To indicate what we mean by a U turn in the learning process, we make use of the Flexibility–Activity Framework from Chapter 1. Figure 5.4 shows the four quadrants of that framework with a 'U' superimposed.

The left arm of the 'U' relates to before activities. This arm is located in the third quadrant of the framework, because these activities have become flexible in a number of ways. Learners make use of a variety of resources, extending the standard texts and even entering extra resources of their own. Learners do activities that give the instructor input into how to focus the upcoming focal-event session, and possibly contribute resources that can be used as a basis for discussion and activity during that session. Not only time and place are flexible, but the nature of the study resources becomes flexible as well. Depending on the nature of the course and students, this left arm of the 'U' can be primarily acquisition in nature or it can move more towards contribution (for example, students with work experience submit short descriptions of episodes in their own experience that illustrate textbook concepts).

The base of the 'U' relates to the focal session. As this is often face to face, for at least some of the participants, or at least involves some sort of event, the flexibility at this part of the U cycle is less than in the *before* or *after* portions. However, the base of the 'U' can still be reasonably high in terms of time and

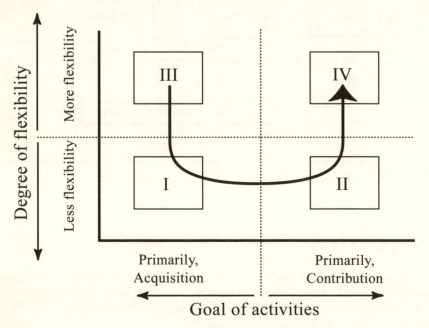

Figure 5.4 *The U Approach as a pedagogical model*

place flexibility if the instructor makes use of the WWW environment to maintain all the resources from the focal session so that those who were not present physically can participate later.

The right arm of the 'U' relates to the follow-up activities. These are again more flexible, in that the use of the WWW environment means that participants can contribute at their own time and place. The emphasis on contribution means that new learning materials will become available for all students, based on participant contributions. The learner gradually takes on a role of co-responsibility for the learning experience of the group as a whole. The emphasis in the course shifts from the content to be studied towards the activities that will be experienced in order to integrate the content into one's larger professional identity.

The location of the 'U' in the Flexibility–Activity Framework grid can vary, depending on the nature of the course, the learners and the instructor. The positioning of the left arm, base and right arm of the 'U' in relation to the four quadrants of the Flexibility–Activity framework symbolizes the emphasis in the course on the aspects flexibility and activity. Figure 5.5 shows a situation where there is little use yet of the contribution idea, for instance in the case of a highly structured subject matter and learners who wish to be as quick as possible in getting through the materials (contribution takes more time for learner and instructor alike than simply going through already prepared materials). There is increased flexibility but not yet much contribution.

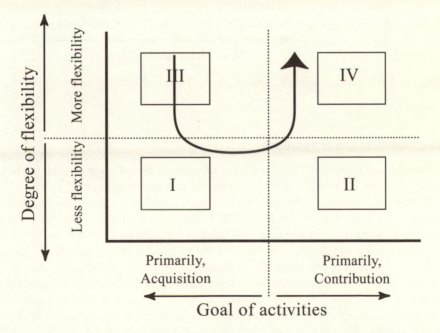

Figure 5.5 *The U Approach, where primarily flexibility increase is involved*

Figure 5.6 shows a situation such as might occur with professionals in a company-learning context, where interacting and supplying resources based on their own experience comes much more strongly in the picture, emphasizing the contribution aspects in Quadrant IV.

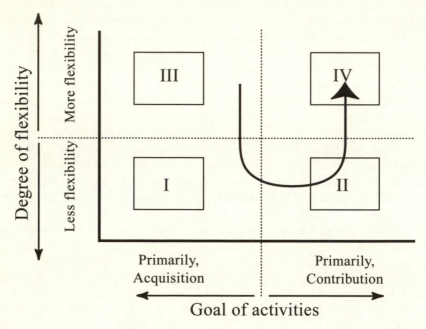

Figure 5.6 *The U Approach, where both flexibility and contribution are involved*

Implementing the U Approach

Examples are beginning to emerge that illustrate different ways in which the U turn idea can be realized. In an analysis of the papers submitted to the ED-MEDIA 1999 conference (http://www.aace.org/conf/edmedia/), we found that over 90 per cent of them involved WWW-based tools, environment, or systems and various forms of flexibility and student engagement (Collis and Oliver, 1999). In order to interpret the value of the U Approach we can relate it to the 4 Es, as described in the previous chapters. From that perspective it is important not to expect too much, too soon, of the instructor. Thus, we recommend the main focus on expanding the flexibility aspects of a course as shown in Figure 5.5 for instructors getting started with flexible learning and the use of a WWW-based system. We call this sort of change pedagogical extension (Collis, 1996d, 1997b). The focus on flexibility and contribution as shown in Figure 5.6 can evolve over time as instructors gain more experience with using the technology to support new forms of learning activities. As more and more use of contribution occurs in a more-flexible learning experience, we say that pedagogical re-engineering has occurred (Collis, 1996d, 1997b). We have found in our own experience (see Chapter 8 and also Van der Veen, De Boer and Collis, 2000) that after some cycles of predominately pedagogical extension (Figure 5.5) instructors start to move toward more contributive forms of student activities (Figure 5.6). Table 5.2 summarizes a small number of the many current examples. Chapters 7 and 8 give examples from our own experiences.

Table 5.2 *Examples of the U turn*

Reference	Description	Relation to the U Turn
Boise State University, USA (Bigelow, 1997)	A course-support WWW site is used to integrate course activites, study material support, discussion and communication, and information about class members.	Figure 5.5, Pedagogical extension, moving towards Figure 5.6, Pedagogical re-engineering
Georgia Institute of Technology, USA (Chinowsky and Goodman, 1997)	An engineering course involves group projects, carried out as virtual teams via communication and groupware tools.	Figure 5.6, Pedagogical re-engineering
California State University, San Bernardino, USA (Oliver and Nelson, 1997)	As a strategy for the study of a second language, students use a WWW environment and CD ROM with interactive resources, video segments and audio files to carry out problem-solving activities using only the second language.	Figure 5.5, Pedagogical extension
Indiana University USA (Bonk, 1998)	A course-support WWW site (*Smart Web*) is used to support a variety of weekly learning activities, such as case reflections, chapter discussions, reports on field observations, and to support and present students' final projects.	Figure 5.5 Pedagogical extension, moving towards Figure 5.6, Pedagogical re-engineering
Henley Management College, UK (Smith and Birchall, 1998)	Students work in distributed groups and use groupware to create electronic case studies.	Figure 5.6, Pedagogical re-engineering
University of Sheffield, UK (Toynton, 1998)	Students make use of a WWW-based resource collection to support problem-solving activities related to geological periods.	Figure 5.6, Pedagogical extension, moving towards Figure 5.6, Pedagogical re-engineering
University of Wales, Aberystwyth (Ratcliff and Davies, 1998)	Network tools are used to facilitate students getting fast help.	Figure 5.5, Pedagogical extension

University of Wollongong, Australia (Lockyer, Patterson and Harper, 1998)	A WWW-based test authoring and administration system supports secure test delivery and administration via a course-support WWW site.	Figure 5.5, Pedagogical re-engineering
University of Sydney, Australia (Gazzard and Dalziel, 1998)	Students, working in groups, use the course WWW site to make available draft versions of their design products and give one another structured feedback via the WWW.	Figure 5.6, Pedagogical re-engineering
Edith Cowan University, Australia (Oliver, Omari and Herrington, 1998)	Instructors can choose from WWW-based resources such as electronic discussion tools, debate tools, personal reflection tools, concept mapping tools and tools for student posting of URLs, to use in their course-support sites.	Figure 5,6 Pedagogical re-engineering
University of Helsinki, Finland (Meisalo *et al*, 1998)	Students use a Java-based interactive algorithm animator to get immediate feedback on their work (in computer science and also in biology)	Figure 5.5, Pedagogicsl extension
Pohjos-Savo Polytechnic and Kuopio Education Centre, Finland (Collis, Andernach and Van Diepen, 1997)	Finnish students work collaboratively with students in The Netherlands on projects, using a WWW-based shared workspace, various other WWW-based tools, and video-conferencing.	Figure 5.6, Pedagogical re-engineering
University of Tampere, Finland (Hietala, 1998)	Students in a computer course use a WWW-based conferencing system for discussions.	Figure 5.6, Pedagogical re-engineering
Katholieke Universiteit Leuven, Belgium (Van der Perre, 1998)	WWW-based tools support student guidance and the development of students' self-study skills, access to network-available resources, groupwork (newsgroups, virtual laboratories) and internationalization.	Figure 5.5, Pedagogical extension, moving towards Figure 5.6, Pegagogical re-engineering

The examples in Table 5.2 are only a small sampling. We could cite several hundred others for which we have reports from professional journals or conferences. The major point is that once flexibility is possible and practised, then new forms of learning involving active-student participation often begin to emerge. However, change takes time. This leads to a new lesson:

Lesson 12: *Watch the speed limit*. Don't try to change too much at the same time. Start where the instructor is at, and introduce flexibility via extending contact sessions to include before, during and after aspects with each of these made more flexible. Move gradually into contribution.

The U turn is happening in many courses in higher education, and in all cases seems to be facilitated by WWW-based tools and resources. There is enough experience to allow guidelines to begin to emerge. We discuss some of these in the next section.

Guidelines for the U Approach

Guidelines for the U Approach can be stated with respect to the sorts of activities that can be used, as well as towards the integration of them into activities for the before, during and after phases. Also, guidelines can be offered for general aspects of activities, such as monitoring and feedback, and problems that occur with group work in flexible activities.

Activities in the U Approach

Activities can take many forms and be carried out both in an individual fashion and by a group. A sample of the sort of activities that can be adapted to the U Approach includes the following (Van der Veen, De Boer and Collis, 2000) (in each case, the WWW environment is used as the workplace for working on, contributing and subsequently accessing the contributions):

- searching for additional information or examples and making these available for others;
- working with a case as a basis for problem solving and contributing some additional materials for the case for use by others;
- participating in a role-play situation and leaving some record of the results for others to consider;
- creating a report to be used as a learning resource by others;
- creating a product, such as a multimedia resource or a design, that is also a resource for others;
- extending and applying theoretical principles in new settings and adding these results to a course repository of extension materials;
- testing one's insight through the development of test questions to be used by others;
- participating in a discussion and leaving a record of key aspects of it for use by others.

The 'others' in the above list of activity types may be other students in the same course or within a student's group in the course. But they may also be other students in other cycles of the course or students in other courses or learners who are not in a course context at all but could refer to the materials via a database rather as they now use a library. The idea of reuse of students' work and of moments of good communication in a course supports flexibility: for those who were not present when a moment of good communication occurred, for example, or to facilitate the development of a substantial database of learning resources that can be reused and combined in many different combinations. Examples of some of these more-flexible and contribution-oriented forms of activities follow (other examples appear in Chapters 7 and 8):

- *Seeking and contributing new or supplementary information*
  Students are given the activity of finding an appropriate example or article on the WWW that relates to a topic under discussion in the course, or illustrates a concept, or extends the references and examples given in the textbook. They enter the URL and name of the resource that they have obtained in a particular location in a course WWW environment, and also add a brief comment to indicate why the resource is relevant. This produces a group-made 'bookmark' list for the course that can be subsequently used as a resource bank, added to, analysed, etc. Students can be asked to select several of the submitted resources (not ones they submitted themselves) and do something further with the resources – discuss, reflect, categorize, relate, etc.
- *Case studies*
  Case studies illustrating issues being studied in the course are uploaded into a course WWW site. The origin of the cases can be the instructor or the students themselves, or they can be found externally (for example, on the WWW). The students then work in groups to discuss the case, using group-ware tools or WWW-board discussion tools in the course WWW site. They are asked by the instructor to follow a certain structure in their discussions. After the deadline for the activities is past, the discussions of each group become open to the other groups. As a follow-up activity, each group compares its main ideas to those of the other groups and comments on points of agreement and alternative interpretations. If students meet face to face, they can have a culmination of this activity as a group discussion; however, their comments are retained on a course WWW site as a resource, for students who were not present at the face-to-face discussion, or for students outside of that particular cycle of the course. The instructor may wish to retain several of the strongest points of discussion, and make those available in the course WWW site for the next cycle of students, as a starting-point for their analyses of the cases.
- *Creating study resources*
  A major project for a course could be that students work in groups and each group be assigned a topic relevant to the course. The group must prepare a report (using whatever type of technology is most appropriate – word processing, HTML, audio, video, or a combination). The intention of the

activity is to extend and complement the textbook in relation to the topic, in a way that is helpful to all of the students in the course. Draft versions of the report are made available via the WWW site, for feedback from the instructor and other groups of students. The final version is also available via the WWW site, in enough time before the end of the course so that students can read and submit comments about one another's work. The reports can be interlinked in the course WWW site, to one another and to the other resources in the course, and can be available for the following cycle of students in the course. Students in the following cycle can update and revise the previous reports, as an activity.

● *Creating test items*
For some or each topic in a course, students have the activity that they must construct several multiple-choice test items, along with a scoring key and appropriate feedback for each of the choices. All items are available via the course WWW site as study materials for other students. As a subsequent activity, students must evaluate the questions that have been submitted. The instructor indicates that the final examination of the course will contain some of the questions, so it is worth the students' time to study one another's questions as a review before the examination.

● *Discussion activities*
Students use a WWW-board or computer-conferencing tool to participate in written discussions relating to issues being discussed in the course where their contributions can be made at a time convenient to themselves but within the deadline for the completion of the discussion. Students can take turns having the role of moderator of the discussion. The instructor sets expectations for how often students should contribute, and for characteristics of the contribution such as length, a requirement that it explicitly mentions the ideas of the message to which it is responding, or that the submission also includes a reference to the course text or one of the course WWW-based resources. Students earn marks for their submissions and moderating tasks.

All of the above types of activities engage the students in a way consistent with either pedagogical extension or pedagogical re-engineering (Figure 5.5 and Figure 5.6). Students are active in a way that directly contributes to the course as a whole, not just their own learning. Also, this sort of approach avoids the problems of lack of fit or the 'not invented here' reaction that accompanies so many computer-based learning products (see Chapter 4). These study materials were 'invented here', in a cost-effective way, as the course proceeds (see Chapter 6 for more about costs and return on investment). The products developed as a result of the process of participating in the course are by definition a good fit to the course and to the local communication norms and culture. It is these reasons that have led to the following lesson learnt:

Lesson 13: *Process yields product*. Through the process of contribution-oriented learning activities, learners themselves help produce the learning materials for the course.

However, as we will see later in this chapter and in this book, this lesson is not simple to realize. One of the problems involves the management of group-based activities and another relates to the problem of appropriate feedback.

Group work in activities

An important aspect of the U Approach is that students will often be working in groups. While group work can also be part of non-flexible (Quadrant I) learning, it has special applications in an approach based on flexibility. Groups can communicate with one another as part of the learning process, and also can as a group give feedback to other groups without needing to be always in the same place at the same time. The *Jigsaw Method* (Aronson *et al*, 1978), where each member of a group has a distinct role and contribution, relates directly to the idea of participation in a learning community within the group and across other groups in the course. Group work makes it possible for a more complicated form of activity to be given than would be the case if each student had to complete the activity on his or her own. Group work can also help instructors, in terms of the number of activities they have to evaluate and projects they have to support.

But group work is not without its problems as a form of activity. In Table 5.3, some of the difficulties with group-based activities (with or without added flexibility) are presented.

The instructor can also have difficulties with managing and monitoring the group work, particularly in knowing when and how to intervene (Winnips, 2000). It is important to realize that the problems exist and can cause burdens for both learners and instructors.

Feedback

The active-student model requires an active instructor as well. One of the forms of activity is the giving of appropriate feedback. There are many possibilities for the form of this feedback (De Boer and Peters, 2000), for example:

1. The instructor gives each student or group an individual comment.
2. The instructor makes a model answer available, against which students must compare their own work to see why they have received the mark that they were given.
3. Students or groups of students give one another feedback.
4. The response is automatically checked by a computer-based tool and feedback automatically given (as with multiple-choice questions).

5. Feedback is given via general comments by the instructor, either in written form to all students or during a face-to-face session.

Table 5.3 *Problems in group-based project work, instructional strategies and WWW-based support (source: Collis, Andernach and Van Diepen, 1997: 112–13)*

Persistent Problems in Group-based Project Work	Instructional Strategies and WWW-based Support in Response to the Problems
Problems in maintaining course cohesion and momentum as students become immersed in their respective projects	– Intregrate all aspects of the course, theoretical and project-related, in a single course WWW environment, accessible to all and making group progress visible to all. – Link student work, in partial or completed form, to the course environment, for use as examples and study material for self-study and for demonstration and comment during lectures.
Problems in motivating and structuring collaboration	– Choose a task where the common product is motivating in itself; where a team approach is needed to handle the various aspects of the task; and where an instructional strategy such as the Jigsaw Methodology (whereby each group member has clearly defined and and separate contributions to the group: Aronson *et al*, 1978) is built into course requirements.
Problems in motivating and structuring communication	– Develop a strategy of having a manager in each group responsible for reporting group progress and group reflection, via the course WWW environment, and with results of this input linked into the course environment so that a group archive is built from the communication.
Problems in maintaining a 'group memory'	– Use tools with shared-workspace functionalities integrated in the course WWW environment so that a common view of notes, partial products and other project-management-related information is available to all.
Problems in organizing and executing self- and intergroup evaluation	– Use the course WWW environment as the product as well as the process environment, so that partial and final products are available for self-, group, peer and instructor evaluation, using structured evaluation instruments also intregrated into the course environment; post and use these various forms to evaluation as the basis for final evaluation of the group product (Collis and Meeuwsen, 1999).
Problems in relating group activities and product outcomes to conceptual aspects of the course, to study materials and to individual assessment in examinations	– Use comparisons of group products, relative to conceptual issues in the course, as questions on the examination; and link criteria for ongoing self-evaluation of group products to study materials and lecture notes also embedded in the course environment.

In general, the options for feedback are: structured or non-structured, process-oriented or product-oriented, and elaborated or short. We are studying the eight combinations of these options in order both to improve the effectiveness of the feedback for the learners and reduce the time demands of feedback for the instructor (Collis, De Boer and Slotman, in press). The option of the instructor giving each student individual written feedback is the most time-consuming for the instructor, and will be less and less feasible when the student numbers are high and as students become more active and participate more flexibly in courses. An example of the guidelines we offer to instructors about feedback includes:

Give the students via the WWW environment:

- personal feedback when they all have to carry out the same assignment;
- public feedback when you want them to learn from one another's answers or maybe use one another's answers for a new assignment;
- group feedback when the number of students in the course is large and could not be handled with personal feedback with regard to time constraints;
- one answer key to all students when many students make the same mistakes in their answers;
- peer feedback when you want to guide the students in learning how to evaluate and give feedback (Remmers and Collis, 2000).

In recent research at our own institution we have found that students do not necessarily need or want lengthy or personal feedback, as long as they get feedback in a timely manner when they submit their work for comments (Collis, Winnips and Moonen, 2000; Winnips, 2000). This is good news for the instructor, because the management of active-student activities is potentially a time and task burden. We discuss this more in the next section.

Implications for the instructor

The U Approach has deep implications for the instructor. These changes relate both to his or her fundamental role and also to the details of carrying out that role, details that include management tasks. We discuss each of these in this section.

Changes in the role of the instructor

Sfard indicated a change in the role of the instructor, from one of delivering, conveying and clarifying in the Acquisition Model to one of 'expert participant' in the Participation Model (1998: 7). Many others have made similar observations concerning the changing role of the instructor. Duchastel (1997), for example, reflects the U Approach ideas when he notes that the instructor should: (a) specify goals to pursue instead of content to learn, (b) accept a diversity of outcomes instead of demanding common results, (c) request the production rather than the communication of knowledge, (d) evaluate at the task rather than at the knowledge level, (e) build learning teams instead of assigning activities that only have meaning to the individual and (f) promote global learning communities instead of remaining localized. What do these ideas mean in practical terms for instructors, following the U Approach? They involve new roles, skills and tasks, and new issues. Instructors move from presenters to managers of activities. Their feedback is given to contributions from the learners, which may include material new to the instructors. They have to study it before they can respond. We discuss this in the next sections. First we state the general lesson that motivates this section:

Lesson 14: *Aim for activity*. The key roles of the instructor are becoming those of activity planning, monitoring and quality control.

Time management and problems

When the instructor is also dealing with new cohorts of students, including those who are participating in varying levels of distance flexibility, the skills needed for this new pedagogy escalate rapidly. The cognitive load as well as the time burden on the instructor can become very high when an institution commits itself to more-flexible learning using technology. Time management becomes a major problem. Table 5.4 shows some aspects of the new role of the instructor with respect to student activities.

The roles and skills noted in Table 5.4 are a mixture of pedagogical insight, technical proficiency and good management. We define management tasks as the activities of the instructor outside of direct content-related interaction with students and outside of the content-specific planning and execution of a course (Collis and Gervedink Nijhuis, 2001). In Table 5.4, tasks (a), (f), (i) and (j) are management tasks, and tasks (c), (d), (e), (g) and (h) involve both instructional aspects and management. As flexibility increases, management tasks can take up an increasing amount of an instructor's time yet they are little studied in the literature. Having a well-designed WWW-based course-management system makes a vast difference in the extent to which instructors can or will be willing to carry out the above roles and tasks.

For the instructor, the time burden is clearly a negative aspect of short-term pay-off. The lack of pay-off in terms of institutional recognition indices (in universities, still primarily research publications in refereed journals) compounds this negative pay-off. While the pay-off aspect could be remedied by institutional decision makers changing their reward systems (see Chapter 3), the time problems remain a serious disincentive. Some of the ways that we are dealing

Table 5.4 *Aspects of new forms of activities and their implications for the instructor (adapted from Brown, 1999; Collis and Gervedink Nijhuis, 2001)*

Types of Change in Activities

When new forms of activities based on the *contributing-student* idea and flexibility occur, they often involve:

- less reliance on lectures and more time spent on new forms of learning activities,where the contract between students and the instructor takes place at least some of the time via a WWW environment;
- more student participation, often via the practice of students entering new resources into the course WWW site or being involved in asynchronous discussions via computer conferencing or WWW boards;
- more group projects or collaborative activities, supported by groupware tools;
- new forms of learning activities involving international aspects such as students in two different courses in different countries working together on some common task;
- new forms of assessment activities, such as electronic portfolios and journals; also more opportunities for self- and peer assessment;
- more time spent on student presentation of the work; work is made for and presented to an audience via the WWW site, and comments are given on it by those in the audience.

Implications for the Instructor

The instructor must:

(a) Select and use appropriate tools to make flexible participation possible and support students in the use of these tools.
(b) Think of new forms of student activities.
(c) Learn how to set up and describe the activities, explaining very clearly what the expectations are both contentwise and also in relation to time, form and method of submission.
(d) Communicate precisely how students will be evaluated on the new forms of activities, particularly for group projects and peer evaluations.
(e) Monitor and appropriately intervene when there are problems within groups with group work.
(f) Handle much more contact with students, via their submissions into the WWW site or e-mail, their comments and discussions, their comments on one another's work.
(g) Develop new methods of grading student performance, so that process is also graded; apply these methods in a consistent way and so that students understand the criteria.
(h) Monitor the quality of what students submit into the course WWW environment for other students to see and study; inappropriate material must be quickly removed and the individual submitting it contacted. *Inappropriate* covers a large number of aspects, from being factually wrong to being potentially offensive to others.
(i) Monitor potential copyright problems with what students submit into the course WWW site.
(j) Keep records relating to student process and participation, to use for monitoring and grading.
(k) Manage incoming and outgoing activities, e-mail, contacts from individual students.
(l) Become an 'expert participant' and co-learner as well as the instructor still responsible for the acquisition aspects of the course.

with the time problem for instructors in our own institution will be discussed in Chapter 8.

Issues related to students' reactions

Not only does the instructor have new tasks, but he or she is confronted by new issues from a number of directions. From the students' point of view, one problem relates to their expectation as to how quickly they will get personal responses and feedback. Whereas before students would have waited perhaps a week for an instructor's office hours, now they complain if an e-mail is not responded to within a short period of time, or if feedback does not appear on their submissions also in a short period of time. Students will send repeats of their e-mails, asking why they did not get a response. The instructor must manage this: who did he or she respond to, saying what, when? How can this communication be archived for handy reference?

A more conceptual issue is the fact that often students do not, in fact, want to become more active and co-responsible for the course. They protest, saying that it is the instructor's job to 'teach them'. They complain that looking for additional study materials 'takes too much time; why don't you just give them to us?' They want to read study materials as being the definitive and last word; having to evaluate materials and decide if indeed they are appropriate is not something for which they have desire or skills. The higher-order skills and maturity needed to assume more personal responsibility for learning need to be developed via a process of scaffolding and monitoring by instructors, over many courses and years (Collis and Meeuwsen, 1999). By and large, students are not intrinsically motivated by change or the use of technology; if activities are not part of the evaluation process of the course (ie if they are not graded), then many students are not likely to take part (Alexander and McKenzie, 1998). Students are pragmatic and busy; they do what they must do to meet the requirements of a course. In terms of the 4 Es (Chapter 3), if an instructor invests time and effort setting up a new type of participative learning activity, and students do not respond positively, then his or her feeling of personal engagement can quickly drop, as well as his or her sense of short-term or long-term pay-off (educational effectiveness). The instructor becomes less likely to try it again.

New roles for the instructional designer

While the majority of instructors in higher education design and develop their own courses, in large institutions and in corporate training there are often instructional designers available for course design or to assist instructors in course design. How does the U turn idea affect their work? We believe, radically. In this section, we discuss some of these new roles for the professional instructional designer.

We have found from our own experience (see Chapters 7 and 8) that a U turn approach brings with it not only new roles for the instructor and student, but also for those professionals who assist the instructors in the design of their courses. The major tasks of these instructional designers and support personnel are no longer to transmit educational content, but to design activities; not to design multimedia learning materials, but to design and develop various sorts of tools that can be used in multiple situations in which students are active, using WWW environments to support and manage that activity. A consequence of Lesson 13, the shift in orientation from product to process, is also a shift for the instructional designer. Most traditional instructional-design approaches are related to the content-acquisition model, where decisions are made, prior to the start of a course and usually by someone other than the instructor of the course, as to how it will proceed. The course is a product, which is presented to the learner. This is not the approach of pedagogical re-engineering, in which some of the products of the course emerge from participation during it. Thus, we believe the label *activity designer* may soon be more appropriate for instructional designers.

In particular, we believe that the new role of the instructional designer is to assist the instructor in the design of activities, activities that relate to the active learner and increased flexibility. The instructional designer will create tools to help support these activities within the context of whatever course-management system is being used. The focus of his or her work will not be to create a course, but to contribute to creating the tools that will allow instructors to design and control their own courses, via their own combinations of external resources, reused student contributions and new resources. We illustrate this in Chapter 8. More ideas about how these developments are influencing instructional-design methodologies can be found in discussions of the *3-Space Design Strategy* (Moonen, 2000e). Because part of our own work is to train instructional designers, we are particularly interested in this change in instructional-design methodologies, and present this as a lesson:

Lesson 15: *Design for activity*. Instructional design should concentrate more on activities and processes, and less on content and a predetermined product.

Summing up

In this chapter we have advocated a *U turn* in pedagogical approach referring to before, during and after activities in a course setting. The U Approach is a pedagogical strategy that makes the Flexibility–Activity Framework concrete in terms of course organization. We have illustrated the approach with a number of examples and guidelines leading to some general design principles:

- Plan for flexibility via pedagogical extension.
- Focus on the design of activities, not of content presentation.
- Plan for a course-support site that initially is relatively empty, to be filled by the instructor and students in their own ways as the course proceeds.
- Plan for a variety of roles for both instructors and students; move towards students being contributors in the course learning community.
- Design for human–human communication, not human–computer interaction.
- Design so that the instructor can be comfortably in control of the course-support environment, before and during the course, shaping and tailoring it to his or her own context.
- Be realistic about what instructors can and will do. Look for strategies to reduce the time needed for management and feedback.

The pedagogy for flexible and contributive learning is complex and involves many new aspects for the instructor. A well-designed WWW system can make it feasible, and even pleasurable (at times!). We conclude this chapter with a review of the lessons developed in the chapter:

Lesson 12: *Watch the speed limit.* Don't try to change too much at the same time. Start where the instructor is at, and introduce flexibility via extending contact sessions to include before, during and after aspects with each of these made more flexible. Move gradually into contribution.

Lesson 13: *Process yields product.* Through the process of contribution-oriented learning activities, learners themselves help produce the learning materials for the course.

Lesson 14: *Aim for activity.* The key roles of the instructor are becoming those of activity planning, monitoring and quality control.

Lesson 15: *Design for activity.* Instructional design should concentrate more on activities and processes, and less on content and a predetermined product.

In Chapters 2, 3, 4 and 5 we have looked at four major aspects of flexible learning and technology from particular perspectives: institutional, implementation, technology and pedagogy. In the next chapter we integrate these together to ask a difficult question: are we getting a return on our investment and efforts?

Chapter 6

When do (or don't) we get our investment back?

In the structure of this book, we began with a general concept – flexible learning – and then looked at this from four individual perspectives: the institutional, implementation, pedagogical and technological. In the previous chapter we integrated these perspectives, but with a core focus on pedagogical change via the *U turn*. In this chapter, we take a different focus. Many times we are asked to advise on cost-effectiveness questions, particularly from decision makers in an

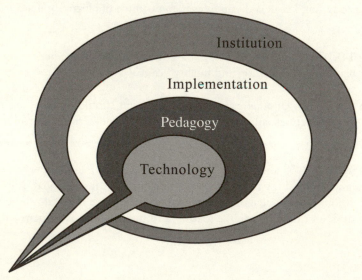

Figure 6.1 *Flexible learning in higher education – return on investment perspective*

institution considering a commitment to a new technology investment. Traditional cost-effectiveness approaches have not been useful. We suggest instead a *simplified return on investment strategy* based on the *4-E Model* (Chapter 3) and involving the institutional, pedagogical and technological perspectives as well as economic, qualitative and efficiency ones. In this chapter, we explain how this strategy works.

Return on investment: getting our investment back

Most people in higher education have little knowledge about concepts such as *cost-effectiveness methodology* or *return on investment* (ROI) or their associated algorithms. Just the same, decision makers, instructors, students and other actors are in fact making implicit ROI judgements about technology and flexible learning as soon as they make a decision or have an opinion about change relating to more flexibility and more technology in their own situations. The most common question we get from instructors or those who work with instructors when confronted with ideas related to the Contributing Student or the U Approach (Chapter 5) is: yes, but how much time will it demand of the instructor? Will it be worth the time and effort? The implicit question is if the investment (of time) will be worth the return, thus it is a return-on-investment question. In general, the return-on-investment questions we deal with are of the following main types. 1) Will the costs of committing to a new technology (in the current situation, often a WWW-based course-management system) in an institution (financial costs, costs in terms of dealing with resistance or problems) pay off in terms of the hoped-for returns, short or long term (technological costs vs institutional return asked by the decision maker)? 2) Will the costs of new ways of teaching or learning be balanced by gains in pedagogical pay-off or other forms of pay-off (pedagogical costs vs institutional and/or pedagogical return asked by the instructor or learner)?

The 4-E Model (Chapter 3) is an intuitive rule of thumb for estimating a response to these sorts of return-on-investment questions. If some or all of the 4-E vectors are very weak, then use of a new technology is not likely to occur and the return on investment in terms of the costs of the technology will certainly be poor. But can this sort of intuitive calculation be done more explicitly? Can we work out a return-on-investment metric for our own situations relating to flexible learning with technology? These questions can be asked at various levels. If we can, when (how long, under what conditions) will ROI be positive? In this chapter we deal with these questions.

What do we expect? Intuitive ROI

In this section, we expand on the general ideas of ROI and relate them to the 4 Es. We will focus on what different players expect to gain or lose (return), and what they expect this will ask of them (investment).

Expected return

In very general terms, reasons for change in higher education involving technology can be clustered around a few general expectations of return (see Chapter 2): improving the institution's economics, usually via increasing student numbers, improving quality, or making procedures more efficient. These three clusters relate to the three components of the 'Effectiveness' vector in the 4–E Model (Chapter 3). These three components are:

- *effectiveness, learning* (generally taken to relate to 'improving quality');
- *effectiveness, short-term pay-off* (relating to tactical gain such as increased efficiency of procedures among other aspects); and
- *effectiveness, long-term pay-off* (relating to strategic gain such as improvement of economic position among other things).

Expectations for return are different depending on the function of the person making the consideration. Managers of institutions emphasize the 'not to lose students' argument, while instructors and students emphasize the 'improve the quality of learning' argument (Chapter 2). All of the actors in the flexible-learning situation (including the students) are interested in efficiency arguments, each from their own perspectives: managers may want to improve the administrative procedures of the institutions, instructors may want to reduce the time it takes to manage their courses and students want to reduce the amount of time they spend on procedural aspects of the course, including travel to the institution. The eventual criteria of success for flexible learning with technology will relate to the incentives for the actors involved as a result of the change process. The instructors and students want to see the incentives in a short time. The institution will probably accept a longer-term perspective. However, for each of the actors, the change process has to be incentive-based (Moonen, in press a).

As we have seen in Chapter 2, there is also the negative expectation: if you don't do it, you will fall behind (*You can't not do it*, Lesson 3). This relates to the inevitability perspective: flexible learning and WWW-based technologies are just inevitable, rather like breathing or taxes.

Expected investments

While the effectiveness 'E' from the 4 Es relates to expected returns, the other Es are related more to the 'investment' or cost/effort perspective. The environment conditions influence the ease of use and to some extent the individual's own personal engagement, each of which is related to aspects that in different ways have to be balanced against the expectation of effectiveness. With strong institutional support relating to technology and flexible learning, the effort involved in moving towards more-flexible learning will be less than if there is not such strong support. With minimal personal engagement, the expectation of effectiveness would have to be much higher to balance out the costs, in this case costs related to personal discomfort.

Thus to relate the 4 Es to ROI concepts, we can think of the effectiveness vector as relating to three important aspects of return (or outcome, or results, or gains); and the three other vectors taken together as relating to 'effort' (or costs or other factors that influence the investment that the individual or institution makes to move towards more-flexible learning) with the environmental factor influencing the others to a large extent. In order to stay consistent with the well-established literature about ROI (see, for example, http://www.astd.org/virtual_community/comm_evaluation/comm_top_page.html), we will use the terms 'return' and 'investment' in this chapter but will elaborate them in terms of the 4 Es.

ROI as formal concept and procedures

In the economic literature, the term 'return on investment' is both conceptualized and operationalized in terms of calculation procedures (Friedlob and Plewa, 2000; Philips, 1997). Conceptually, ROI can be expressed in simple terms as a ratio (outcomes/input), or a difference (gains less costs) (Horngren, Foster and Datar, 1997). Formal ROI procedures are much more complex, and tend to be used in educational contexts only in certain training situations (Shepherd, 1999). Partly it is the complexity of the procedures that is the reason they are rarely used to support decision making in higher education (Gustafson and Watkins, 1998). More fundamentally, it is the difficulty in obtaining the data to enter into the calculations. Also, there is considerable disagreement about the variables on which one should attempt to collect data. Yet another problem is the weighting of whatever variables are used. While long lists of variables tend to be standard in formal return-on-investment procedures, in practice in educational contexts involving technology, a few key issues dominate an individual's opinion or decision, and these key issues will vary among individuals. We discuss these points further in this chapter.

Intuitive ROI

Despite the lack of use of formal methods for understanding or calculating ROI, we have noticed that an *intuitive ROI* approach none the less guides predictions and decision making about technology and flexible learning, similar to the way that the 4 Es also operate as an intuitive construct. For example, the management chooses a policy for more-flexible learning, predicting that this will lead (eventually) to increased quality and/or quantity in its educational programme. But two major costs or inputs to balance against the expectation of the future gain are time (the extra time that is likely to be required of instructors and others in the institution in terms of handling this more-flexible learning) and costs (the costs of the production of new study materials and resources). The institution decides that the costs of the instructor do not count (the instructor is paid the regular salary no matter what amount of time he or she spends on feedback with students via the WWW), and that the costs of producing new instructional materials can also be shifted down to the instructor (who in turn shifts some of them to the students). Thus, it is intuitively predicted that the eventual ROI is going to be positive and the decision for the technology is taken (Moonen, 2000c).

But an intuitive ROI approach should be based on more than a string of assumptions. How can we make a compromise between formal methods for ROI and informal intuitive approaches? First we need to think more deeply about each of the key concepts: return (in terms of impact or effectiveness) and investment (in terms of costs). Then we can describe a relatively simple approach to estimating ROI.

Measuring effectiveness

The general assumption when the term 'effectiveness' is used in ROI contexts in education is that gains directly related to student learning are intended. In this section, we will look at problems involved with using student-learning gains as a measure of effectiveness for ROI. Then we will suggest effectiveness measures that can be used, in addition to student learning, in relation to tactical gains such as efficiency increase (related to short-term pay-off) and in relation to strategic gains such as flexibility increase (related to long-term pay-off).

Effectiveness related directly to student learning

Twigg (2000) is one of many who assume that in a return-on-investment approach what is being measured and compared is learning and financial costs. She indicates that the question to address is 'Did they really learn?' and describes four assessment techniques to answer the question. These techniques are: 1) matched examinations, with students in the redesigned course compared to students in a non-redesigned version of the course; 2) student work samples, similar to the above but using a sample of student papers and problem sets rather than examination scores; 3) behavioural tracking, in which students in both redesigned and non-redesigned versions of the course are followed afterwards to see what happened to them later in terms of variables such as programme completion and grade performance in subsequent courses for which the course in focus is a prerequisite; and 4) attitude shifts based on student testimony, relating to their own levels of confidence and/or motivation to continue study in the area.

These seem reasonable comparisons. The problem is that such comparisons are limited in value, even if they can be made. Most of the time they cannot. The reasons for this are the same as those we discussed in Chapter 4 related to the traditional media-selection research ('Which is better, X or Y?'). There are too many local, contextual variables that confound the results of any comparison.

There is not just one aspect of a course that has changed (for example, 'more flexible'), but what Salomon, Perkins and Globerson (1991: 8) call a 'whole cloud of correlated variables – technology, activity, goal, setting, teacher's role, culture – exerting their combined effect'. Using the analytic-experimental approach to compare X to Y is not valid where all variables are interdependent. Salomon (1995: 5) notes that in the complex systems in which change involving technology takes place in higher education, the variables are not only interrelated, but also 'mutually defining, each being "independent", "mediating", and "dependent" at the same time'. Thus, for example, in comparing a course which had been redesigned so that a group project making substantial use of groupware technology was the core activity:

> team work, motivation, interaction, effort expenditure, general atmosphere, affiliation, quantity and quality of communications, perceptions of tasks and activities, are all strongly interrelated and give meaning to each other... Obviously, although the computer technology is a crucial element in these processes (serving as the yeast), responsibility for the success or failure of the project cannot be attributed to the computer alone. The orchestration of variables leads to the observed results.
>
> (Salomon, 1995: 5)

Even assuming that an 'X vs Y' comparison does show some difference in student learning outcomes, for example higher final examination performance for 'X' compared to 'Y', how should this be weighted in an ROI sense? If the score difference is only a few points higher, it may not justify the efforts and costs.

Instructor's impressions

Because of the difficulties in doing the sorts of measurements that Twigg suggests, many learning-effectiveness studies rely on other measures, such as the instructor's or students' perceptions of how much they have learnt. For example, Alexander and McKenzie (1998) reviewed 104 out of 173 centrally funded projects relating to network technology for teaching and learning in Australian higher-education institutions between 1994 and 1998. The benefits found for students based on the instructors' impressions were:

- improved attitudes to learning;
- improved quality of learning (not shown by test scores but in a more nebulous sense);
- improved productivity of learning (it is not defined what 'productivity' means);
- improved access to learning;
- the opportunity to interact with others internationally;

- enhanced communication between students and instructors;
- the development of information and technological literacy.

In particular, when focused directly on the impact of the technology applications on students, 51.6 per cent of the 128 instructors responding to the evaluation indicated that the major result was improved attitudes to learning: that students enjoyed using the information-and-communication (ICT) technology applications, that the ICT use was related to a more positive attitude towards learning and that a positive perception of the use of ICT in learning occurred. The next-highest response, given by 30.8 per cent of the instructors, was improved learning outcomes. However, these were defined in a large number of ways, such as 'an improved understanding of the need for a mathematical approach', 'they are now aware of the cause of the problem that they had when talking or listening to native speaker conversation' and 'better skills in the analysis of practical problems'. The instructors did not mention higher performance on test scores or grades in the courses involved. These results are not what the instructors predicted at the start of their technology-application projects. At that time 87 per cent of the instructors expected that there would be improved learning outcomes, and only 16 per cent indicated that improved student attitudes would be a result. Thus, the effectiveness gains that were perceived to occur were generally not measurable.

Students' impressions

Alexander and McKenzie also asked students involved in the projects to give their own perceptions of the value of technology for learning. The following are the major results (1998: 234):

- Students' perceptions of assessment are a major influence on their approach to using technology. Will they earn points for the technology use? Will it be counted in their grades?
- Students' experience of working in groups with technology is often more negative than positive.
- Students' previous experiences of the teaching and learning situation influence their acceptance of new learning approaches with or without technology.

The students did not indicate that they felt learning gains had occurred from their technology use, in a sense that could be quantified and entered in a formal ROI calculation.

Pay-off to instructors?

There is not evidence from the Australian study that new uses of ICT led to pedagogical change (Chapter 5) outside the persons directly involved in the (short-term) projects. Also interesting is that while 31.4 per cent of the instructors believed at the start of their projects that the ICT use would lead to an improvement of the quality of the teaching and learning process, only 3.5 per cent felt this was the case after the project was concluded. None of the instructors indicated at the start of the project that they expected negative impact/problems/difficulties; at the close of the projects 20 per cent indicated this to be the case. One result stayed consistent: only 2 per cent of the instructors at the start of their projects believed that the experience would led to personal academic gain, such as academic recognition, promotion, or tenure; at the close of the projects 0 per cent indicated this to be a result.

In our own analysis of information and communication technologies in The Netherlands, USA, UK, Finland, Belgium and Australia, we surveyed a considerable amount of literature looking for learning-specific gains (as indicated by the sorts of measures used in an institution, generally tests: Collis and Van der Wende, 1999; Moonen, 1999). We were not able to conclude in a general way that students using ICT do better on traditional measures of learning such as tests than students not using ICT, although certainly individual examples here and there in individual courses can be found. What can be claimed at a general level is that students experience new forms of learning, that instructors are making new types of contacts with their students and that new resources and types of learning activities are occurring. Perhaps these indirect effects are what we should be measuring but how do we quantify them against costs in an ROI sense?

Effectiveness related indirectly to student learning

There are many indicators that relate not directly to learning, but indirectly, such as 'more group work takes place', or student attitudes, or new types of learning experiences that students are having. In terms of a *Contributing Student* pedagogy (Chapter 5), many different types of learning experiences related to the guiding metaphor of contribution-oriented learning are valuable. The indicators given in the 'Participation' column of Table 1.5 (Sfard, 1998) include 'the process of becoming a member of a community', 'the constant flux of doing', 'the dialectic nature of learning interaction', 'community building', 'belonging', 'participating', 'communicating'. These are worthy goals, but the problem is how these indirect gains are to be measured. They are all concepts in which growth is desirable, but virtually impossible to measure. And even if for some of them evidence can be found ('the students communicate more with one another'), how does one quantify this in order to compare it to costs and effort? How much communication is enough? Is more better? (See Lesson 10, *Don't overload.*) Does a student fail a course because he or she has not succeeded in 'community building'? How do we give grades on 'belonging' so that we differentiate among students in a consistent and fair way? As a general conclusion, measuring gains indirectly related to learning and claiming their causal relationship with a specific pedagogical approach or a specific technology is difficult, to say the least.

Effectiveness related to short-term pay-off, in particular efficiency gains

While effectiveness in terms of learning gains, direct and indirect, is difficult to measure for ROI purposes, there are better possibilities with other aspects of effectiveness, such as *efficiency*. Efficiency is a complicated concept, particularly when discussed from an economic perspective. We want to deal here with efficiency as used casually in conversation: improving the speed or lowering the effort or frustration level of carrying out tasks and procedures. We differentiate it from learning in the same way that we differentiated the management tasks of instructors from their pedagogical activities (see Chapter 5). We see efficiency as doing things that relate to management and instruction in a way that saves time and energy, when saving time and energy is desirable. For example, saving time and energy is desirable when giving feedback to a general assignment and to an entire class, but it may not be an instructor's chief priority when a student having difficulties comes to him or her for help and support.

Many gains in efficiency are possible when using a well-designed WWW-based course-management system (Chapter 4), but the term 'well-designed' is important. Another 'if' relates to the competency of the instructor to handle the technology in order to take advantage of the efficiency-gain potential. Table 6.1 shows some possibilities for increased efficiency in teaching and learning, using a well-designed WWW-based course-support system.

As another aspect of efficiency (as well as the contribution-oriented approach to learning), the instructor for some or all of the categories in Table 6.1 can reuse materials, including student work from previous versions of the course, with ease (again, if the WWW-based system is appropriately designed). All of these aspects can increase the efficiency of the tasks of the instructor.

Interestingly, efficiency-related aspects are not often mentioned in the literature (with exceptions, such as Rada, 1998, and Whittington, 1998 and current research going on in our own institution, Collis and Gervedink Nijhuis, 2001) despite their importance to instructor acceptance and short-term pay-off. While such gains may not be directly related to learning, they are directly related to short-term pay-off, for both instructor and students.

Effectiveness related to long-term pay-off, in particular strategic goals

Long-term pay-off can be seen from the perspective of the institution, the instructor and the learner. For the institution, flexibility increase is a major institutional goal. Thus, being able to document increases in flexibility can be good input for an ROI approach. However, flexibility is not an end in itself, but presumably a means to reach other ends, such as more students, or better quality learning. With these, in terms of measurement, we have the problem of time. These are benefits that will take time, which complicates the ROI problem for the decision maker who must make a decision within a short period, long before data to estimate return can be available.

As with indirect learning-related benefits, how to weight the value of various

Table 6.1 *Potential efficiency gains from the pedagogical use of well-designed WWW-based systems (Collis, 1999b)*

Pedagogical-Activity Category	Ways in which a WWW-based Course-Support Site Can Lead to More Efficiency
1. Course organization	– All course information, and updates, needs only to be entered once in the site; students learn to check the site rather than come to the instructor to ask procedural questions. – All e-mails are handy to access in the course site, including collective e-mail addresses for groups of students. – Overviews of what students have handed in are directly available via the site. – All student submissions are grouped togther in the course site, not as individual pieces of mail in the instructor's e-mail inbox; all feedback is available from the same location to the students. – If the system is so designed, the instructor and the students can access the site from any location where there is an Internet access, and check course information, upload and download assignments, send messages and do all other course-related activities.
2. Lectures, contact sessions	– Lecture notes and demonstration materials are all available in the course site; students do not have to be given handouts and absent students do not need to come to ask for handouts later.
3. Self-study, exercises	– If the system is so designed, the instructor and students can add additional study materials to the course site without photocopying simply by uploading (copyright is a constraint here). – If the system is so designed, the instructor can access the site from any location where there is an Internet access, and check the assignments that students have submitted, look at them directly from the site, give feedback and record marks, all in the same WWW environment.
4. Major assignment	– Detailed information about expectations for the major assignment, as well as links to examples of student work from previous years (if the system is so designed), can save many questions from students.
5. Testing	– Frequently asked questions and sample questions from previous years can be available via the site, saving many student contacts.
6. Mentoring, communication not specific to Items 1–5	– The instructor can contact students whenever he or she wishes and answer questions at his or her convenience, can save previous communication with students for reference, can forward the same message to other students and can contact the students when he or she is out of town.

gains over the long term remains a problem. In the Australian study conducted by Alexander and McKenzie (1998), short- and long-term benefits for instructors were also examined. These, according to the opinions of the instructors, were mainly:

- increased job satisfaction;
- increased understanding and skills in the use of information technologies;
- improved understanding of student learning, student needs and student difficulties;
- an improved understanding of their own discipline area;
- enhanced enthusiasm for teaching (Alexander and McKenzie, 1998: ix).

How can these be quantified? A first step is to state strategic goals in measurable terms (remember Lesson 1). But even when measured, what is their value, compared to costs?

Effectiveness: searching for the measurable

The research on output effects in the literature mainly reflects the context and goals of traditional educational systems. Many claim, however, that specific approaches integrating flexible learning and well-designed WWW systems lead and are often focused towards new kinds of outputs, in particular in the affective domain (feeling good and self-confident about technologies), the psychomotor domain (being able to handle new technologies with confidence) and with respect to higher cognitive and meta-cognitive skills (having insight into global and complex problems, being able to locate and use available information, being able to solve problems, participating in a new way in the learning process). Traditional measurement methodologies are less or not appropriate to capture such outputs. Therefore, other measurement methods will have to be developed and applied, and criteria for effectiveness expressed in measurable terms (Moonen, 1997). Or as another approach, measurable changes such as efficiency improvements and tangible measures of the goals of flexibility initiatives (for example, more students) should be used. We conclude this section with the following lesson:

Lesson 16: *Get a new measuring stick.* What we are most interested in regarding learning as a consequence of using technology often can't be measured in the short term or without different approaches to measurement. Measure what can be measured, such as short-term gains in efficiency or increases in flexibility.

If we need a new approach to measuring effects, do we also need a new approach to measuring investment, or costs?

Measuring costs

Just as effectiveness and effects are context-specific and thus difficult as a base for generalizations, so are costs. In this section we will look at different categories of costs that relate to ROI for flexible learning. A first issue is deciding the units for which costs are considered.

Cost units

There are various approaches to cost specification in the ROI literature (Moonen, 1999). One approach relates to fixed versus variable costs, where the latter depend on the number of students. In the typical acquisition-type course (Chapter 5), the cost of developing the course is considered fixed, and the variable costs of the course in operation depend on the number of students. In contribution-oriented learning, as we have seen, the development of at least part of the course occurs as a result of the input of the students, so the concepts of fixed and variable costs need redefinition.

Another issue is the unit for expressing costs. Typically in the cost-effectiveness literature relating to distance education (see, for example, Bates, 1995), costs are standardized per student and contact time. The meaning of contact time, however, is also changing in the context of flexible learning with technology, for example as when an instructor spends time via the WWW site with his or her students. In contrast, although many traditional higher-education institutions are moving toward more-flexible learning, there is still the tendency to use older models to calculate teaching load and compensation for teaching load, for example basing load on lecture hours in the lecture hall. For a contribution orientation, this sort of approach is meaningless.

Also, what to include as costs is difficult to specify. We will focus on two major categories: technology and instructor costs, although the costs of instructor support and of the students themselves should also be counted.

Costing models

Many costing models have been developed in order to measure the costs of educational delivery, in particular in relation to the use of new technologies (Bacsich *et al*, 1999). Bacsich concludes however that 'there are organizational barriers to accurate costing' (p 75). There is indeed a significant difference between a strong rationale for costing models and the applicability of such models in practice (Moonen, 1998).

To get an idea about potential cost items involved in maintaining a WWW-based system for flexible learning in an organization, Table 6.2 identifies some of the ongoing costs related to adopting such a system in an institution moving toward more-flexible learning supported by technology. Some of the costs are tangible, and thus can be estimated in advance. Many, however, are intangible, even when they can eventually be expressed in financial terms.

Table 6.2   *Costs involved in maintaining a WWW-based system for flexible learning in an institution*

Cost Category	Aspects
Technology (assuming a WWW-based system is licensed or bought)	– Licence or purchase costs for the system – Costs involved in time and effort to come to the decision about what system to purchase – Costs in terms of servers for the system – Costs related to impact on other network facilities in the institution – Costs related to increasing access to network technology for instructors and students – Increased printing costs; increased network-use costs – Costs related to maintenance, updates, expert help for system problems – Costs relating to adequate printers, back-up storage, projectors for display of computer screen during contact sessions
Technology-support personnel	– Help-desk personnel costs – Costs involved in training technical personnel to maintain the system – Costs involved in maintaining staff to support instructors in changing their teaching and making use of new technologies – Costs involved in having an adequate location for instructor support, such as a teaching and learning centre – Costs related to learning about and adapting to updates
Instructor costs	– Costs involved in time and effort needed to get started with and use the system – Costs (time and energy) involved in preparing a course, using the technology – Costs involved (time and energy) in supporting students during the course using the technology – Costs involved (financial) in accessing the technology when working at home – Costs related to learning about and adapting to updates
Student costs	– Costs involved in network access – Costs involved in obtaining and maintaining an adequate computer installation, including modem, printer, etc – Costs involved in extra time spent on new forms of computer-based activities

Problematic aspects

There are also problematical aspects. How to quantify and express as a cost the time and effort of the instructor when he or she starts to use a WWW-based system is not only difficult to judge ahead of time, but also difficult to express in terms of financial units. Many instructors in traditional universities are paid on a salary scale in which the amount of teaching, research and other responsibilities in which they are involved is not differentiated. If these instructors spend more time on their teaching because of flexible learning and new technologies, they are not paid more, nor in most cases are their other responsibilities decreased. They are just meant to fit it in. The issue of instructor cost, then, is not particularly a variable for the institution (unless new persons are hired) but certainly is for the instructor. In addition, many of the standard cost-effectiveness calculations relating to technology in education seem to assume that reducing lecture time reduces personnel costs. This is a strange assumption for regular full-time employees, both in terms of the nature of their monthly salaries (paid by monthly lump sum, not in terms of individual activities) and the fact that they may be spending more contact time with students in the type of activities we described in Chapter 5 than they would in presenting a lecture.

More complicated than direct financial costs are other sorts of costs – time, energy, frustration, anxiety, opportunity. For the instructor confronted with a computer that does not work minutes before a contact session in which he or she had planned to make extensive use of resources in the course WWW site as demonstration and discussion materials, the costs of the frustration are not quantifiable in terms of salary, but very much make an impact in terms of anxiety and stress level, and general attitude about using technology in instruction.

Thus, for the input side of ROI, more than financial costs needs to be considered; all factors relating to investment need to be balanced against the results, including those relating to time, energy, stress and effect on one's self-confidence and concentration. When equations become this complicated, however, the question of quantification becomes impossible to manage. In that respect the NCHEMS project (2000) reports that 'the ability of instructional technology to reduce costs in higher education is unknown'. Current costing formulae suffer from several drawbacks: they cannot be generalized beyond a campus or set of institutions; they require a level of detail and specificity that is not easily adapted; or they view technology implementation in isolation from the remainder of the campus.

However, with respect to costs, there is one constant that can be indicated. This constant appears whenever educational innovation involving technology occurs. Even the efficiency gains we noted as possible in Table 6.1 don't occur immediately when a WWW-based system is introduced in an institution. There is always a learning curve and start-up time. With the continual changes in technology it is difficult for instructors to get competent with a particular technology product so that the efficiencies it affords can start to be enjoyed. A new version of the software, a new system, a new feature, a new type of technology altogether, start the learning curve anew. This constant is expressed in the following lesson:

Lesson 17: *Be aware of the price tag*. It is not going to save time or money to use technology, at least not in the short term.

Simplified ROI

Thus, ROI-type thinking is important, but trying to be specific about ROI leads directly into problems, and into discussions beyond the patience level of decision makers. It is also theoretically complex. How to proceed?

The way we recommend is to abandon the idea of ROI calculation in an absolute and exhaustive way, and instead concentrate on a more intuitive (but still systematic) calculation that emphasizes the relative comparison of ROI in one situation and another. We call this a *simplified ROI*, comparing costs (investments) and benefits (returns) on a small number of key issues that matter most to those involved (Moonen, 2000a, in press a). The approach is based on the following principles and steps:

1. Keep the focus on a specific local context.
2. Consider only those items that will be or are changing in ways that are *meaningful* and will make a difference to those involved when moving from one way of operating to another. Keep this list as short as possible to be manageable and focused.
3. Concentrate those items in three major categories: items relating to and expressible in economic (often monetary) terms, items relating to and expressible in qualitative terms (often attitudes) and items relating to and expressible in efficiency terms (often in terms of time or effort to do a given task). Identify also the kinds of data you can obtain: tangible economic data (already known amounts of money), intangible economic data (costs will be involved but amounts are not yet known), qualitative (attitudes, beliefs, percentage of change, etc) and subjective ('fuzzy' data relating to general perceptions and expectations without basis in fact).
4. Identify the major actors that will be involved in the change; often these actors can be labelled as groups with an institutional interest (the management of an institution), instructors and students.
5. Consider, for each of the actors, the perceived impact with respect to the items in the three major categories: those related to economic aspects (often in the context of long-term results – benefits and costs), those related to qualitative terms (often in the context of learning and instruction – better or worse), or those related to efficiency aspects (often in the context of short-term results – more or less).
6. For each item and for each actor make a simple estimate of how the change will be perceived by that actor, for example on a scale from –5 to +5, where

−5 relates to an absolute disaster in comparison to the original situation, and +5 relates to a golden opportunity in comparison to the original situation. Use the most accurate data available.
7. Tally the results and use the totals as a basis for discussion.

The purpose is not precision (unless, of course, one can obtain tangible data on the items involved) but rather a guide to more systematic thinking about intuitive feelings and expectations. As an example, consider the following situation:

A decision maker in an educational institution announces that the institution is going to take a major step forward in terms of being a 'wired university'. A WWW system will be set up through which any prospective student considering enrolling can find out information about the courses at the university and see an example of a typical assignment or activity from each course. Instructors therefore must make these examples available via the WWW. If the prospective student wants more information about the course or about enrolling, all he or she has to do is submit a form via the WWW site and the institution promises that someone will make contact by e-mail the next day. The institution does not yet have a standard practice relating to putting course-related materials on the WWW and many instructors have not yet made use of a WWW environment in support of their teaching. The motivations for the university are potential growth in enrolment and marketing value, as well as reducing the time needed for personnel in the education office who now have to respond by mail and telephone to requests for information from prospective students.

Will this initiative have a good ROI? Table 6.3 shows the calculation using a simplified ROI approach. The items for which meaningful change is expected to occur are mentioned in the left-hand column. The groups of actors involved are stated in the first row. For each group, estimates for each of the items in the column are expressed subjectively and in relative terms on a scale from −5 to +5. The estimates can be made by a consultant or researcher after interviews or surveys with representatives of the different actors. Or they could be made by the representatives themselves. To illustrate the general flavour of this approach, the three major categories of economic, qualitative and efficiency returns have not been split up in separate tables. This is also reflected in the kind of data used: most of the data in the table are fuzzy and subjective regardless of the category.

In Table 6.3, only a small number of potentially meaningful benefits and costs are identified (selecting these is a useful exercise in itself to clarify thinking) and a score between −5 and +5 is given for each cell, to indicate an approximation of the meaningfulness of the item to the party involved compared to the current situation. A blank means the aspect has no particular meaning one way or the other to that actor. Other comments relating to Table 6.3 include:

Table 6.3 *ROI prediction for prospective-student WWW site example*

Actors	Institution	Educational Office Personnel	Instructors	Prospective Students
Meaningful aspects				
Potential growth in enrolment	+3	+3		
Marketing value; status of the university as a 'wired' university	+2	+1	−2	+2
Efficient way to maintain information on prospective students and their interests	+3	+3		
Depth of information for student decision making		+3		+4
Time and effort reduction for educational office personnel	+2	+3		
Time and effort for instructor to make the information available			−3	
Effort, time, for keeping the information in the system up to date	−1	−3	−3	
Problems when system malfunctions or information is not complete or not up to date		−4	−2	−4
Totals:	+ 10 −1 = +9	+13 −7 = + 6	−10	+6 −4 = +2

Numbers in the cells show an estimate of direction and amount of importance (−5 to +5), from the perspective of someone in the group represented in the column involved. Estimates are subjective, as no tangible base of comparison is available, for example to express expected percentage differences. The text gives the rationale for some of the estimations.

- The −2 for *marketing value/instructors* reflects the annoyance of many instructors at the perceived 'hype' of the notion and way of phrasing it, and also their annoyance that other initiatives are not being pursued while this one is.
- The −1 for *effort, time, for keeping the information in the system up to date* from the institutional perspective is probably a gross underestimate of what the costs will actually be for the institution. The −4 value for instructors relates to their awareness that they will have to keep submitting updates, which they anticipate to be a tedious and time-consuming yearly activity.
- The negatives for *instructor* and *students* when the *system malfunctions* represent the lost time and annoyance for the instructor if he or she has to resubmit information, and the annoyance for prospective students if they can't find something they think they would like to see, or worse, find out later that it is out of date or incorrect.

This simplified ROI exercise should be helpful in alerting decision makers to potentially vulnerable aspects of their plan. In particular, the negative total with respect to instructors and the weak-positive total relating to the group that was supposed to be impressed by the initiative (the students) should lead the decision makers at least to examine the potentially most problematic aspects of the innovation, in this case the time and effort for the instructor, and thus concretely to look for alternative ways for the course information to be input into the system before launching the idea to instructors.

The simplified ROI analysis can be made more sensitive by incorporating weighting factors with the various values. For example, in Table 6.3, the item relating to *marketing value* would probably be weighted highly for the institution but not the instructor, while in contrast the item *time and effort for the instructor* would be weighted highly for the instructor but (unfortunately) not for the institution.

There are a number of practical advantages of the simplified ROI approach. These include:

- The number of items chosen to consider is short. Only those that really matter to the actors involved are included.
- The approach takes in the perspectives of the different actors.
- Data of different types can be used with the approach. If specific amounts or percentages are available, they can be used, associated by a weighting coefficient. However, if data are no more than informed opinions, the approach can still be used (with, of course, weaker results).
- The approach can be used at different times: in the decision-making period to help predictions and decisions, to support formative evaluation after some experience has been accumulated, or for a summative assessment if data are known.
- The approach can steer discussion and analysis, in terms of what items to use for the rows, what sorts of data could be available, which actors are most affected by change in the row items and how the input from these actor groups should be expressed and weighted.

We are finding the simplified ROI approach to be a manageable strategy to help decision makers move intuition-based decisions about technology and flexible learning one step forward towards more systematic thinking. A more extensive example of a simplified-ROI analysis applied to a real situation in our own institute is given in Chapter 8. This section concludes with another lesson:

Lesson 18: *Play the odds.* A simplified approach to predicting return on investment (ROI) that looks at the perceived amount of relative change in the factors that matter most to different actors is a useful approach.

Summing up: who wins, who loses?

Using simplified ROI as a basis to predict what will happen after introducing more-flexible learning using technology in an institution suggests a number of speculations, focusing on the institution, student and instructor. We close this chapter with a few:

ROI for the institution
- We predict that the institution in the long run will win or at least not lose, in that it will shift its costs to instructors and to students whose 'time' and 'efforts' are perceived by the institution as free.
- The institution in the long run will win or at least not lose, in that it will fund the new initiative with special short-term funding and thus will not have to sustain these particular technology-related costs over time. If an investment after the special funding is sustainable, it will bring in enough money to pay for itself. The responsibility for the continuation will eventually rest with some unit within the institution; the unit will stop if the sustainability fails.

ROI for the student
- Students win, but in a complicated way. They will probably have to have more costs relating to acquiring and using networks and computers, but with increases of flexibility they can travel less, spend less time on campus, be more efficient in terms of course procedures. Also, there is the potential, if they take advantage of it, to pull out better quality (more contacts, more interaction, more resources, even courses or learning experiences at other universities), thus a gain.

ROI for the instructor
- The instructor has the potential to be the loser in terms of ROI, particularly in terms of having the expectations of the students heightened about more interaction and participation, and needing to spend more time to move into new ways of teaching. This can be balanced if the instructor learns to exploit the efficiency of the technology system, if he or she feels a benefit from the

increased contacts with the students and the new forms of interaction, or if the institution rewards him or her in some way for the new efforts.

● The instructor also can move to a positive ROI if some of the costs of the production of course resources and some of the costs of interactivity in a course can be shifted from him or her to the students. The instructor still has to maintain quality control, but can have the benefit of new ideas and resources for the course even if he or she does not have to create them.

For the institution, we predict that the question of 'When do (or don't) we get our investment back?' is likely to be answered in a positive way in the long term, if gains in enrolment or other desirable changes in operating procedures or perceived institutional stature occur related to the flexible-learning initiative. For the instructor, a positive ROI is most likely to come from a combination of increased efficiency and a belief in the value of new forms of teaching and learning. For the student, a positive ROI is most likely to reflect more flexibility and more quality.

After so much abstraction, it is time to turn to actual examples of the concepts and ideas in Chapters 1-6 in terms of our own experience in the last three years (1997–2000). In the next two chapters we show how we are practising the lessons that we preach, in our own institution. We conclude this chapter by reviewing its lessons:

Lesson 16: *Get a new measuring stick.* What we are most interested in regarding learning as a consequence of using technology often can't be measured in the short term or without different approaches to measurement. Measure what can be measured, such as short-term gains in efficiency or increases in flexibility.

Lesson 17: *Be aware of the price tag.* It is not going to save time or money to use technology, at least not in the short term.

Lesson 18: *Play the odds.* A simplified approach to predicting return on investment (ROI) that looks at the perceived amount of relative change in the factors that matter most to different actors is a useful approach.

Chapter 7

Practising what we preach: getting started

In the previous chapters we have developed a set of 18 lessons, which we predominately argued via literature references and general statements about our own experience. In this chapter and the next, we make that experience explicit. In particular, we focus on our experiences since mid-1997 in leading our faculty to more flexible learning with technology. Do we practise what we preach?

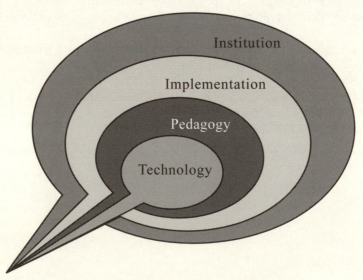

Figure 7.1 *Flexible learning in higher education – initiation experiences*

These illustrations will involve a case from our own institution, the University of Twente in The Netherlands, during the years 1997–2000. We are both members of the same department in the same faculty (the Faculty of Educational Science and Technology, abbreviated as 'TO' from its Dutch name) in this institution, and have been since the late 1980s. Many times we have worked together on the same projects, other times not. For convenience in Chapters 7 and 8 we will not differentiate who did what, but just use the general 'we'.

The purpose of the chapter is not only to illustrate the lessons, but also to give practical examples that others hopefully can shape to their own situations. The chapter will be a success to the degree to which others can say, 'Yes, this is like our situation; I have an idea of how to apply the experiences in my own situation.' The structure of the two chapters is as follows:

Chapter 7
- the pioneer phase: 1990–97;
- the initiation phase: 1997–98, Year 1 of TeleTOP;

Chapter 8
- the implementation phase: Year 2 of TeleTOP, 1998–99;
- from implementation to institutionalization: Year 3 of TeleTOP, 1999–2000;
- institutionalization: 2000 and beyond.

Throughout, we will refer to the lessons in terms of the short phrases that begin each lesson. For convenience, we group the lessons together in Table 7.1.

Table 7.1 *The lessons learnt*

Lesson 1 *Be specific.*	We need to define our terms and express our goals in a measurable form or else progress will be difficult to steer and success difficult to claim.
Lesson 2 *Move from student to professional.*	Learning in higher education is not only a knowledge-acquisition process but also a process of gradual participation in and contribution to a professional community. Pedagogy should reflect both acquisition and contribution–oriented models.
Lesson 3 *You can't not do it.*	The idea whose time has come is irresistible.
Lesson 4 *Don't forget the road map.*	Changes takes a long time and is an iterative process, evolving in ways that are often not anticipated.
Lesson 5 *Watch the 4 Es.*	An individual's likelihood of voluntarily making use of a particular type of technology for a learning-related purpose is a function of the 4 Es: the environment context, the individual's perception of educational effectiveness, ease of use, and sense of personal engagement with the technology. The environmental context and the individual's sense of personal engagement are the most important.

Lesson 6 *Follow the leader.*	Key persons are critical.
Lesson 7 *Be just in time.*	Staff-engagement activities to stimulate instructors to make use of technology are generally not very effective. Focus on just-in-time support for necessary tasks.
Lesson 8 *Get out of the niche.*	Most technology products are not used in practice beyond developers. Keep implementation and the 4 Es central in choosing any technology product.
Lesson 9 *After the core, choose more.*	Technology selection involves a core and complementary technologies. The core is usually determined by history and circumstances; changing it usually requires pervasive contextual pressure. The individual instructor can make choices about complementary technologies and should choose them with flexibility in mind.
Lesson 10 *Don't overload*	More is not necessarily better.
Lesson 11 *Offer something for everyone.*	A well-designed WWW-based system should offer users a large variety of possibilities to support flexible and participative learning not dominated by any one background orientation. If so, it is the most appropriate (core or complementary) technology for flexible learning.
Lesson 12 *Watch the speed limit.*	Don't try to change too much at the same time. Start where the instructor is at, and introduce flexibility via extending contact sessions to include before, during and after aspects, with each of these made more flexible. Move gradually into contribution.
Lesson 13 *Process yields product.*	Through the process of contribution-oriented learning activities, learners themselves help produce the learning materials for the course.
Lesson 14 *Aim for activity.*	The key roles of the instructor are becoming those of activity planning, monitoring and quality control.
Lesson 15 *Design for activity.*	Instructional design should concentrate more on activities and processes, and less on content and a predetermined product.
Lesson 16 *Get a new measuring stick.*	What we are most interested in regarding learning as a consequence of using technology often can't be measured in the short term or without different approaches to measurement. Measure what can be measured, such as short-term gains in efficiency or increases in flexibility.
Lesson 17 *Be aware of the price tag.*	It is not going to save time or money to use technology, at least not in the short term.
Less on 18 *Play the odds.*	A simplified approach to predicting return on investment (ROI) that looks at the perceived amount of relative change in the factors that matter most to different factors is a useful approach.

The pioneer phase: early 1990s to 1997

We begin by reviewing a sampling of our pioneer experiences at the University of Twente that contributed to our current faculty-wide use of the TeleTOP WWW-based course-management system. We had both been pioneers with the use of technology in our own teaching for many years (for example, Collis, 1982, 1988; Moonen and Gastkemper, 1983; Moonen, 1989a, 1989b) but will pick up the story in the early 1990s at the University of Twente.

Pioneers, pre-WWW

In our faculty in the early 1990s, our work evolved to the application of data-communication tools and systems for educational purposes into our own teaching, with our regular on-campus students. What we and some of our colleagues were doing was revolutionary, in The Netherlands at least, because we were using tools such as e-mail, computer-conferencing systems and then, in 1994, WWW sites, not for distance education but to extend and redesign our teaching with students whom we saw face to face and who saw one another regularly. We evolved the term '*tele-learning*', the application of information and communication technology (called telematics in The Netherlands and several other European countries) for learning-related purposes (Collis, 1996d) to relate to this broad context. But for many years (and even still) we had to explain that there was more to flexible learning than only distance flexibility and more to the use of network technology than only distance education. The next three subsections give an overview of this pioneer period.

Early experimentation: e-mail and collaborative tools

Our pioneer work during this period was partly with our own courses, but also via a number of special projects in which we were involved. In terms of examples from our regular, on-campus courses in the early 1990s, we used the annotation tools available in Windows so that students could contribute reflective comments to scientific articles and make these comments available to the instructor and one another via a type of shared electronic workspace. We began using e-mail and a listserv as tools for weekly assignments involving students locating extra course resources in the library and telling one another about what they had found. Along with another pioneer colleague, we used the computer-conferencing system *First Class* (http://www.softarc.com/) for several years, to support discussion, collaborative learning, and general course organization for our students. From these initial experiences and also our work in the 1970s and 1980s with computers in education, we learnt many of our lessons. A first-year compulsory course in multimedia design called *ISM-1,* in which we have been instructors for many years, is a prime example. We will now discuss it in some detail (summarized from Collis and Gervedink Nijhuis, 2001).

ISM-1, pre-WWW phase

Lesson 14: *Aim for activity.*

The course ISM-1 was a requirement for first-year students in our faculty, which introduced them to the specialty of educational technology. In this course students learnt to design and develop various media products for learning support in a group-based project setting based on the *Jigsaw Method* (Aronson *et al*, 1978). This method involves each student having his or her own role in the group so that they learn from one another within their groups. In addition, they learn from those who share their specialisms in other groups.

The ISM-1 course evolved from an approach of teacher-guided practical sessions in the computer laboratory with extensive individual face-to-face communication between an instructor and students, to an instructional form of self-guided work within group projects and using computer communications (to begin with, computer conferencing) to support individual students as well as project groups (Collis and Breman, 1997; Collis and Meeuwsen, 1999; Collis *et al*, 1996). The role of the instructor changed, from 'teacher' to planner and monitor of student activities designed to be carried out by students working together on their own (with appropriate instructions and support materials).

Although the students had been using computers to create their media products for many years in this course, it was in the academic year 1995–96 that computers were for the first time used to support the overall teaching and learning processes in the course itself. The computer-conferencing system First Class was used. Using this system made it easy to present assignments to all students via the computer so that an archival version was always at hand, to communicate in a structured way between the instructors and the students as a whole, and in informal ways within the groups. Separate from the folders in the computer-conferencing system was the private e-mail sent among the course participants. Some of this (over a thousand messages!) was in the First Class e-mail area, but others came via the ordinary e-mail system used in the faculty and thus were not archived in the First Class environment.

Lesson 17: *Be aware of the price tag.*

While the use of First Class helped us to make the conceptual jump towards the idea of using a networked system to serve as a communal communication, work and archival area for students who otherwise were in regular face-to-face contact, it also taught us some major lessons. It was difficult for us as instructors to manage all of the course materials, as they were scattered among First Class folders, First Class e-mail, ordinary e-mail and also in materials not submitted electronically (videotapes and desktop-published materials of various sorts produced by the students). We had over 3,000 items in First Class by the end of the course, and we did not even try to quantify all the other materials. We could barely manage all this activity. Having the print and video materials submitted by the students available in a central location where any member of the instructor team could access them when needed was cumbersome, and organizing and handling the management of all of the course materials took an enormous amount of time. We needed one integrated electronic environment in which communication, student projects, archival material, course information, course resources and also our own internal team communication could all be conveniently managed. And we needed strategies to cut down on the amount of communication and material we needed to manage, even while keeping the richness of what was going on.

Research developments

Lesson 5: *Watch the 4 Es.*

Our pioneer work during this pre-WWW period was also of a research nature. For example, we carried out a project for the Ministry of Education on the state of the art internationally of educational uses of computer communications (Collis and De Vries, 1991). It was in this project that we first developed the *4-E Model* (Chapter 3; in those days it was the *3-G Model*, using Dutch words beginning with 'g' for the vectors relating to educational effectiveness, ease of use and personal engagement; we added the 4th E for the environment later). In subsequent national and international studies in 1992 and 1993, we urged decision makers to apply the 3-G approach to guide the implementation of network technology and illustrated ways for this to occur, in Dutch education (Collis, Veen and De Vries, 1994; Moonen and Kommers, 1995), and more generally (Collis and De Vries, 1993). Also, at the same time, in national and international projects focused on cost-effectiveness of technology in education relating to technology (Moonen, 1994, 1997), the roots of the simplified ROI approach (Chapter 6) were established.

Lesson 8: *Get out of the niche.*

We also continued to be involved in national projects relating to the development and stimulation of educational software use (Collis and De Diana, 1990; Moonen and Beishuizen, 1992). From these experiences, the observation that most educational-software products developed in such special projects were rarely used beyond the project was re-enforced.

Pioneers with the educational use of the WWW

A major breakthrough occurred in early 1994. A radical new form of network interconnectivity called the *World Wide Web* had been emerging at the CERN Institute in Switzerland and *browser* software began to be available. We began using WWW functionalities in our own courses, in particular a course called *On-Line Learning* (later *Tele-Learning*) and the course ISM-1 (described above).

The Tele-Learning course

Our course On-Line Learning in March 1994 was one of the first courses anywhere not only to make use of WWW functionalities, but also to support new types of learning activities that extend the regular on-campus course via those functionalities. This course, now called Tele-Learning, has gone through seven yearly cycles, and remains a source of pioneering activities integrating advanced WWW-based technology with new forms of pedagogy (Collis, 1997b, 1998d).

Lesson 13: *Process yields product.*

We began using the term 'pedagogical re-engineering' in this course to describe the redesign of teaching, supported by the WWW, for new forms of student engagement (Collis, 1997b). Among the ideas that evolved in this course were: the use of the WWW for support of a collaborative writing project involving participants in other countries, working together with our own students, to produce WWW-based study materials that would be reused and further developed by students in the next cycle of the course, an example of *process yields product*. We also began the use of a matrix-like structure that we called a *roster* integrated within a WWW site as a way to organize the content and assignments of a course and combine these with communication and instructor and student contributions to it, the support of group-based projects with various WWW-based groupware tools and the use of WWW-based fill-in forms to simplify and structure student and instructor communication. All of these helped us gain ideas and experience with the idea of students' creating study materials that could be reused by others.

ISM-1, early WWW uses (1996–97)

From the experiences in the Tele-Learning course, we knew we wanted to apply WWW functionalities to remedy our management problems as well as enrich the learning processes in the ISM-1 course. Thus, in the academic year 1996–97 a WWW-based environment was built to support the students in all aspects of the ISM-1 course. We replaced First Class with a *Netscape* browser as the interface to integrate all aspects of the course. Figure 7.2 shows part of the *Week-by-Week Centre* that we designed for the WWW environment, showing the way that it

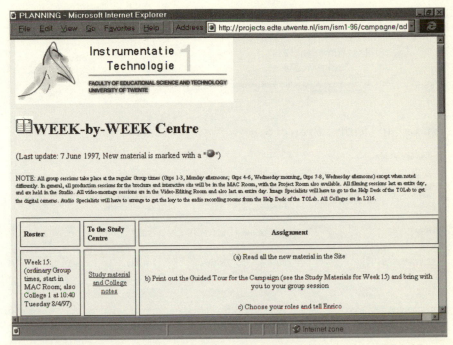

Figure 7.2 *Week-by-Week Centre of Project 3 of the ISM-1 course, 1996–97 (http://www.edte.utwente.nl/ism/ism1–96/campagne/admctr/planning.htm)*

served as an integrated entry point for students for both their theoretical study and their group-based project work.

Figure 7.3 shows what we called a *Group Centre* for one of the projects. Via this page, there was an integration of instructions from the instructors and links to planning documents of the group; to the group's final projects (an interactive, multimedia WWW site with video); and to different forms of evaluation related to the products, from the group as well as the instructors.

The main advantages were the user-friendly WWW interface, the fact that all course information and materials were directly available in the same environment, and the ability to integrate visualizations and the multimedia products made by the students in a hyperlinked way to the overall course-support environment. All materials were presented using a menu structure available via a navigation frame, and icons clarified the functionality of specific areas of the WWW site.

For us as instructors, all of this helped enormously with a number of management burdens associated with the course, particularly through the integration of all course resources via one WWW site. But at the same time these ways of using WWW functionalities added new management burdens. We still spent a large amount of time on the course, but now much of that was going into the management of the site instead of leading face-to-face sessions with students. It

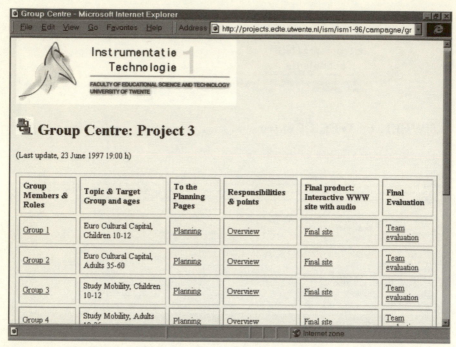

Figure 7.3   *Group Centre page for one of the projects in ISM-1, 1996–97 cycle, showing the integration of materials from the instructors, groupware tools, the multimedia products made by the groups themselves, and feedback (http://www.edte.utwente.nl/ism/ism1-96/campagne/groupctr/groupcen.htm)*

was very helpful that student submissions were linked directly to the Group Centre pages so we could compare them with previous planning and feedback via a mouse click, but it took us a great deal of time to make these pages consistent in detail and layout and usable for the students. A database-driven system was needed so that pages would be generated in a consistent way, and without an instructor needing to enter page content and set-up more than once. This led to our awareness of the value of a WWW-based course-management system.

In the 1997–98 cycle of the ISM-1 course a revised version of the WWW environment was designed and used. A new technology approach made it easier for students to contribute materials to the environment as their answers were not only posted automatically to the WWW site, but also in the correct layout. Students were then able to see the results, for example of the peer evaluations, and compare their reactions on assignments with the reactions of other students and with a model answer. This was another step forward towards a contribution-oriented approach in which student work is used as part of the study materials (Lessons 2 and 13). In Figure 7.4 an example of an assignment of this kind is

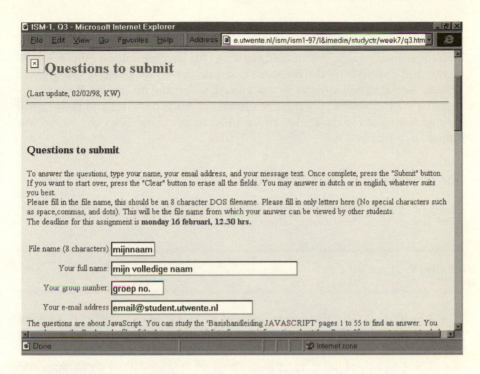

Figure 7.4   *Exercises in the use of JavaScript in the 1997–98 cycle of ISM-1, whereby the answers of the students were immediately archived within the course WWW environment, after which the student could compare his or her answer to those of other students and to a model answer*
(http://projects.edte.utwente.nl/ism/ism1–97/I&imedia/studyctr/week7/q3.htm)

shown in which students submitted a small JavaScript code that was automatically tested when submitted.

From pioneers to initiation

As our own courses evolved in their use of WWW sites, tools and resources, so also during the period 1995-97 did the use of WWW-based resources, tools and systems in several other courses in our faculty as well. In addition, experience with the WWW and more-flexible forms of teaching and learning accumulated through being the focus of a number of Masters' theses and externally funded projects (for example, European Union-sponsored *TeleScopia Project* (Collis, Vingerhoets and Moonen, 1997) involving the design and development of innovative uses of WWW technology to support different forms of flexible learning). By mid-1997 there was a solid base of experience in our faculty in the application of telematics tools, systems and resources for learning-related purposes. The faculty had moved from the pioneer phase into the *1,000 flowers blooming* phase (Collis, 1997a). Then a major step occurred: a decision by the faculty management to use the WWW as a tool for systemic, managed change and pedagogical re-engineering throughout the entire programme. The *TeleTOP project* was launched in August 1997.

The pioneer period and lessons learnt

What lessons emerged or had major impact during this pioneer period? Several have already been mentioned; others are described below.

Lesson 5: *Watch the 4 Es.*

The 4 Es (then, 3 Gs) helped us understand a number of experiences during this period. First, although eventually seven faculty members became involved with the use of the WWW or non-WWW computer conferencing, the remainder did not. The 4 Es helped us interpret this. Those of us who did use technology had high personal-engagement levels and were convinced of the value of the new sorts of learning activities that we needed the WWW sites to support. Ease of use was certainly negative for us, but we persisted. Our colleagues, with low or negative values for all three of these variables (personal engagement, learning effectiveness, ease of use), did not.

   The period also taught us that students need concrete incentives to respond positively to the use of technology and to new pedagogies. For our students, the effectiveness vector is expressed in terms of what they can earn points for in their courses (Collis, 1997c; Moonen, 1994). Students especially are annoyed if the use of technology forces them to spend time on procedural tasks that they didn't have to do before, such as printing study materials from the WWW site (Van Rennes and Collis, 1998). They much prefer printed text for their primary readings, and do not like to read from the screen. Even with multimedia and interactive resources, they still want to print out the text, take it away and read it at home or on the train. Ease of use is more compelling than (potential) learning effectiveness. This can be disappointing and frustrating to the instructor who has put considerable effort into a new learning activity involving technology, and adversely affect his or her level of personal engagement. Only the pioneers will go on.

Lesson 11: *Offer something for everyone.*

Several major lessons came out of our courses that made use of e-mail and list-servs and computer-conferencing systems. These tools were not enough. It was frustrating that there was no convenient way to archive e-mail, and that everyone had to read e-mail via their e-mail programs which were not integrated with other tools and environments. Also, while communication and discussion were important, they were not the only forms of student participation we wished to support. Computer conferencing in itself did not provide a good way to support group work on design projects, where the partial products needed to be referred to for discussion. WWW functionalities evolved quickly to offer not only all of the individual sorts of tools we had been using before in an uninte-grated fashion, but also to offer the tools integrated with one another, and with student work and submissions as well as with other study materials.

Lesson 10: *Don't overload.*

Another lesson we learnt during this time made a major impact on us. Having students communicate was good, but soon became overwhelming for the instructor. More is not better, after a point. One year we had over 3,000 items in the computer-conferencing environment for one of our courses, a mixture of entries from the instructor that were important course resources, student submis-sions and feedback from the instructors, general instructions and course informa-tion, and messages from students and from the instructors about procedures. We learnt that communication should be structured, and stored in convenient, well-defined locations where it is accessible to everyone but not a bother to them. The folders in a computer-conferencing environment soon were too constraining. Either we had too many, or too many levels of nesting within folders. Also, we found that a certain amount of communication was procedural only, and could be avoided if we wrote instructions and expectations very clearly in the WWW site, even if we saw students regularly. We had to teach the students to 'check the WWW site' first, before sending us an e-mail to ask a procedural question.

Lesson 9: *After the core, choose more.*

Yet another important lesson we learnt from these pioneer experiences was the importance of a good choice of core and complementary resources. In our courses, the course WWW site quickly became the core technology, but this did not mean that it should be the only technology. In particular, the WWW was not the best technology to present the primary reading materials for the course to the students. We learnt over time to use the WWW site to supplement those printed reading materials with student- and instructor-submitted extra URLs, with structured communication about the readings, and with interactive applets or self-test questions to help students with understanding the study materials.

Lesson 13: *Process yields product.*

We started to talk about pedagogical re-engineering in 1996 (Collis, 1996d). We became aware of the distinction in our use of our WWW sites and before that, computer conferencing, between uses that were primarily aimed at the efficiency and flexibility of procedures, and uses that related to new types of student activities. The main examples became 'active-learner', contribution-oriented activities (Chapter 5) in which the students themselves create and contribute study resources for one another, to build upon, to discuss and to become part of the course resources for subsequent cohorts of students. Without well-designed technology, we could not have managed these sorts of activities in any feasible way.

Lesson 12: *Watch the speed limit.*

Lesson 14: *Aim for activity.*

Finally, a major lesson from our pioneer days related to the change in our own roles as instructors. We shifted, from primarily being the facilitators of student acquisition to primarily being the designers and moderators of student activities, particularly in collaborative groups. This brought new tasks, and took more time than before. Interestingly, we also had to spend time defending these new approaches, to students, to our colleagues, to faculty committees, all of these distrustful that this was 'real teaching', or that students could learn with these approaches, or many other fears. Students feared they were being short-changed by having to take more responsibility for learning. Many worried that quality would unacceptably decline if the instructors were not always the source of course materials. Thus we learnt from our experiences that new forms of student activity were possible, and exciting, but that the evolution towards them would have to take time and a culture change.

The culture change took place in the academic year 1997–98.

The initiation phase: 1997–98, Year 1 of TeleTOP

The *1,000 flowers blooming* in our faculty were bringing the faculty recognition from both within and outside the university. At the start of the academic year 1997, the faculty leadership decided to commit itself to a tele-learning initiative. By the end of the academic year 1997–98, this initiative, named *TeleTOP*, had moved rapidly, with all the first-year courses in the curriculum redesigned for more flexibility and ready to begin in September 1998. A new WWW-based system had been designed, built and used for an initial set of courses as well as forming the core technology for all of the courses that were ready to begin.

How did we do all of this within a year? In this section we summarize this initiation phase and relate it to the lessons. The following were key aspects of the initiation year with the approximate times that the aspects were of major focus:

- setting goals and making fundamental strategic decisions (Months 1–3);
- developing key principles (Months 1–3);
- developing and using an implementation model (Months 2–4);
- developing a WWW-based system (Months 2–6, initial; Months 6–12, Version 1);
- developing and carrying out an instructor-engagement strategy (Months 3–12);
- developing and using the *TeleTOP Decision Support Tool* (Months 3–12);
- getting all first-year courses redesigned for pedagogical extension (Months 9–12).
- dealing with unexpected and expected problems (Months 3–12).

We will discuss these in the following subsections of this chapter, relating our decisions in each to a key lesson.

Goals and strategic decisions

Lesson 1: *Be specific.*

The faculty management launched the TeleTOP project around several goals: to make our instructional practice more efficient for the students, and more flexible, and to build on the faculty's reputation as a leader in tele-learning. What was a key factor to the initiation of TeleTOP was the fact that the major goals were also expressed in specific, measurable form. The faculty committed itself to a new cohort of mature working students who would like to do our unique educational technology curriculum in a flexible way while primarily remaining in their homes and jobs. This cohort would be advertised for during 1997–98, and would begin in September 1998.

A critical point was that the strategy for this cohort would not be one of typical distance education, with parallel courses for regular and distance students, but rather that our entire pedagogical approach would be redesigned, so that more-flexible learning, based on an instructional principle of the active student, would be available for all students. Thus, the goal for TeleTOP was to do what was necessary for this to happen. We had a concrete goal: get ready for the new cohort of students, who primarily would not be physically present, but not treat them as a separate stream of 'distance education' students.

Lesson 6: *Follow the leader.*

Having the specific goal of preparing for the new cohort and the more flexible approach to course delivery led to an important spin-off. The faculty management decided that all instructors would have to be involved, not just volunteers. All of the first-year courses would have to be redesigned for the new approach by the start of the next academic year. The following year, all of the second-year courses would have to be redesigned. After that would come all the third-year courses, and then the fourth-year, elective courses. Everyone had to do it.

This was essential for the development of a critical mass and culture change within the faculty. It was an unusual decision; usually if institutions do move toward managed, systemic change, they begin with some pilot experiences and work via encouraging volunteers to participate (De Boer and Collis, in press). It required commitment and courage from the faculty leadership. It also required a strong team with strong leadership.

As a key strategic decision, the faculty leadership supplied start-up funding in order to form the TeleTOP team. In addition to one of us as the leader, funding was available to hire five new team members. Those hired were all recent graduates of our programme who had chosen a technological orientation for their Masters' theses. Four had also trained as teachers before coming to our programme. All were experienced in the design and development of innovative WWW environments to support learning situations. It was important to have leadership and a team who were in tune with our instructors and who had personal experience themselves in the sorts of activities that the instructors were going to be encountering.

Key principles

Lesson 5: *Watch the 4 Es.*

Even though it was the case that all instructors were told that they were going to change, in a university environment, without instructor commitments, such an order would not be successful. A top–down/bottom–up approach, based on the 4 Es, was essential. An important first step was to articulate the key principles of the initiative in a way that was convincing educationally. After several weeks of discussion with key members of the faculty, we indicated the following key principles, and began the process of consensus-building around the principles, all of which we derived with the 4 Es in mind (Carleer and Collis, 1998):

1. Learning arises from the *active engagement* of the learner, and a *communication-oriented* pedagogy. The active student is our base.
2. Because of changes in society, students are increasingly diverse. Thus, our courses must become more flexible, not only in location but also in programme, types of interactions, types of communication, and learning materials. A combination of new pedagogies and the use of a well-designed WWW system would make these flexibilities, as well as the active-student principle, concrete.
3. We will use technology to extend good teaching, not to replace the instructor but rather to amplify what he or she does well. 'Extending the good instructor' will be one of our mottoes.
4. We will use a 'teach once, adapt within' approach whereby the general timetabling of all courses is the same for both cohorts of students, in terms of when the course begins and ends and when certain key events occur, such as the final examinations.
5. There will be a 'common day' approximately every second Friday, when all students who can, come together physically on our campus. Each course begins with an introductory whole-group session of approximately one hour during those common Fridays, so that the instructor can efficiently communicate his or her view of the course, and the students can better visualize the instructor when receiving electronic communications. Also, social contacts among the students can be facilitated.
6. In place of traditional lectures (now to be only 3 instead of 10 or 12 per course), the instructor will focus on new forms of student activity, primarily through the use of the WWW site and techniques such as fill-in forms for structured communication and reflective activities.
7. The WWW system will be a core technology, but complementary technologies, particularly textbooks, are also important. The instructor, not an instructional designer or technician, is the shaper, developer and manager of his or her own WWW site. He or she uses it as a personal tool, not as an instructional product pre-made elsewhere.

These principles were rooted in the 4 Es (Lesson 5):

● To win instructor (and student) *engagement*, we needed to emphasize that instructors were not being undercut or replaced by technology, but that it was to be a tool to amplify what they already do well. Textbooks do not have

to be abandoned. The opening lecture of a class where the instructor estab-
lishes his or her rapport with the students continues as a face-to-face event
(with provision via the WWW site for students who are not able to be
present). Instructors work from a process of redesign of existing courses for
pedagogical extension, building on what they already do. (This was a start-up
step; later, in Year 3, more focus on pedagogical re-engineering occurred.)
The aspect of fit to the instructor's comfort level with regard to teaching was
strong.

● To argue *effectiveness*, we stressed both the learning aspects of the active
  student and the long-term pay-off aspect related to the institution serving
  more students.

● To strengthen the *environmental* context, we redesigned the organizational
  structures for course delivery, particularly in limiting the number of lectures.
  An overall approach was chosen, in which the institutional practice itself was
  changed (fewer lectures, 'common Fridays', etc).

● Key to facilitating all of this was an *easy-to-use* WWW system designed to
  support the above principles, and a process by which the WWW system
  comes to be used in as easy-as-possible steps, taking a minimal amount of the
  instructor's time and fitting with the instructor's way of working.

Implementation model

We knew from all of our experiences with the implementation of technological
innovations in educational practice (see Chapter 3) that we as the team responsible for making TeleTOP succeed needed a comprehensive view of the implementation process, to remind us at all times of the many variables that needed
our simultaneous attention. Based on the literature, we evolved the (first version
of the) *TeleTOP Implementation Model* shown in Figure 7.5 (Collis and De Boer,
1999a). The model has since evolved further, but the one shown in Figure 7.5
guided us in the initiation phase. The emphasis in 1997–98 was on the transition
from initiation to implementation; thus the majority of the change entities in the
model related to that period.

All of the change entities shown in Figure 7.5 were critical for us. But such a
theoretical analysis had to be translated into practical processes. We translated our
TeleTOP Implementation Model into the *TeleTOP Method*. Table 7.2 shows
how we mapped the change entities into our operating procedures.

Many if not most of our lessons can be related to aspects of the TeleTOP
Method as outlined in Table 7.2. We will illustrate this more specifically by
expanding on a number of aspects of the method as the chapter progresses. In the
following portions of this section, we focus on three: the TeleTOP WWW-
based course-management system; and two aspects related to instructor engagement: the TeleTOP Decision Support Tool and the TeleTOP rapid-prototyping
approach.

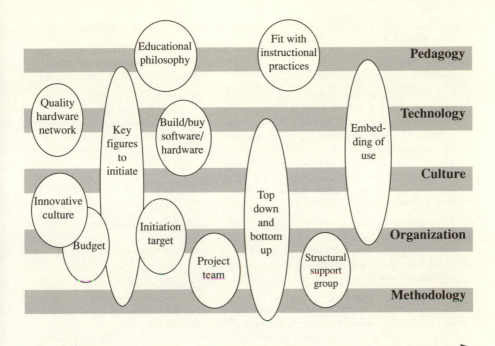

Figure 7.5 *The TeleTOP Implementation Model, Version 1, from initiation to institutionalization (Collis and De Boer, 1999a; De Boer and Collis, in press)*

The TeleTOP WWW system

Lesson 11: *Offer something for everyone.*

Lesson 8: *Get out of the niche.*

Given the above method, based on our fundamental principles of supporting and extending the good instructor, not expecting him or her to drop effective teaching approaches but instead extend them, we identified some critical requirements for the WWW-based course-support system we would use for our implementation period. These requirements relate not only to Lesson 11 (*Offer something for everyone*) and Lesson 8 (*Get out of the niche*) but also to Lesson 5 (*Watch the 4 Es*), Lesson 9 (*After the core, choose more*) and Lesson 15 (*Design for activity*). These requirements included the following (see also Chapter 4; and Collis, 1999a; Tielemans and Collis, 1999), each of them referenced to the 4 Es:

Table 7.2 *The TeleTOP Method, related to the initiation phase (see Figure 7.5)
(Collis, 1999a)*

TeleTOP Method (listed in order of importance)	Circles in the Initiation Phase (listed in order of importance)
1. The TeleTOP educational philosophy underlying all aspects of the TeleTOP Method: (a) extending, not replacing, the good instructor and the good textbook; (b) increasing student participation and communication; and (c) redesigning the nature of lectures to have fewer of them but more student activity and instructor feedback before, during and after contract sesssion, for both regular and part-time students.	Educational philosophy Top down and bottom up Fit with instructional practices Key figures to initiate
2. The strategic principle for the 'multiple use' of courses: of designing a course to *teach once, adapt within for individual differences*, via re-usable units of learning materials contributed by students and the instructor.	Educational philosophy Top down Key figures to initiate
3. An educationally grounded analysis approach used for the course-redesign process, involving six categories of course components and two focuses for adaptation (pedagogical extension, re-engineering).	Educational philosophy Fit with instructional practices Bottom up
4. The WWW-based *TeleTOP Decision Support Tools* (Version 1, for use during initial decision making by the instructor relating to functionalities for his or her course-support environment, and Version 2, for final decision making about the functionalities) (see later in this section).	Fit with instructional practices Quality hard/software and network project team Top down and bottom up Innovative culture
5. The *TeleTOP rapid-prototyping approach,* whereby each instructor goes through an eight-step sequence of contact sessions, involving successive prototypes and partially to fully finalized versions of the instructor's course-support environment (see later in this section).	Fit with instructional practices Project team Top down and bottom up Budget Quality hard/software and network
6. The technical environment created for TeleTOP that consists of the code developed by the TeleTOP team for the integration of a Domino server, a Domino database engine and an HTTP server, and that generates the user-friendly WWW based user interface characteristic of TeleTOP course-support sites (see later in this section).	Quality hard/software and network Budget Project team Key figures to initiate Innovative culture Fit with instructional practices Top down and bottom up Educational philosophy
7. The *roster* as the integrating area for course-support activity within each course's WWW environment (see later in this chapter).	Fit with instructional practices Quality hard/software and network Project team Top down and bottom up Educational philosophy

8. A technique for synchronizing the replay of-captured presentations via the combination of video, audio and PowerPoint slides-on-demand and in any sequence for lectures-on-demand as well as other instructional purposes (see later in this chapter).

Quality hard/software and network
Innovative culture
Key figures to initiate

---

1. To make the threshold of use as low as possible for the instructors, so that the WWW environments are as easy for them to handle as a word processor, without having to have a special training course. The instructor should be able to choose the features he or she desires to support the course, and only has to type into various fill-in forms to organize the notes and other material that are to be put into the WWW site as well as the feedback to be given to students. (E = ease of use; E = effectiveness, short-term pay-off – efficiency)

2. Students also must be able to use the system without instruction, and with no more support than a small manual. Once they are familiar with the interface of one course-support environment, they should have a consistent interface in all their other courses, reducing the need to learn to handle new environments with each new course. The environments are to be accessed through familiar WWW browsers: no new packages to learn, and nothing that requires them to come to the computer laboratory to use it. (E = ease of use)

3. Similarly, the instructor must be able to do everything he or she wishes with the course through an ordinary WWW browser: no special authoring software, no special client. An instructor travelling out of the country can work on his or her course wherever there is access to the Internet via a standard browser without needing to have access to the server. (E = ease of use; E = effectiveness, short-term pay-off – efficiency)

4. By the principle *extending the good instructor*, instructors must be able to choose for themselves the way that a WWW site will be used to support their courses (**Lesson 11:** *Offer something for everyone*). There is no standard pedagogical model that all are expected to follow. With this in mind, there should be a decision support tool available to the instructor that offers examples of what fellow instructors have done with the large number of options possible in a course WWW site. A system must allow the instructor to be the decision maker about the course site, but these decisions should be alterable over time, as the instructor gains more experience. (E = environment; E = engagement)

5. The course-support sites do not replace the textbooks in the courses or make lectures unnecessary (**Lesson 9:** *After the core, choose more*). Instead, the course-support sites help the instructor add extra opportunities for student reflection, for communication, for student contribution of additional learning resources, for peer interaction and peer evaluation, and to add a

'preparation for' and 'follow-up from' activity to each face-to-face session. Thus we conceptualized our course-support environments as social collaboration environments as well as information-communication exchange environments that were also coupled with other information systems of the faculty such as the bureau responsible for student issues and administration. (E = effectiveness, learning; E = environment)

6. The course-support environments must be capable of supporting a large variety of different types of instructional approaches, from courses focused on reading and written assignments with classic final examinations, to courses with complicated approaches to group work and project-based education (**Lesson 11:** *Offer something for everyone*). Tools to support any instructional approach must be available, including shared workspaces, test banks and discussion boards. (E = effectiveness, learning; E = environment; E = engagement)

7. The system must work with all other WWW products, for example Java applets and plug-ins. (E = effectiveness, learning; E = ease of use)

8. The instructor must be able to put in and take out whatever is necessary in the course site without needing direct technical support. Uploading and downloading attachments of a variety of types is particularly important. (E = ease of use; E = effectiveness, short-term pay-off – efficiency)

9. The course sites must help instructors organize the information streams within a course; instead of student messages coming to the instructor's e-mail address, for example, they can be posted directly into the course site, either as private (only for the instructor to see) or public (for all in the course to see). Feedback from students or the instructor must follow the same principle (**Lesson 17:** *Be aware of the price tag*). Also, there should be easy-to-set-up ways for messages to be sent to a group of students, or all the students in the course, or other groupings within the course, all from the same WWW environment. (E = Effectiveness, short-term pay-off – efficiency)

10. Access to the system must be organized on the basis of in-log data, which are used by the system database to tailor what can be seen and not seen by each individual. Also, it must be easy to leave the system and go to an external site on the WWW and then return to the system, without leaving the browser. The author of an item should be able to decide him- or herself who has rights to a submitted item. (E = ease of use; E = effectiveness, learning; E = effectiveness, short-term pay-off – efficiency)

11. The system must be efficient to maintain, thus no labour-intensive hand-made HTML pages, but pages generated dynamically out of a database (**Lesson 5:** *Watch the 4 Es*). (E = ease of use)

12. The system must handle multimedia resources the same as text resources. Video and audio must be streamed over the bandwidths available to the students (**Lesson 5:** *Watch the 4 Es*). (E = effectiveness, learning; E = ease of use)

Choosing to make our own system

On the basis of our prior experiences, including a detailed market research of available course-support systems and participation in an international evaluation of several such systems, we came to the conclusion that none that were commercially available met all of our requirements, even those still in the advertisement stage. We needed to proceed quickly; thus we created our own system, *TeleTOP*, which is now in its third version (see http://teletop.edte.utwente.nl for an overview). Each version adds more features, based on instructors' and students' needs (see later in this chapter and Chapter 8).

The TeleTOP system, Version 1

On the basis of a WWW database that is optimized for free-format data (because we did not want to decide in advance what an instructor or student might want to include in a course environment) and that can support a large number of simultaneous users (a Domino server, 4.6), we created an environment that from the instructor perspective is as simple as a great number of hierarchically ordered WWW-based fill-in forms. If anyone with the privileges of an instructor logs in, he or she sees not only the site as the students see it, but also a number of extra edit icons whereby on any page he or she can do tasks such as making changes in the content, making changes in text or HTML, adding links to external WWW sites (and also to other materials in the database) and adding files as attachments to any page. Anything entered by the instructor or student (to the extent to which the student has privileges) is placed on the server and in the database. This concept is carried out on all pages, for consistency and learnability, even the most complicated pages. Also critical to the TeleTOP system is that the instructor can choose just the tools and functions that he or she wishes, and can alter this choice at any time including during the running of the course (**Lesson 7:** *Be just in time*). We offered more than 60 tools and resources at the start-up period of TeleTOP, plus instructors could always ask the team for a new tool or feature that was not in the core collection, from which point-and-click choices can be made.

The roster

Lesson 11: *Offer something for everyone.*

A particularly popular WWW-based tool among our instructors was a matrix-type construction called a *roster*, to indicate the organization of a course and bring together study materials, lecture notes, student assignments, assignment submissions and feedback, all in one convenient table. Figure 7.6 shows an example of the instructor's view of a roster page in Version 1 of TeleTOP. The instructor decides how many rows and columns he or she wants and labels the columns (the number of columns possible is limited because of the width of the screen). The instructor chooses the number of rows, and can add new rows or delete rows according to his or her needs. The rows do not have to be organized chronologically, but can also reflect different topics in the course, or different groups of students, or anything else that can serve as an organizing principle. Once a cell in the matrix is labelled with text (the instructor just types it in), a linked pageview is directly generated. This new linked page can be used for presentation of text or HTML resources or images or video or audio, as well as for student submission of assignments and instructor submission of feedback directly linked to the student's submission.

Figure 7.7 shows a page from the 1997–98 roster ready for the students to submit an assignment. The instructors can also decide if they wish the students' assignments to be readable by everyone in the class or only by the instructor or members of the student's group.

Students can move through the course-support site pages, sometimes to submit assignments or ideas through the fill-in-form system, can add files to the site and can use the e-mail tools for general e-mail communication (standard Internet addresses, sendable within the intranet or over the Internet).

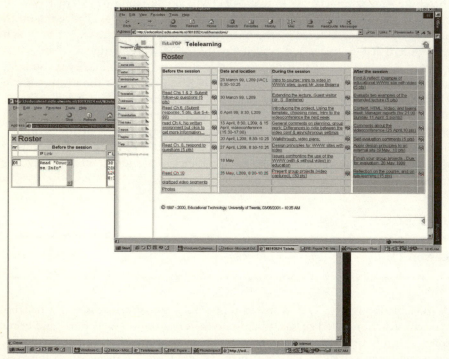

Figure 7.6 *Instructor's normal view and edit-view of a roster page in TeleTOP, Version 1*

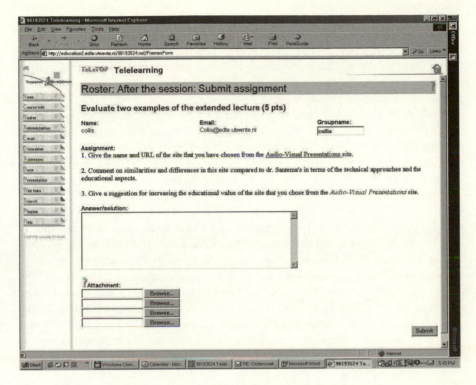

Figure 7.7 *Student submission tools in TeleTOP, Version 1*

Because of these features, the TeleTOP system relates well to Lesson 11, *Offer something for everyone*. We will discuss this in more detail later in this chapter, including what instructors and students chose to do with the system. A key tool in this choose process is the TeleTOP Decision Support Tool that is part of a larger instructor–engagement strategy.

Instructor-engagement strategy

Lesson 7: *Be just in time.*

The need for an effective instructor–support strategy was critical. Instructors needed to be made aware of possibilities for pedagogical change toward more flexibility and more contributions from their students (Chapter 5). They needed to be supported in planning for the redesign of their own courses. They needed to be supported in the actual redesign process as well as the creation of their own WWW environments. Many of them needed training in some aspects of computer and network use. More fundamentally, they needed to become part of a culture change: a critical mass of reflection and discussion about flexible learning. And they needed to express and discuss their fears and opinions. But on top of this, they were busy, overloaded with appointments and time commitments.

Against all of these needs, we had only a team of five, who also had to build the TeleTOP system and tend to all of the change entities in Figure 7.5. Thus, we developed the *TeleTOP rapid-prototyping method* as our instructor-engagement strategy (Fisser *et al*, 1998). The eight steps of this method as we applied them in our initiation-implementation year are shown in Table 7.3. We use the term 'rapid prototyping' because that is a well-known approach to software design. The essence of such an approach is that the designer does not attempt to create a full design of a product before realizing it as an electronic product, but instead gets his or her initial ideas into a simple electronic form as soon as possible in order to get feedback from the intended users and revise the ideas in the product before the next round of prototype-feedback-revision (Moonen, in press b). Rows 2–8 of Table 7.3 are all related to *just-in-time* support, just in time for the instructor to redesign his or her course. The first row relates to weekly voluntary meetings that the TeleTOP team organized, over the Wednesday lunch hours. The purpose of these meetings was as much informational and strategic as it was related to instructor support; after the initiation year we no longer had regular meetings but focused our support directly through just-in-time contacts and instructor-support tools integrated within TeleTOP.

Table 7.3 *The TeleTOP rapid-prototyping approach to instructor engagement (initiation year, end of 1997 to mid-1998)*

Step 1	Activity in TeleTOP
1. Wednesday orientation sessions	1. Become familiar with the overall TeleTOP approach for more-flexible learning, and with possibilities for the use of the WWW to support instruction; attend the weekly optional instructor sessions run by the TeleTOP team, Wednesdays, 12.30–1.30 pm.
2. First DST (Decision Support Tool) session	2. With two members of the TeleTOP team, and using the TeleTOP Decision Support Tool (DST), Version 1, participate in a one-hour interview in which initial choices are made for the instructor's WWW site. A tailor-made WWW site with examples of all these choices is immediately generated by the DST and a print-out given.
3. Office follow-up	3. Two members of the TeleTOP team will come to the instructor's office, discuss the initial choices made with the DST (by walking through the WWW site generated by the DST). The instructor can indicate changes in the choices. Following this visit, the first prototype of the tailor-made course-support site is ready for the instructor within a few days.

4. Practice, and initial filling of sites	4. During the weekly Wednesday instructor sessions, instructors work with their own first prototypes, filling in various materials and getting familiar with the use of the technology. Different forms of workshops are also offered, such as sessions in how to use TeleTOP to manage assignments.
5. DST, Version 2	5. Each instructor works together with an individual TeleTOP team member to walk through a second version of the TeleTOP Decision Support Tool, to make the final choices for his or her course-support site. From this, the site is generated.
6. Preparation of the sites	6. With the help of TeleTOP student assistants and members of the TeleTOP team, instructors are supported in their filling and preparation of their sites.
7. Visit prior to start of course	7. One or two TeleTOP team members and the education dean visit each instructor approximately two weeks before the start of his or her course, to walk through the course and course site and discuss last-minute refinements.
8. Support and visit during the course	8. During the course itself, one or two TeleTOP team members visit the instructor and discuss expeiences. In addition, any problems or wishes of the instructor that arise during the course can be immediately considered, and if possible responded to, by making contact with the TeleTOP team.

A key aspect of this just-in-time support is the *TeleTOP Decision Support Tool* (DST).

The TeleTOP Decision Support Tool (DST)

Lesson 9: *After the core, choose more.*

The TeleTOP DST is a WWW-based environment consisting of a series of more than 60 questions related to the six major generic course components that are our basis for course analysis for more flexible learning: course organization, contact sessions, self-study/ongoing assignments, major assignment, testing, and additional communication (Collis and De Boer, 1998, 1999b). For each of these categories questions were available on a WWW-based questionnaire integrated with the TeleTOP system that led the instructor to think about possibilities for increasing flexibility in his or her course or making the course more efficient or increasing student activity (see Chapter 5).

Using the TeleTOP DST

The questions in the DST are very short and deal with the normal questions that an instructor has to ask him- or herself when setting up a course, such as: 'What kind of presentation formats will I use in my lectures? How, when, and to what detail will I provide feedback on assignments?', etc. Each such consideration is presented in terms of a question such as:

- For *course organization*: do you want to give short updates and announcements and have these available for students to check, regardless of their locations?
- For *communication*: do you want your students to participate in group discussions where they can enter their reflections at a time convenient to themselves?
- For *lectures*: do you want to make additional information available to your students relating to material in the lectures?
- For *self-study*: do you want to give occasional personal feedback to the students based on their progress with self-study?
- For *major assignments*: do your students work in groups on a major assignment, and if they do, do they sometimes have problems managing themselves and staying on tempo?
- For *testing*: do you want to give students access to previous test questions, along with feedback and overviews of previous students' answers?

In order to help the instructors to consider better their answers to these questions, and at the same time relate the answers to the range of new pedagogical and technical possibilities, examples were available from courses already in the system and could be studied in relation to each question that the instructor might still have had from the DST session. The examples were all taken from existing TeleTOP environments in the faculty (to begin with, from the pioneers). Seeing examples from one's own colleagues is an important strategy for stimulating change (Collis and Moonen, 1995).

Each of the questions in the DST was answered by entering a yes-or-no choice. Instructors were encouraged to answer 'yes' if they were potentially interested in an option; changes could be easily made in later rounds of prototyping. After completion of responses to all pertinent questions in the DST, the database that underlies the DST automatically generated a unique WWW page with the specific answers and the chosen options made by the user. In this way, users immediately could see via the WWW browser or a print-out what they have chosen, and could continue to examine the examples in their own offices simply by loading the WWW page that was generated for them. The TeleTOP team also obtained information from the DST session, allowing the team to keep an overview of which features were being selected by instructors and which were not. In Year 3 we expanded the DST based on these data (see Chapter 8). Figure 7.8 shows the interfaces for one course redesigned for TeleTOP: (a) the DST environment; (b) the output from the DST; (c) the first prototype site; and (d) the site as in use with a full group of students.

The DST was a key tool for us in our initiation year, to structure the

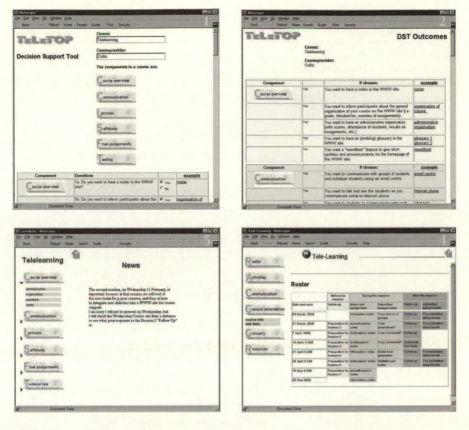

Figure 7.8 *Interfaces of four stages – 1) DST session; 2) DST output; 3) first prototype of the course; 4) final course environment – of realizing a WWW-based course-support environment using the TeleTOP rapid-prototyping method, illustrated with the course named* Tele-Learning *(Collis and De Boer, 1999b)*

instructor-engagement process and make it streamlined for both instructors and the TeleTOP team. It also was the basis of our 'just-in-time' strategy for instructor support (Lesson 7): the instructor learnt to use TeleTOP not before but during the process of setting up his or her own environment for upcoming courses.

Instructors' choices with the DST

We showed examples of over 60 different sorts of tools and approaches for course-support sites in the DST. After their experiences during the rapid-prototyping process, which of these possibilities did the instructors actually choose? Table 7.4 gives an overview of the options selected for the first set of courses being redesigned during the initiation year. It is clear that many of the

Table 7.4 *The options chosen for the WWW-based course-support environments by the instructors in the initiation year of TeleTOP*

Course Component	Options and Percentage of Instructors (n = 24) Choosing this Option	Description
General course information, self-study, lectures and support	News (100%)	A place for up-to-date information.
	Roster (100%)	Here, instructors can put their study materials, assignments, sheets, notes and feedback related to the lectures. Also, the roster provides a convenient way to have students enter follow-up reflections or assignments after each class session, for these submissions to be directly posted in the site and for the instructor and the students to give feedback.
	Quiz server (29%)	This option enables easy-to-make (self)-tests.
	Course information (100%)	A course description stating the objectives, organization of the course, assigned texts, etc.
Communication	E-mail (100%)	In the mail centre, addresses of individuals and groups can be found. E-mails can be sent from here.
	Discussion (43%)	The discussion area can be used for asynchronous discussions.
	Question and answer (5%)	Same as the discussion area, here with the focus on questions to the instructor.
	Chat (15%)	Synchronous communication.
Groupwork	Groupware I (19%)	An easy to-use file-management area, for collaborative work.
	Groupware II (58%)	A more advanced file- and communication-management shared workspace area, for collaborative work.
	Presentation (52%)	Presentations and other products can be presented in this part.
Resources	Glossary (55%)	Area where concepts can be explained. Relations with other areas can be made clear as well.
	WWW links (53%)	Resources: links to sites on the WWW.
	Multiumedia (47%)	Resources: links to a multimedia database maintained within the faculty.
	Search (43%)	A search centre within the course environment or the WWW.
Other	(53%)	Variety, including some tailor-made options.

options were not taken up by the instructors, based on their current level of experience.

The options *newsflash*, *roster*, *course information* and *e-mail centre* were chosen by all the instructors in the 1997–98 cycle, and thus were advised as the basic environment for the new round of courses being tailored during the 1998–99 academic year.

Results of Year 1

By the end of Year 1 (June 1998), we had designed and developed Version 1 of the TeleTOP system and of the TeleTOP DST as well as the conceptual and methodological models underlying TeleTOP as an implementation initiative. We had conducted 15 Wednesday sessions and many other demonstration sessions, in our faculty and outside of it. We had gone through the DST/rapid-prototyping process with over 30 instructors, and worked with them to redesign all of the first-year courses and several other courses whose instructors did not want to wait until their point in the planned change-over. Several courses had already been offered in the March–June 1998 period and had gone well (Dijkstra, Collis and Eseryl, 1999). Ideas relating to our new educational philosophy were in the mainstream of discussion. TeleTOP had become a well-known name not only in the faculty but throughout the university and nationally.

Lesson 4: *Don't forget the road map.*

However, this does not mean that there were no problems and no concerns. Change takes time, and some reactions occurred that distracted the team now and then from its methods. Fortunately, the faculty leadership was always solidly in support of TeleTOP. Table 7.5 shows the major issues that had to be confronted during the initiation year.

Fortunately, most of the challenges faded away in Year 2. We discuss this in Chapter 8.

Summing up

Of our lessons learnt (Table 7.1), Table 7.6 shows the set that appeared to be the most important in the initiation year of TeleTOP. The set is not in rank order, because of the interrelationships between the lessons. The lessons marked with an asterisk (*) are the subset that had the most steering power for the start-up.

Table 7.5 *Some challenges during the initiation year of TeleTOP (Collis, 1998c)*

Challenge	Reflection
Conservatism of the students	Surprisingly, some of the regular-programme students reacted negatively, and in an over-reactive way. They said that they would have to spend all day at a computer, in a tone that made it clear this was totally unacceptable; that they would never have contact with the instructor, that lectures were going to disappear. The fact that none of these was accurate did not stop the rumours.
Persistence of stereotypes	Despite a vast amount of ongoing activity and examples, those with stereotypes ('I am not going to be replaced by the computer...)' hung on to them tenaciously.
Difficulty in integrating the pioneers with the mainstream	In order to support better the majority of instructors, and provide WWW-based resources to the students that were consistent and integrated among themselves, a database approach with a standard interface was chosen. Instructors with prior experience of doing WWW sites their own way were not always happy with this imposition.
Students are pragmatic, not necessarily interested in extra resources and enriched possibilities	If points are given, or the activity is known to be directly related to a test, then the activity is done. If points are not given, then few do it. Students have time constraints and suspected that all these new tools would cost them time and effort.
Persistence in seeing the lecture as the core of the course	Even in a Faculty of Educational Science and Technology, there was a deeply rooted belief among students and instructors that lectures were the best and core form of teaching and that TeleTOP would diminish the lecture.
Students are not necessarily charmed by telematics applications or computers	They saw computers, on the one hand, as their own personal tools for using the WWW, word processing, etc, but, on the other hand, not as a tool for studying. In particular they did not like to read or study from the screen.
One's head 'sticking out above the crowd' is uncomfortable	Because of all the attention the project got, many requests came to the team for interviews and meetings and to request support. But the more that this was done, the more others who were also active with other forms of technical innovation felt overlooked.

We believe it was our attention to the lessons that brought the TeleTOP initiative so quickly through its initiation phase.

Perhaps it is Lesson 15 that distinguished us most from other start-up initiatives with WWW-based course-management systems. We did not start with the idea that instructors should be transforming their content into digital form, nor did we particularly encourage this (instructors already had textbooks and readers, which were efficient ways of transmitting large amounts of formatted text). Also, our students had told us many times that they did not appreciate doing their study of primary course readers off the computer screen, but instead wanted a

Table 7.6 *Lessons that had the greatest impact on the initiation year of TeleTOP*

Lesson 1 *Be specific.*	We need to define our terms and express our goals in a measurable form or else progress will be difficult to steer and success difficult to claim.
Lesson 3 *You can't not do it.*	The idea whose time has come is irresistible.
Lesson 4 *Don't forget the road map.*	Changes takes a long time and is an iterative process, evolving in ways that are often not anticipated.
★Lesson 5 *Watch the 4 Es.*	An individual's likelihood of voluntarily making use of a particular type of technology for a learning-related purpose is a function of 4 Es: the environment context, the individual's perception of educational effectiveness, ease of use, and sense of personal engagement with the technology. The environmental context and the individual's sense of personal engagement are the most important.
Lesson 6 *Follow the leader.*	Key persons are critical.
★Lesson 7 *Be just in time.*	Staff-engagement activities to stimulate instructors to make use of technology are generally not very effective. Focus on just-in-time support for necessary tasks.
★Lesson 8 *Get out of the niche.*	Most technology products are not used in practice beyond developers. Keep implementation and the 4 Es central in choosing any technology product.
Lesson 9 *After the core, choose more.*	Technology selection involves a core and complementary technologies. The core is usually determined by history and circumstances; changing it usually requires pervasive contextual pressure. The individual instructor can make choices about complementary technologies and should choose them with flexibility in mind.
Lesson 10 *Don't overload.*	More is not necessarily better.
★Lesson 11 *Offer something for everyone.*	A well-designed WWW-based system should offer users a large variety of possibilities to support flexible and participative learning not dominated by any one background orientation. If so, it is the most appropriate (core or complementary) technology for flexible learning.
★Lesson 12 *Watch the speed limit.*	Don't try to change too much at the same time. Start where the instructor is at, and introduce flexibility via extending contact sessions to include before, during and after aspects, with each of these made more flexible. Move gradually into contribution.
★Lesson 15 *Design for activity.*	Instructional design should concentrate more on activities and processes, and less on content and a predetermined product.

Note ★ = lessons with strongest steering power during the initiation period print copy. Thus, instead of focusing on content transformation, we put our attention right from the start on to activity design for the contribution-oriented student (thus, Lesson 15).

While *active-student* approaches are not new in themselves, what was possibly unique was our attention to the lessons (Table 7.6) in an approach that involved all the instructors in the first-year courses of our programme. In a subsequent survey of other higher-education institutions also having experience with change toward more-flexible learning involving WWW-based technology, we found that this involuntary aspect was the major difference between them and us (De Boer and Collis, in press). And the involuntary aspect could only work because of a clear, shared goal ('Get ready for the new type of student, by September next year': **Lesson 1:** *Be specific*).

In the next chapter we continue this case study, moving from the initiation through the implementation phases and into the institutionalization phase and beyond. The lessons were certainly relevant for us during the initiation phase reported on in this chapter.

Chapter 8

Practising what we preach: keeping going

In Chapter 7 we showed how a successful initiation process involving more-flexible learning and technology took place in our faculty during the academic year 1997–98. By the end of the first year of the TeleTOP initiative, an implementation strategy based on the ideas of the active student (Chapter 5), flexibility (Chapters 1, 4 and 5), and the 4-E Model (Chapter 3) and involving a specially

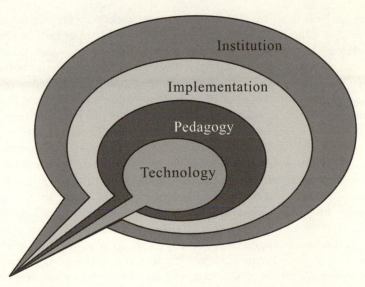

Figure 8.1 *Flexible learning in higher education – scaling-up experences*

developed WWW-based course-management system (Chapter 4) were all made concrete. We were ready to open the doors to a new first-year group of students, some of whom would be regularly on campus, while others, working people, would only come physically once every two weeks. In this chapter we tell more of this story. We look at the subsequent implementation process, not only in our own faculty but in other faculties at our university and beyond. We also look at a transition that not many institutions have yet gone through: the move from implementation to institutionalization with a WWW-based course management system. In this chapter we also tell about the institutionalization of TeleTOP and our current work. Throughout the chapter we refer to the lessons.

The implementation phase: Year 2 of TeleTOP, 1998–99

This section gives highlights of the second year of the TeleTOP project. This summary involves a general overview of the implementation process, instructor choices, results of evaluation studies of TeleTOP, transfer to other institutions and the mixture of implementation with new aspects of pioneering work.

Results of the overall implementation process

Lesson 16: *Get a new measuring stick.*

To sum up Year 2 briefly, TeleTOP's primary tasks – to prepare the faculty so that the new educational approach could be fully in operation at the start of September 1998 and would run smoothly throughout the year, incorporating new forms of student activity and flexibility into all of its first-year courses – were successfully executed. The entire first-year programme in our faculty (21 courses or independent portions of courses), as well as 4 additional courses at the second- and third-year levels, ran during the September 1998 to June 1999 period using TeleTOP-based course-support environments and reflecting in different ways a move towards the U Approach (Chapter 5) and new forms of student activity. There were as many working students attending physically only once per two weeks as there were the traditional on-campus students. All of the TeleTOP-supported courses operated under the 'one course, adapt within approach'. There was little drop-out among the working students, a strong difference from the faculty's earlier attempts at offering an evening and Saturday version of its programme as an approach to dealing with working students who needed time flexibility (Van Rennes, 1998). Thus, our specific goals of making our programme ready for the new cohort of students via more-flexible courses, but without the instructors having to teach the same course twice, were met.

Lesson 9: *After the core, choose more.*

No disruptive technical problems involving the TeleTOP system occurred. Instructors as well as students in both the part-time and full-time variants of the programme made extensive use of the TeleTOP system, with about two-thirds of the use occurring on weekdays and the other third at weekends, a reflection of the flexible use of the system in terms of time. The system was visited by instructors and students approximately 500,000 times in the first eight months. The average session length for students was 11:07 minutes, several times a day. This shows that students were using the course environments not as the primary study source for content material, but as support for short interactions and communications. In terms of our goal of a blend of core and complementary technologies, we were not using the system to replace books and readers but to support more interaction and communication in a flexible way. Thus, in regard to content TeleTOP was primarily a complementary medium, with textbooks and readers as the core (see Chapter 4). For other aspects of the learning experience, those related to the active, contribution-oriented student, the TeleTOP-based course environments became the core technologies.

Instructor use of options

Lesson 11: *Offer something for everyone.*

Lesson 14: *Aim for activity.*

To study how instructors made use of the features in TeleTOP that they chose for new forms of contact with and among their students, the course environments and the instructors were involved in a one-year evaluation study (Bloemen, 1999). In addition, there were ongoing interviews with instructors and students as sources of data (see the evaluation results in the next section). Given many options (60 specific options and others that could be tailored on request) to choose from using the TeleTOP Decision Support Tool (see Chapter 7), what did our instructors actually use? Figure 8.2 shows an overview (Collis and De Boer, 1999a).

All instructors chose the *news* option, with 84 per cent using it often and 16 per cent using it marginally. The *course information* option was another popular option, with 92 per cent of the courses using it to give an extensive overview of the course, and the remaining 8 per cent using it minimally. All but one (96 per cent) of the courses used the e-mail centre to have efficient access to the e-mail addresses of all course participants as well as the instructor(s) of a course. Some used the group option in the e-mail area to send different messages to different

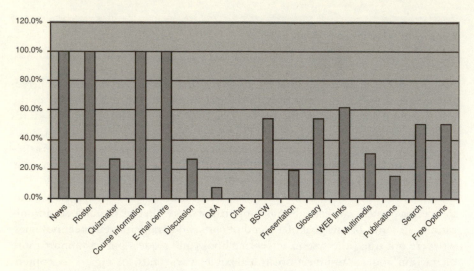

Figure 8.2 *Choices made by instructors of 25 courses in our faculty offered between September 98 and April 99 from options suggested in the TeleTOP Decision Support Tool*

groups of students, small but useful indicators of increased flexibility and efficiency.

The *roster* became one of the most important options in the TeleTOP system. Every instructor chose to use the roster as an organizational structure. Table 8.1 gives an overview of various ways in which the instructors made use of the roster in 25 courses supported by TeleTOP during the 1998-99 academic year.

The roster was used by 92 per cent of the instructors for access to some kind of study material including (PowerPoint) slides, assignments during and after face-to-face sessions or relating to particular topics, and the provision of WWW links to related topics. Two instructors integrated video segments of portions of their presentations and of student presentations in the roster for review and discussion via the WWW site. These are examples of flexibilities and efficiencies afforded by the TeleTOP system as well as the beginning of the U Approach in many of the courses (Chapter 5; see also Dijkstra, Collis and Eseryl, 1999).

Lesson 14: *Aim for activity.*

In addition to these sorts of uses of the system for increased flexibility, examples of increased levels of student activity began to emerge. When contact sessions were held for on-campus students, some of the instructors began to structure

Table 8.1 *Use of the roster in 25 redesigned courses during September 98 to April 99 (first implementation year of TeleTOP)*

New Forms of Contact Supported in the Roster	Yes	Minimal or No Use
To provide instructor-produced material for self-study	52%	48%
To provide instructor-produced materials for a face-to-face session (and for use by the part-time students after the session)	65%	35%
To provide instructor-created PowerPoint slides	80%	20%
To provide instructor-selected links to external resources	20%	80%
For student submission of results of small activities during face-to-face sessions in our combination lecture-room/computer-room (or after the session for part-time students)	56%	44%
For student submission of work via the course site	72%	28%
For reuse of student work submitted in the course site as study materials for others in the course	18%	82%

these not as lectures, but as guided-activity sessions, so that students who were not present could do the same activity later and submit the results via the course site. The average number of assignments submitted via the roster was about five per (8- to 12-week) course per student. For many courses, there had not been any such 'small' assignments previous to TeleTOP; the emphasis had been on reading the textbook, attending lectures, perhaps doing a major course project or essay, and a final examination. Thus, the switch from lectures with marginal feedback to a series of small assignments with personal feedback as part of the U turn had begun.

There were also a number of interesting examples of contribution-oriented learning. For example, one instructor made extensive use of multiple-choice questions produced by the students themselves relating to major topics in the course and submitted within the roster. Each row of the roster was organized around a topic in the course (covered as a chapter in the course textbook); contained cells via which the instructor added some brief motivational comment related to the chapter to be studied; made available his or her PowerPoint slides from previous years relating to the topic as a background resource (the instructor no longer lectured, but did meet three times with the students, focusing on motivation and discussion of examples and applications of course theory); and provided a link to an external WWW site that illustrated some aspect of the topic in process. Each row also contained a cell describing the assignment for the topic (the creation of the two multiple-choice items), a link to the quiz tool that the students could use to produce those items, and the *submit* function via which they uploaded their questions and responses to the site. The questions of the students were thus directly linked to the same row of the matrix as contained the other study materials about the topic. The students studied one another's questions as preparation for the final examination.

In another example of students as contributors to a course learning resources, students in a required second-year course worked together in groups of three (often with some of the group members in a different physical location from one another) to create supplementary study resources for each topic in the course. These were made available via the TeleTOP course site, were assigned reading for the other students in the course and were included in the material required for study for the final examination.

Lesson 12: *Watch the speed limit.*

Thus, although the data in Table 8.1 show that the majority of uses of the roster were for making aspects of instruction more flexible or efficient, use of the roster as a tool for contribution-oriented pedagogy also began to emerge. This progression is what we expected: the instructors were going at a comfortable speed in terms of change, with the first step primarily toward Quadrant III in the Flexibility–Activity Framework of Chapters 1 and 5, as indicated by more-flexible learning and an increase in student activities. But the increase in student activities was leading the way to a contribution orientation, and thus towards Quadrant IV. It was enough for the first cycle of experience that the instructors made use of the system for more flexibility and efficiency as well as more student activity.

Evaluation results

The first-year courses were extensively evaluated during the entire academic year via three information streams (see Table 8.2). An evaluation team of six persons carried out portions of the evaluation with the remainder of the evaluation informed by expert input and by the ongoing data collection of the TeleTOP team itself (Bloemen, 1999; Maslowski *et al*, 2000).

Evaluation in relation to the 4 Es

Lesson 5: *Watch the 4 Es.*

The results of the evaluation (Bloemen, 1999; Maslowski *et al*, 2000) showed no significant difference between the regular and part-time students in achievement and in their appreciation of the courses. For courses in which there were comparative data from earlier versions, there were also no significant differences between the 1998–99 TeleTOP version of the course and previous versions in

Table 8.2   *Information streams for formative evaluation of the TeleTOP WWW-based course-management system (abbreviated here as a 'W-CMS') (Maslowski* et al, *2000: 12)*

Information Stream	Major Instruments	Major Focus	Evaluation Type (Sweeney, Maguire and Shackel, 1993)
1. Instructor choices and behaviours	(a) Decision Support Tools (DST) and interviews in which the DSTs are used. (b) Options for instructors to choose from in W-CMS and data about choices made.	What do instructors choose when using a W-CMS? Why? How do they think about their instructional conditions, and how can these be reflected in the W-CMS?	User-based; theory-based
2. State-of-the art inventory and analysis	(a) Ongoing contacts with others using W-CMS and with literature and research about W-CMS. (b) Participation in national studies about W-CMS.	What are the major international and national trends with respect to W-CMS and their implementation? What implementation model is most appropriate?	Expert-based; theory-based
3. Field reactions (in addition to input related to instructor choices and behaviours, Item 1 above)	(a) Questionnaires and interviews, instructors and students. (b) Reactions from implementation teams in other faculties making use of the TeleTOP W-CMS. (c) Reactions given during demonstrations to persons from other institutions.	What are opinions about the implementation process as it is being carried out? What aspects of the W-CMS are most important in the local context? How well are instructors making use of the W-CMS? What are the major differences in TeleTOP and other W-CMS with which persons are familiar? How should TeleTOP be revised?	User-based; expert-based

terms of student performance and attitudes. Thus, replacing lectures with TeleTOP-supported activity did not lead to measurable declines in learning, as had been feared by some (see Table 7.5 in Chapter 7), but it did not lead to measurable increases either. Among the results of the evaluations relating to instructor and student reactions and expressed in terms of the 4 Es were: 1) *ease of use* – the user friendliness of the TeleTOP system was evaluated by the instructors and students as good; and 2) *effectiveness* – students made considerable use of the system and indicated that it was for them the most important resource (not necessarily as content provider, but as a stimulus and guide for activities) for their courses.

Thus, with the *environment* 'E' so strong in the faculty, the fit with the instructors' chosen ways of working also good (relating to the development of a sense of *engagement* as well as the perception of educational *effectiveness*), the fact that the new flexibility allowed us to double our number of students (educational *effectiveness*, long-term pay-off) and the above two Es, the 4-E combination of our first implementation year can be seen as shown in Figure 8.3. Likelihood of use was 100 per cent.

In addition to helping guide us to our implementation process, the 4 Es also helped us categorize areas for further improvement that had been clarified by the evaluations. These included:

- *Ease of use*. Students need a clearer way to get an overview of what is expected of them in all their courses, not just in each course separately. (This was subsequently done in the third version of TeleTOP.)

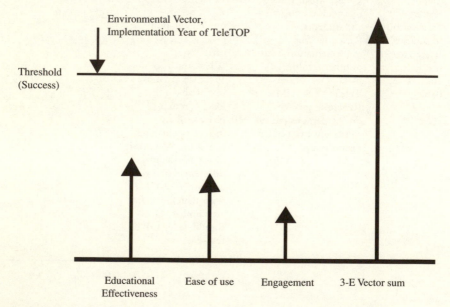

Figure 8.3   *The 4-E Model in terms of the implementation year of TeleTOP*

- *Effectiveness, short-term pay-off.* Instructors were concerned about the higher time investments that they perceived were needed on their parts, not only for direct student contacts but also for the preparation and management aspects of using a WWW-based learning environment. (Attention to this was a major focus of Year 3 and continues in Year 4.)
- *Effectiveness, short-term pay-off.* The giving of feedback was identified as a problem area: instructors felt that they were spending large amounts of time in giving personalized feedback, while at the same time students did not always perceive the feedback as helpful or timely enough. (Attention to this was a major focus of Year 3 and continues in Year 4.)
- *Effectiveness, long-term pay-off.* Instructors need to continue to develop their ideas about how to use the TeleTOP system for added value educationally. (This will be an ongoing task, with a new decision support tool based on activities for the U Approach being developed in Year 4.)

Evaluation of the TeleTOP system

Lesson 11: *Offer something for everyone.*

We also were regularly involved in the systematic evaluation of the TeleTOP system itself. In Year 2 we used our 12 criteria for a WWW-based course-management system (see Chapter 7 and Tielemans and Collis, 1999) as a framework for evaluating our progress so far with the TeleTOP system. Table 8.3 reviews those criteria and the results of the implementation-year evaluation in reference to those criteria.

Thus, while the TeleTOP system was clearly off to a good start, it was far from a finished system. This was by design: we wanted to continue to shape the system, based on input from our users. Thus, the technology of the TeleTOP course-support system continued to evolve during 1998–99. Continuing with its combination of Domino database technology and HTTP server technology, TeleTOP evolved from Version 1 to Version 2 during the 1998–99 academic year without any disruption to instructors or students. Version 2 was primarily Version 1 with more features added, based on instructors' comments and experiences and ongoing improvements in the ease of use. Of particular importance were improvements in the way the instructor could modify portions of the roster as well as the choices of tools in the environment as a whole. Also, workspace tools were simplified and made more flexible.

Institutional support: the TeleTOP PC Plan

From an ease-of-use perspective, a major activity during 1998–99 was the implementation of the *TeleTOP PC* plan. All first-year students were given the chance, at a highly favourable rate (and via a loan that they do not have to pay

Table 8.3   *Dimensions for formative evaluation of the TeleTOP system (from Maslowski et al, 2000: 17)*

Requirements	Type of Dimension	Standards and Performance Indicators	(Ongoing) Results of the Formative Evaluation
1. Threshold of use as low as possible	Usability	Measured by the skills needed, those of using a word processor, file handling, using a WWW browser.	Minor revisions in editing/typing-in procedures based on observations of use and expert analysis.
2. Only an ordinary WWW browser is needed	Usability	Measured by the extent to which all system functions can be accessed via only a WWW browser regardless of location and computer used to access.	System in itself succeeds; some problems with network capacity and access especially for video.
3. Instructor makes choices about features to include	Utility, scientific basis, usability	Measured by the extent to which instructors' wishes can be accommodated.	In most cases successful, but ongoing enhancements occur; difficulty in accommodating changes in user interface.
4. Extend, not replace, books and lectures	Utility, usability, effectiveness	Measured by quantitative and qualitative measures of use of the roster.	Data (see Table 8.1 and Figure 8.2) show the functionalities are being used; more attention now needs to be given to how the functionalities are used.
5. Tools to support any instructional approach must be available	Utility, scientific basis, usability	Measured by ability to supply whatever instructors request, and by instructors being able to make use of what is supplied.	Supply has been successful; usability is being improved for some tools, such as the quiz tool and shared workspace.
6. Expansion to include any product accessible via the WWW	Utility	Measured by ability to call up any WWW product requested by instructors.	Difficulties with student products involving multiple files in folders, such as projects involving WWW sites.
7. Uploading and downloading must be simple	Usability	Measured by the problems encountered by users.	Some revisions to uploading and downloading have occurred.
8. Instructor can organize communication streams	Usability, effectiveness	Measured by usage, instructor and student satisfaction.	Complaints by students most related to deficiencies in instructors' practice, such as slowness in responding, unclear responses, etc.

9. Access organized around log-in data	Utility, effectiveness	Measured by accuracy of access, based on user characteristics.	Revisions needed for external users, persons having different roles.
10. Maintain-ability	Utility, usability	Measured by opinion of system master.	Hand entry of registration; individual templates were most time-consuming; extensive upgrade occurred.
11. Multimedia data need to be handled in the same way as text data	Utility, usability	Performance indicators: speed, quality.	Full compatibility with video server; network access problems for persons outside of The Netherlands.
12. Instructors and students are using the system	Usability utility	Measured by usage and robustness.	All first- and second-year courses, as well as others; no technical crashes or slowdowns, but continual improvements in back-up and other back-office features.

back if they maintain good grades), to obtain a powerful personal computer with fully installed applications and tool software to support all of the courses in the first year, and other features such as a writable CD ROM drive, choice of an ISDN, modem or network connection, and audio- and video-handling capabilities. The PC offer was highly attractive to students, with almost all of those using TeleTOP (regular and working cohort) taking advantage of it. Because of demand, the TeleTOP PC Plan was also made available to other students in the faculty and to instructors and staff. Connectivity for students from anywhere in The Netherlands to the university network (and thus to TeleTOP as well as the Internet) was subsidized by the university and cost home users no more than a local phone charge. Our faculty also subsidized this home ISDN connectivity for our instructors, so that they could work on TeleTOP from home with minimal personal cost. In terms of the 4 Es, these are *environmental* and *ease-of-use* factors that we believe offered a good return on investment (ROI, see Chapter 6), in that without them barriers and frustrations for use of TeleTOP would certainly have occurred for many instructors and students.

Transfer to other institutions

Lesson 8: *Get out of the niche.*

A major activity for TeleTOP in 1998–99 was the generalization of the TeleTOP Method to other groups and settings. Was TeleTOP going to be a niche product (Chapter 4), fitting its own context but not likely to be useful in others? In particular, would TeleTOP's roots in a faculty with educational-technology expertise transfer to a technical faculty? The first tests of this occurred in Year 2 with a new curriculum in the computer science faculty of our university and in a law faculty in another university. The new curriculum in the computer science faculty was in the area of telematics (applications of network technology from a technical perspective). The motive of the new Telematics Department to want to use TeleTOP was that they felt that it was valuable to the profile of their programme to be able to indicate that they were using a state-of-the-art telematics platform (the TeleTOP system) in their courses. During Year 2, the TeleTOP team thus also focused on a method for moving TeleTOP out of its niche in our own faculty (Collis and De Boer, 1999a). The general approach developed by TeleTOP for the transfer of the TeleTOP Method to other faculties, based on the experiences in the first half of 1999 with the Telematics Department and the Law Faculty adaptations, has the timeline shown in Table 8.4. The time periods can be different for any particular case; they depend on the level of readiness and organization in the target institution, and the persons involved.

Using the method indicated in Table 8.4, the TeleTOP team supported the redesign of all of the first-year courses for the 1999-2000 academic year in the Telematics Department, and an evaluation study was carried out among the telematics instructors as to their expectations and initial impressions relating to working with the system. In general, the telematics instructors had similar expectations and concerns as our instructors had had one year earlier: that a major problem would be the time management for instructors, particularly in the handling of feedback for an increased number of student assignments (Fisser, Van der Kamp and Slot, 1999). Perhaps because they are a technical faculty or because the experience in the Faculty of Educational Science and Technology was well known, there was no expression of concern among telematics instructors or students about too much computer dependency or loss of contact between instructors and students. The time needed for instructors to be comfortable with using the system was also quicker than had been the case in our faculty, probably because many of them had already been using technology in a variety of ways to support their teaching.

The transfer to the Telematics Department went so well that discussions began about the systematic implementation of TeleTOP throughout the entire university. This would be under the responsibility not of ourselves in a faculty but of

Table 8.4 *Timeline for transfer of TeleTOP to another institution*

Time Period	Activities (Collaboration between TeleTOP Team Member and Local Team)
Months 1–3	Define target group, analyse context in terms of 4 Es, set concrete goals, carry out planning, appoint at least two implementation-team members (technical and educational), decide on technical infrastructure, build awareness in target group.
Month 2	Set up the technical infrastructure.
Months 2–3	Train the implementation-team members.
Month 2 onwards	Put into place technical support, help-desk.
Months 3–4	Instructor sessions, focused on redesign of their own courses.
Month 3 onwards	Redesign of courses, use of decision support tool with instructors for design of their course-support environments.
Month 4	Student orientation session.
Month 4 onwards	Start first courses, put into place ongoing educational support, begin internal evaluation.
Month 5	End of support by the TeleTOP team.

the central teaching-support centre called the DINKEL Institute. Considerable time was spent in 1998-99 in discussions with the DINKEL as to the generalizability of the TeleTOP Method to the rest of the university. The TeleTOP system was extensively studied by a work group (of which we were not members), and recommended for university-wide adoption. Proposals were submitted independently of this decision for collaborative activities with TeleTOP from two other faculties (electrical engineering and applied mathematics). Much interest was coming in from other institutions and much time was spent on demonstration sessions and meetings with parties interested in potential collaborations.

Pioneering work

TeleTOP was funded as an implementation project. But we, and other pioneers, also saw TeleTOP as a test bed for new ideas, research and experimentation even while implementation was just beginning. This led to new, small-scale cycles of initiation and implementation within the larger overall implementation progression and several research-oriented experiments (Collis, Winnips and Moonen, 2000). Major new pioneering interests during Year 2 were student portfolios as part of the TeleTOP system, and investigation of the use of video-on-demand within TeleTOP. The practical reason for the interest in video-on-demand was to provide students who are not regularly present at the faculty with access to the experiences available to students who are present. Doing this as other than a 'talking head' capture of instructor presentations began to be one of our interests in TeleTOP. Also, the use of video explanations or demonstrations in reusable units of learning material in course sites was seen as a growth area for TeleTOP, and preliminary work was done (Collis and Peters, 1999).

Preparing for Year 3, 1999–2000

Lesson 4: *Don't forget the road map.*

In addition to the courses successfully offered during the 1998–99 academic year, the TeleTOP team was busy throughout 1998–99 with preparation for more than 50 courses for the academic year starting in August 1999, in particular the revision of the second-year courses to begin in September 1999, and not previously planned, the courses in our Masters' programme.

A major and unexpected event affected our planning. The university decided to adopt a new approach called the Major–Minor system, which meant that much of the third year of each faculty's programme had to be made free so that students could take a minor in another faculty. This led to the decision in our faculty to reconsider not only the third year, but the entire curriculum. Consequently, much time was taken up with curriculum review, with TeleTOP and pedagogical change moving out from the central point of attention in the faculty.

In some ways this turned out for the good: TeleTOP was moving quickly to being accepted as ordinary procedure in the faculty, and thus stimulated less debate compared to the initiation year. Instructors just got on with it. Also, the instructors could see that TeleTOP would allow them to tailor versions of their courses for students from other faculties taking the courses as part of their minors, and thus a new long-range benefit became clear. As a direct consequence of the time being spent on curriculum-change activities in the faculty, our rapid-prototyping method (see Table 7.3) was abbreviated (although still including the decision support tool sessions) and only a few workshop sessions relating to pedagogy and TeleTOP were held. There was a risk of forgetting the pedagogical road map.

Thus, Year 2 tested the strength of TeleTOP's approach in two major ways: by moving it (perhaps prematurely) into the start of institutionalization in our own faculty, and by moving it successfully out of its niche in our faculty into other settings. Both appeared to be succeeding, although it would have been better for pedagogical change to have had another year of attention in the faculty. Instead, the flexibility aspects of TeleTOP became the major focus, in terms of redesign of courses for the new curriculum and student groups.

From implementation to institutionalization: Year 3 of TeleTOP, 1999–2000

In Year 3 of TeleTOP the major focuses were course redesign, instructor support and pedagogical analysis, time and effort costs for instructors, transfer to other settings and the institutionalization of the system within our faculty.

Continued course redesign

All courses in the first and second year of our programme were re-redesigned in TeleTOP to reflect the new curriculum, and TeleTOP was used without technical problems to support the two cohorts of regular and working students. A number of third- and fourth-year courses were also redesigned. And a number of courses in different variants of our Masters' programme were redesigned and offered in TeleTOP, including all the courses in the totally-at-a-distance variant. The remainder of the courses in the old curriculum and the majority of the remaining courses for the Masters' programme were in the process of redesign for the 2000–01 academic year. Over 80 courses were supported in the TeleTOP database for our faculty during the third year. Thus, the implementation process in our faculty, in terms of the redesign of courses for more-flexible participation using the TeleTOP system, was nearly complete. The redesign of pedagogy for the U Approach (Chapter 5) will be a longer process. In addition, all of the first-year courses in the Telematics Department ran using TeleTOP.

Evaluation, instructors in two faculties

Lesson 14: *Aim for activity*.

An evaluation was carried out at the end of the academic year 1999–2000 with 22 of the instructors in our faculty (in their second year of actually using TeleTOP and in their third year of contact with it) and 13 of the instructors in the Telematics Department (in their first year of using TeleTOP) relating to their experiences with it during the 1999–2000 academic year (Messing, 2000; Collis and Messing, in press). Among the focuses in the evaluation, instructors were asked what was new in their teaching as a result of using the system.

The majority of the open-ended responses to this question focused on improved opportunities for feedback provision, both qualitatively in terms of new ways of providing feedback (for example, peer evaluation) and also procedurally (faster, via the course site, with feedback available in the course site, feedback to groups via the site). Other new teaching aspects included (in the words of the instructors):

- 'Reuse of student work as models.'
- 'The rich supply of links and attached files is very handy and beneficial for students' learning.'
- 'Change in teaching style (more interaction) has been forced – I am less an information giver, more a problem solver.'
- 'Via the roster I was able to organize the background information for each week.'
- 'Improved presentation including of feedback.'
- 'The possibility to answer students' questions and have these answers available to all students.'
- 'More flexibility and up-to-date teaching.'
- 'More personal communication.'
- 'Easy to provide the students with relevant information.'
- 'You learn as a teacher to prepare lessons for students more thoroughly.'
- 'Providing a more encompassing database (not only texts but also WWW links, glossary of concepts) to students.'

Despite their different amounts of experience with TeleTOP and their different subject-matter backgrounds, there were no particular differences in the responses of the educational science and technology instructors and the telematics instructors.

Both groups of instructors also noted that their use of TeleTOP resulted in 'more activity and instruction of students' accompanied by 'a better overview of the tempo of the learning and level of participation'. Students are 'stimulated to react/comment more intensely' with new options added to the learning process, for example 'giving students the opportunity to exchange information – greater student interaction'. The course becomes 'more personal for students'.

Thus, the instructors in both faculties were moving towards an approach more focused on student activity than had been the case before using TeleTOP. In addition, two-thirds of the instructors felt that their courses were now a better learning experience for their students. Of the one-third who felt that the learning experience was no different than before (no one felt it was worse), almost all admitted that they were only making marginal use of TeleTOP, predominately using the system for flexible provision of course information.

Lesson 17: *Be aware of the price tag.*

The majority of the instructors also noted efficiency gains. Some of their comments were:

- 'All materials are handy and reusable.'
- 'More materials (WWW-based) are available and there is better access to the materials.'
- 'Overcomes the hassle of having readers in stock, etc.'
- 'Students have a uniform interface to courses (saves time; avoids confusion).'
- 'Helps organize the communication with students.'
- 'It provides a uniform user-interface with helpful features that can be easily reused.'
- 'I can let students work and hand in assignments that force them to process the literature studied. I can provide them feedback on their work more flexibly'.

In terms of the features chosen by instructors to use within the TeleTOP system, there were more similarities than differences between the two groups of instructors. Figure 8.4 compares the features chosen and used in these two samples of instructors in our faculty and the less-experienced Telematics Department instructors (Messing, 2000).

Lesson 12: *Watch the speed limit.*

Lesson 11: *Offer something for everyone.*

Analysis of the reasons provided for choosing or not choosing a particular feature revealed that the decisions were based largely on the current practices of the instructors. While comments were made that indicated that the TeleTOP implementation was an opportunity to redesign the teaching strategy, instructors still largely tried to adapt existing practices to TeleTOP so that these practices would become more flexible and efficient. Instructors are most likely to begin by choosing aspects of a system that reflect their current ways of teaching, and then gradually move to new instructional approaches and new features. A system should be flexible enough so that instructors can find a comfortable starting-point, but are stimulated rather than constrained by the system in moving beyond that starting-point. TeleTOP appears to offer these characteristics.

Instructor support and pedagogical analysis

For just-in-time support, a TeleTOP environment was created as a resource for instructors. It contained a variety of hints, examples, resources documents and links to course sites illustrating new approaches to flexibility and to student

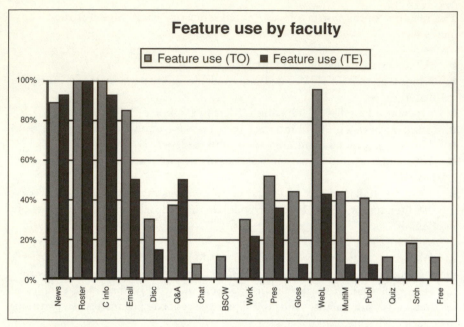

Feature use by faculty

□ Feature use (TO)   ■ Feature use (TE)

Note: *BSCW* and *Work* refer to two different groupware tools. *Pres* is *Presentation area* (where highlights of student work can be presented). *Glos, WebL, MultM, Publ* and *Srch* are *Glossary, WebLinks, Multimedia* and *Publications* areas (in all of these, both instructors and students can make entries) and *Search*, a collection of search tools for inside the TeleTOP database as well as externally.

Figure 8.4   *Use of TeleTOP features, by faculty (Note: 'TO' is the Faculty of Educational Science and Technology, in its third year of involvement with TeleTOP; 'TE' is the Telematics Department, in its second year of involvement)*

contributions. In particular, ideas relating to the use of TeleTOP to support new forms of assignments and feedback, which as a topic was given particular attention during the year, were also supported in the TeleTOP instructors' environment. The time and effort costs for instructors of new forms of student activities became a topic of considerable interest.

Lesson 15: *Design for activity.*

To support the instructors with respect to assignments and feedback, that is, to help them 'design for activity', we first made an inventory of what they were currently doing with respect to learning activities, particularly in terms of assignments. Table 8.5 shows the types of assignments and feedback in 31 of the courses in our faculty during the 1999–2000 academic year. The table is not

Table 8.5   *Forms of assignments and feedback, Faculty of Educational Science and Technology, a sample of 1999–2000 courses (n = 31) (Van der Veen, De Boer and Collis, 2000)*

Type of Feedback	Instructor Gives Feedback	Model Answer	Students Give Peer Feedback	No Feedback TeleTOP	Computer-generated	Total
Searching for new information	5		1			6
Case studies	3	1				4
Role play		1				1
Reports	1					1
Production of multimedia products	2		1	3		6
Assignments related to theory	6			2		8
Skill practice	1			3		4
Testing, quiz					1	1
Total	*18*	*2*	*2*	*8*	*1*	*31*

exhaustive: it only indicates the major approach per course, not the number of assignments. Also, if more than one approach was used in a course, the table only reflects the one used most often or given most emphasis.

In the TeleTOP instructor site, examples from existing courses were used to show how different instructors were managing different types of assignments and feedback. Also, Table 8.5 was available in hyperlinked form in site, so that instructors could examine examples in their own time and just in time.

Also available to them was a set of guidelines for handling assignments, but also for other aspects of designing and managing their TeleTOP environments (Remmers and Collis, 2000). The guidelines mix pedagogy and efficiency aspects and each includes a hyperlink to an example from one of our own courses, so that instructors can see what is meant as made concrete by a colleague. For example, some of the guidelines relating to feedback are:

Give the students via the WWW site:

● personal feedback when they have to carry out personalized variations of the same assignment;
● public feedback when you want them to learn from one another's answers or maybe use one another's answers for a new assignment;

- group feedback when the number of students of the course is large and could not be handled with personal feedback with regard to time constraints;
- one answer key to all students when many make the same mistakes in their answers;
- peer feedback when you want to guide the students in learning how to evaluate and give feedback.

As can be seen in Table 8.5, the majority of instructors were using the most time-consuming form of feedback, individualized comments to each student entered via the course environment. A goal for TeleTOP in its fourth year became helping instructors further on the pedagogy of student activity, particularly focused on making that pedagogy manageable for them as well as the students. It is interesting that in Year 3, there was one complaint being voiced by the students, not the fears from Year 1 about depersonalized education, but rather the opposite. Students complained that they were being expected to be too active, that it was costing them too much time to carry out all these activities, certainly more time than they had spent on their courses in the previous lecture orientations (although no more than they were meant to be spending on the courses, according to the number of credit hours involved). The *contribution approach* is not as time-efficient for students as the previous acquisition approach. It is also more time-consuming for instructors.

Time and effort costs of TeleTOP for instructors

Lesson 17: *Be aware of the price tag.*

Particular attention was paid during Year 3 of TeleTOP to the time and effort costs for instructors, not only for assignment and feedback management, but also other aspects of course redesign and delivery using the system. In the evaluation carried out by Messing (2000), the instructors who were interviewed, from both our faculty and the Telematics Department, were asked to estimate their time expenditures for course preparation and delivery. Because the issue of time demands is so important as a potentially negative effect of using TeleTOP (**Lesson 5:** *Watch the 4 Es*), these time estimates are reproduced in Table 8.6. Unfortunately, we do not have comparative data for non–TeleTOP time investment in course preparation and delivery.

All instructors indicated great difficulty in estimating their time investments and gave their perceptions rather than specific data. However, two observations are still useful. First, the four second-year users estimating that they spent more than 80 hours (two weeks) in the delivery of their courses were also all pioneers in terms of doing innovative things in their teaching. They were likely to be

Table 8.6 *Preparation/delivery workload, estimated by instructors, comparing first- and second-year users of TeleTOP (Collis and Messing, in press)*

First-Year Users of TeleTOP (n = 18)		Second-Year Users of TeleTOP (n = 14)	
Preparation	*Delivery**	*Preparation*	*Delivery*
0.5 week = 13	0.5 week = 5	0.5 week = 8	0.5 week = 3
1 week = 3	1 week = 4	1 week = 2	1 week = 3
1.5 weeks = 0	1.5 weeks = 2	1.5 weeks = 3	1.5 weeks = 2
2 weeks = 2	2 weeks = 0	2 weeks = 0	2 weeks = 2
More than 2 weeks = 0	More than 2 weeks = 2	More than 2 weeks = 1	More than 2 weeks = 4

* Several courses were still in progress at the time of the interview.

spending considerable time on their courses, with or without TeleTOP. For the majority of instructors, it cannot be said that their estimated time involvement is excessive, but in the perception of many it was. A number of instructors indicated that they only gave the time that they felt they had available: if this meant that they didn't give feedback, that was just the way it had to be. Thus, there seems to be a natural ceiling on time and energy investment, based on the willingness of the instructor to make these expenditures in teaching. But this has always been the case, well before TeleTOP.

While overall time spent on a course is important, the ways that time is spent within a course making use of TeleTOP to support more-flexible learning and some forms of student contributions to the course learning environment also were studied. Figure 8.5 shows one instructor's estimates of the percentages of time he spends on different aspects of the course preparation and delivery process with TeleTOP.

Some of the main management problems encountered by our instructors and the main responses that they have found helpful include (Collis and Gervedink Nijhuis, 2001):

● Preparation becomes less time-consuming because there are many resources that can be reused, and instructors know better what to do or to leave out. However, it still takes time to find good references on the WWW because there are so many sites and pages. Quality control of what students find and submit to the course WWW site is a new and major time concern. Making WWW site selection and evaluation an assignment for the students saves us considerable time and also considerably enlarges our own resource collections.

● Communication among students and between instructor and students is no longer a technical problem, but how to handle and archive communication in an efficient and effective way is still a problem. It is useful to try to avoid

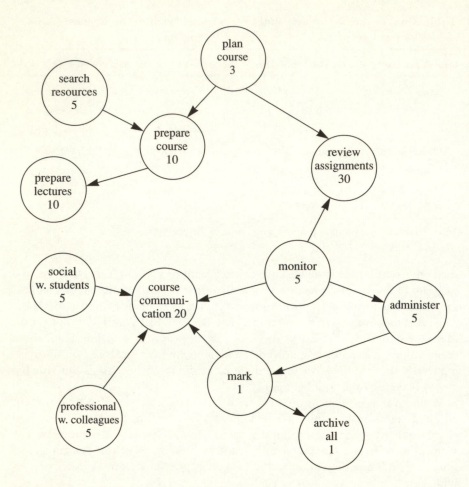

Figure 8.5 *Estimate percentage of instructor time spent on various categories of course-related tasks (Colis and Gervedink Nijhuis, 2001). 'w' stands for 'with'*

unnecessary communication by writing instructions clearly so that students do not have to send messages to ask for clarification. Another good idea is to structure the communication that is to occur via the use of forms.

● Assignments and feedback still take much time, although it is foreseen that using techniques such as *frequently asked questions* and standardized feedback will help to decrease the burden for instructors (Van der Veen, De Boer and Collis, 2000). (Well-structured) peer feedback can help so that the instructor does not have to provide all feedback, but instead only needs to respond to that given by others (Winnips, 2000).

● Monitoring group work still needs attention, firstly to be able to handle the progress of activities and secondly to be able to signal problems within a group before the problems escalate (Van der Veen, 2000). It is valuable if each member in a group has a specific task, and if progress on these tasks is easy to monitor via the TeleTOP site.

● Keeping student records is becoming an ever greater burden for instructors as individualization and diverse types of students call for more and more exceptions in course planning. It is useful to keep records of all agreements with students about exceptions to assignments, changes in dates, etc, archived in the course TeleTOP site for immediate reference when needed.

In order to get some quantitative measures about the impact of TeleTOP on the main actors of a faculty, a simplified ROI approach (Chapter 6) was applied to one of the courses using the system in the Telematics Department. Actors that provided data were (a) the education manager of the faculty representing the institutional perspective, (b) the instructor of the course and (c) a sample of 60 students. Simplified ROI tables (as the example in Table 6.3) were used for economic, qualitative and efficiency aspects. In Table 8.7 the results of the analysis for the efficiency aspects are given.

Table 8.7 *Simplified ROI with respect to efficiency, for a specific course running in TeleTOP (adapted from Mombarg, 2000: 13)*

Actors:	Institution (Education Dean)		Instructor		Students (n = 60)	
Aspects:	*Weight*	*Score*	*Weight*	*Score*	*Weight*	*Score*
Flexibility	1.0	+5 ('Can serve students at a distance')	0.6	+2 ('Can work on the course at home or when travelling'	1.0	+3 ('Time can be used more efficiently, don't have to come to lectures, but you need to work at a computer')
Studying course content via TeleTOP					0.6	−2 ('What's there is not important, only the textbook')
Efficiency in terms of student results	1.0	+5 ('Students stay on tempo, finish the course on time')	1.0	−4 ('Costs too much more time to look at and give feedback on all the extra assignments, handle e-mail, etc')		

Finding information and literature on line	0.8	+2 ('Useful for final projects')	0.8	+2 ('Information, also via WWW, always available, but students can waste time and find irrelevant info on the WWW')	0.6	+2 ('Glad to have the lecture notes, but don't make much use of extra information')
Doing and submitting assignments					1.0	+1 ('Saves time and is handy, but there are more assignments now, and you have to use a computer')
Assessing assignments and giving feedback			0.8	−3 ('Easier and faster to give feedback with a red pen, directly on paper')		
Feedback on assignments via TeleTOP			1.0	+1 ('Despite above, it is handy to give feedback directly on to the WWW site')	0.8	+1 ('Good that you can read feedback, even at home, as soon as the instructor puts it there, but the instructor is slow at entering the feedback')
Communication	0.8	−3 ('Not flowing as expected')	0.8	−1 ('Good for streamlining communication but students don't use them')	0.8	−2 ('Options, ie Q&A, are sensible, but we just don't use them')
Support of group work			0.8	−2 ('Much better if students do it face to face')	0.6	−2 ('Easier to get together face to face')
General information about the course available via TeleTOP	0.8	+ 1 ('Handy, also handy that integrated with the university news')	0.8	+1 ('The news is handy, but students don't look at other information')	0.8	+2 ('Always up to date and handy')
Technology skills and competencies	0.8	+2 ('Everyone will benefit from having more technology experience')	0.8	+2 ('Has got much more handy with the computer since using TeleTOP')	0.8	+2 ('Improves your skills at using the Internet; stimulates you to get your own computer)
ROI: efficiency (weighted total)		+11.6		−2.6		+5.2

In Table 8.7 a number of relevant items with respect to efficiency are mentioned in the first column. The following columns represent the points of view of the education dean, the instructor and the students. Furthermore, a weight factor is mentioned in order to represent the importance of each aspect as reliably as possible. The data in the cells (on a scale from −5 to +5) represent the relative amount of loss or gain that was perceived by the respective actors in the new situation using TeleTOP in comparison with the original situation. For instance, +5 in the first cell means that the education dean has the opinion that from the perspective of efficiency, the flexibility provided by the TeleTOP system had really made a difference.

The last row gives the weighted sum of the data in the respective columns and can be interpreted as the simplified ROI with respect to the efficiency category from each of the actors' perspectives. As has been said in Chapter 6, the importance of this simple calculation is not to get absolute results, but to come to comparative results between the main actors. In this example, it became clear that the institution and the students got a relatively good ROI from the TeleTOP investment, while the instructors are not that lucky. This empirical result confirms the conclusions brought forward at the end of Chapter 6. Of course, this result is influenced by the choice of items selected in the first column. But again, as has been said in Chapter 6, selecting those items of which the expectation is that they will make a difference is an essential part of the discussion. The simplified ROI leads to more explicit thinking about return on investment that should take place in order to come to valid decisions.

Transfer of TeleTOP to other settings

As Messing's (2000) survey data show, the transfer of TeleTOP to a technical faculty has proceeded smoothly, with results similar to our own experiences. During Year 3 of TeleTOP several other transfer activities absorbed much of the team's time. These included transfer to two other universities as well as transfer to the remaining faculties in our own institution.

Lesson 6: *Follow the leader.*

A major event for TeleTOP in Year 3 was the official transfer of it as a technical system and an implementation and pedagogical method to the DINKEL Institute (the institute for teaching and learning support at university level). The board of the university decided during 1999 to support TeleTOP as the common course-management system to be used throughout the university in order to provide a consistent and common environment for all students. The transfer took place in January 2000. Since then, the DINKEL Institute is assuming all responsibility for implementation of TeleTOP within the faculties of the University of Twente (including, eventually, for support of our own faculty), and also for the licensing of TeleTOP by external parties. The DINKEL also has the task of commercialization of the system, a task that culminated in September 2000 with the signing of an agreement between the University and IBM that TeleTOP will be marketed and supported internationally by IBM under the name *TeleTOP powered by Lotus*. For the TeleTOP team, this year of transition to the DINKEL has meant continual interaction and collaboration with the institute in a variety of ways. This transition has still continued in 2000–01.

Institutionalization of TeleTOP

Throughout the year additions to the TeleTOP system were developed to reflect the wishes of instructors and students. Considerable time has been spent in Year 3 by the TeleTOP team on designing and developing a TeleTOP-based support environment for the educational-affairs office of the faculty to handle student registrations, the making of student accounts and other administrative functions. Also, the team began working with others at the university level on the integration of TeleTOP with other administrative information systems supported by the faculty and university. These activities have had little or nothing to do with pedagogy, but rather have been primarily information-systems tasks relating to efficiency.

As a complementary process to the transfer of implementation responsibility to the university level, within our own faculty TeleTOP was also moving to insti-tutional status. We discuss this more in the next section, relating to the academic year 2000-01. Procedural issues relating to the transfer to institutionalization took up much time. While this is the price of success, there are also few models to guide us, as not many implementation projects of the scope of TeleTOP (technology, new pedagogies, flexibility) have made it to the institutionalization level in such a short time.

Institutionalization: 2000 and beyond

This section is relatively short, as at the time of preparation of this book, the academic year 2000–01 had only just begun. Thus, the illustration here is of the planning and anticipation of issues for the completion of the institutionalization of TeleTOP rather than a description of what has already occurred. The main points in our institutionalization year relate to stimulating the continual develop-ment of flexibility and contribution-oriented activity within an institutionalized process, further developing the U Approach, and more generally blending inno-vation with stability.

Two major focuses are under way in 2000–01 to continue the development of systematic methods for pedagogical change and more flexibility. One focus is on a different way of thinking about a course, as a view of a database with reusable objects. A second is on new support tools for instructors. One of these tools will be to help them consider ideas for new forms of contribution-oriented student activities as well as see examples of how to implement the activities within TeleTOP and manage the support and feedback process for the activities. A second tool relates to tailoring a new environment and copying objects from one environment to another.

A major focus in 2000–01 is to design a systematic way for instructors to build a database of resources and components related to a subject domain, and then have simple-to-use tools within TeleTOP to designate various alternative views (ie different course environments) for different categories of students, such as regular students and working students, different variants of our Masters' programmes and other possibilities. We are developing this approach for all the instructors in a programme, bringing new opportunities for collaboration and sharing of resources, and new challenges for instructors used to developing their courses in relative isolation from other courses. A new tool for copying objects from one database to another makes it easy to list all the resources in the underlying database in a variety of orders, and then select the components for reuse in the new view. This will enhance the efficiency for tailoring variations of a course for different groups of students, an ongoing goal of flexible learning. Strategies for tagging objects in the underlying database to designate their key attributes are being developed (Strijker, 2000), coupling international standards such as IMS with locally relevant attributes.

Lesson 14: *Aim for activity.*

A second focus in 2000–01 is on support for instructors for assignments and feedback, not only to move towards new forms of contribution-oriented learning but also to improve the efficiency and thus time demands of assignment management. Based on the inventory done in Year 3 of types of assignments and feedback currently being used by instructors (see Table 8.5), we are developing and testing a new decision support tool, this one to focus on helping the instructor systematically consider different types of learning activities and types of feedback and see examples of how these types are being or can be carried out within TeleTOP. This new TeleTOP DST will be a complement to the first TeleTOP DST (see Chapter 7), the first one most appropriate for instructors at the transition between initiation and implementation phases and the new one most appropriate for instructors with some experience, at the transition between the implementation and institutionalization phases. In addition, we are planning to adapt both decision support tools for corporate-university environments, to study similarities and differences between the needs of instructors in those settings compared to university instructors.

Summing up

In this chapter, we have continued our illustration of how we apply our lessons in our own practice. All the lessons have been represented explicitly or implicitly in Chapters 7 and 8: we do practise what we preach. And we are continually evolving the lessons, based on new rounds of experience.

How we will combine institutionalization with new rounds of pioneering will be one of our challenges for 2001 and beyond. The transition to institutionalization and the gradual mainstreaming of the approach and system for maximal involvement and ownership are critical, and after a point a special team and project can be a barrier to this transition. So, the time has come for us as the TeleTOP team to phase out. We will continue as researchers, and probably as always, as pioneers ourselves in the use of technology in our own learning settings.

We can also have a role as visionaries. In Chapter 9, we look at some future developments for flexible learning and technology that show that this combination of innovation and stability will be critical.

Chapter 9

A new economy for education?

Major changes are occurring in society: in the ways that we work, produce wealth, spend our money, interact and amuse ourselves. Collectively, these changes are leading to a new system for human commerce and communication that is being called the new economy. Is there a new economy emerging for education? In this chapter we argue that this is so, and use the lessons to suggest

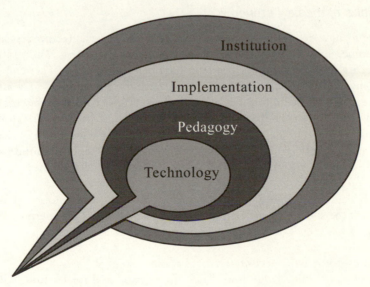

Figure 9.1   *Flexible learning in higher education – future perspective*

its characteristics and implications. We begin by taking some major characteristics of the new economy in the business and consumer world and speculate on the forms those might take as a new economy for education also emerges. We also look at several routes towards this new economy for higher education, routes which can differ in a number of ways but which we sketch in terms of four scenarios (*Back to Basics, The Global Campus, Stretching the Mould* and *The New Economy*). Key issues associated with the scenarios for different actors related to the institution, implementation management, pedagogy and technology perspectives are predicted, and recommendations linked to the lessons learnt are given. Regardless of the scenario or the manner of reaching the new economy, flexible learning and technology will be its key attributes.

Characteristics of the new economy

The phrase 'the new economy' began to appear regularly in the mass media in 1999 and 2000 (just as the phrase *the information superhighway* appeared several years before). The phrase *information superhighway* was a metaphor to capture the discovery of the power of the Internet that occurred in society in the mid-1990s. Although the phrase does not appear much any more, the idea it expressed is now firmly grounded. Similarly, the phrase *new economy* emerged more or less in 1998 and became a buzzword in 1999. As with many metaphors, the phrase has a variety of meanings. In this section we extract some of the major attributes of the term and then apply them to the educational setting.

Principles of the new economy

The term new economy is multifaceted. It refers to a change process as well as the components of that process and the results of the process. Within this broad basis many different definitions and ideas are being expressed. In general, the new economy 'has three distinguishing characteristics: It is global. It favours intangible things – ideas, information, and relationships. And it is intensely interlinked. These three attributes produce a new type of marketplace and society, one that is rooted in ubiquitous electronic networks' (Kelly, 1998: 2). Kelly goes on to argue that networks are the central entity and metaphor around which the new economy is organized and that communication is what the new economy is about (pp 3–5).

Kelly's three distinguishing characteristics give rise to a number of associated aspects of the so-called new economy that was established or emerging in degree of impact in 2000. These include (Moonen, in press a, in press b):

● Access to network technology has become essential.
● Interrelated knowledge is available on demand and new knowledge can be rapidly disseminated.

- Technology is fundamentally changing the ways in which business, communication and other forms of human recreation and interaction occur and new opportunities for market growth are rapidly arising.
- The traditional chains for products are changing; middlemen are being eliminated or emerging in new forms, transactions are quicker and more efficient, and transaction costs can be reduced. Whether cost benefits are being passed directly to the consumer is less clear.
- Because of technology, the buyer has access to an oversupply of products and services. The issues now are gaining attention and selection.
- Organizations are rapidly changing because of these aspects; they must adapt. Often, adaptation involves mergers or alliances.

These aspects have been summarized in the popular press in terms of sets of lessons for businesses, such as those given in the magazine *Business 2.0* (10 driving principles, 2000). Some of these principles are given in Table 9.1.

These changes did not happen overnight. For more than a decade before the new economy became developed enough to be noticed and described in the popular consciousness, there was debate about why productivity was not showing up in the business world despite the huge expenditures on information technology that had occurred (Brynjolfsson and Yang, 1996). There are several key reasons why the impact of the new economy took time to show up in society, but finally has. Among these are: new methods and processes are needed for measurements related to technology and its impact (lack of progress may be a 'mirage created by outdated measuring tools' – Gibbs, 1997: 84); a critical mass both in terms of humans and infrastructure needs to develop in practice; the

Table 9.1 *Principles for success in the new economy (from 10 driving principles, 2000: 220)*

Principle	Implication
'Matter: it matters less.'	The value of a company is in its key people, ideas and information-driven assets.
'Space: distance has vanished.'	'The world is your customer and your competitor.'
'Time: it's collapsing.'	Instant activity and response are critical and force constant change.
'Efficiency: the middleman lives' (but in a new form).	' "Infomediaries" are replacing intermediaries.' 'Traditional intermediaries... are seriously threatened by a networked economy in which buyers can deal directly with sellers.'
'Transactions: it's a one-on-one game.'	Consumers will demand tailoring.
'Impulse: every product is available everywhere.'	'The process for marketing, sales, and fulfillment are merging.'

incubation time that is needed for an innovation to occur, in complex processes in which organizations and humans are players, is lengthy; and many applications of technology were poorly chosen, for example trying to replace human skills with computerized routines (Gibbs, 1997; Moonen, in press b). The fact that technology now is used to facilitate human communication rather than replace skilled humans is seen by many as a critical change (Kelly, 1998).

Principles of a new economy in education

We believe that higher education will eventually show the characteristics of the new economy that are now appearing in other sectors of society. For the same reasons that an impact of technology took a decade to show up in the commercial world, this impact and thus preparation for the new economy will take time to show up in the educational sector. The pace of the change will be different from that in the business world, in that most higher-education organizations are not (yet) so overtly profit-oriented and thus are slower to be motivated toward change.

In addition, the impact of change towards the new economy will be tailored to the sector. Some of our expectations for the new economy in education are given in a general form in Table 9.2. In the subsequent sections of this chapter we expand upon these expectations from the perspectives of different actors who will be involved.

The expectations in Table 9.2 have far-reaching implications for all aspects of post-secondary school learning, in terms of the market sector involved, the participants and the learning process itself. What configurations might be present in higher education as a result of the expectations in Table 9.2? We see at least four scenarios, varying on two major dimensions that are now emerging based on key developments in both society and education. We introduced some of these developments in Chapters 1 and 2, but return to them now in the context of integrating all the aspects of this book towards an eventual new economy for education.

Identifying dimensions for change

In this section we extract two main dimensions for change and from these project four scenarios for higher-education institutions in the future. One of these scenarios is *The New Economy*.

Trends in the organization of teaching and learning in higher education

In Chapter 2 we discussed how changes occurring in the primary processes of higher education – courses and degree granting – are closely related to the contextual trends of virtualization, internationalization, lifelong learning and customer orientation that are part of change in society in general. We also iden-

Table 9.2   *Expectations for the new economy in higher education (Moonen, in press b)*

Aspects	Implication for Higher Education
Global	International orientation will grow; students will be from, or even still living in, many different regions and countries. There is global reach, and global competition.
Ubiquitous electronic networks	Electronic networks are ubiquitous, even to support face-to-face contacts.
Knowledge on demand	The textbook, instructor and library are becoming supplementary forms of information, not as up to date and easy to access as that on the WWW. Knowledge overflow is the problem.
Technology changes market players and opportunities	New services and new sources of courses and other types of learning experiences are available via the WWW.
New roles for the middleman	Instructors, librarians, even institutions are becoming middlemen. Consumers (students) can go directly to sources of knowledge; instructors are becoming facilitators of circumstances for student learning and participation, not bringing the information but setting up situations so that the student can find and assimilate information him- or herself. New middlemen are appearing both in and outside the university to offer services of various sorts.
Consumer demand	Customers will demand tailoring of lessons and courses to their own circumstances and will easily 'click and switch' around alternatives. Consumer loyalty to an institution will fade.
Efficiency	Efficiency will be sought in various ways, such as eliminating duplicate or costly courses and facilitating students to participate in similar courses offered by other parties. Another layer of efficiency will relate to the processes involved in the learning experience itself.
Winners and losers	At the institutional level, there will be a relatively few market winners (although translating this into financial profit for the institution will not be so easily seen) and a larger number of institutions that must adapt in new ways such as fusions and consortia in order to survive. Investors seeking short-term windfall profits will be likely to crash once the market stabilizes.
Producers of traditional resources (textbooks, media, laboratory products, etc)	Producers of traditional resources will have to reposition their resources as products, or redesign them as complementary technologies for on-demand access.
Regulations	Governmental or institutional bodies that accredit eduction will have to relax standards and norms on what is accredited. Society will come to accept new forms of competency-based degree programmes. New funding mechanisms will have to develop.

tified key questions relating to the value and academic rigour of an *online* degree or a *virtual university*; problems relating to learner engagement and persistence; issues relating to instructors; and issues relating to ownership, quality control and acquisition of learning resources.

Looking at these questions, two main lines of development can be noticed. One relates to the local vs global issue. Should the university move towards strengthening itself as a home base for its learners, or move towards a future in a multinational partnership? What if the individual university decides to go it alone? Can it compete? Will the big partnerships dominate client attention? Or will a swing *back to the basics* occur, as a backlash against failed attempts at globalization if these should occur?

A second line of development relates to the programme and content to be offered. How should this be obtained, and offered to clients? As total programmes? As individual courses? As portions of courses (modules, or learning events of different types) that can be combined in different ways? What if the *choose-your-own-combination* idea takes root, stimulated by competition for fee-paying professional clients? Can the local institution handle this sort of individualization itself?

Trends related to services related to education

At least two major trends can be spotted in the category of secondary services. The first one is the *commercialization* of education as an online market. The second relates to the emergence of portals and brokers, some of which may also be commercial enterprises. The many new permutations of services relating to more-flexible learning suggest some major issues. One is *quality control*: who controls what is available via portals, or what is chosen in enterprise services? What if there is no assurance of quality: to whom does the purchaser turn? Another issue relates to the *location and management* of these services: can the sort of help that is needed be obtained by typing questions or pointing and clicking at alternatives on a WWW site? Which services are best done locally by personally known and trusted supporters, and which can benefit by economy of scale?

These developments show the sort of overlap that is now occurring between primary educational processes and secondary services. In all cases, technology is essential.

Trends in technology

In Chapter 1 we noted trends in networks and access and trends in products and tools as all being important to flexible learning. In addition, 'tele-immersion' and 'virtual laboratories' as well as techniques such as information visualization are all seen as bringing educational value to Internet2 (Lan and Gemmill, 2000). But many questions also are of concern with regard to increasingly ubiquitous or pervasive computing. Are we becoming too vulnerable with respect to networks and computing? What if servers are overloaded or fail for other reasons? What if new technologies keep changing so fast that users cannot settle down to a dependable habit of use? What if standards cannot be agreed about?

These questions represent two lines of concern. One is that technology is rapidly changing, but is it moving to a point where it is too exotic for the average user. (Think of the 4 Es.) Does the average instructor want to plan educational uses of *virtual reality rooms* or *pervasive 3-D* settings? Will there be a backlash? The dimension is one of less technology vs more technology.

A second dimension relates to the vulnerability that comes from depending on a server, system (such as a WWW-based course-management system) and networks for so many important learning-related transactions. What if these systems crash or are mismanaged or misused?

Extracting two key dimensions

These questions suggest two main lines of development. One relates to *quality control*. Who does it? By what criteria? Using what forms of control interventions? On one extreme, the Internet can be seen as a *free* channel, allowing anyone to access and contact anyone else. On the other extreme, the Internet can be seen as needing to be ordered; made secure; made a place to do business with consumer confidence; made a place to go for entertainment, with confidence that one's norms will not be offended. A second line of development relates to the *local vs global* aspect. Will one shop at the corner store or via a virtual portal whose server may be continents away? Where will one go to meet friends and socialize? What language will be spoken? How expensive is each alternative?

Many different ways could be found to zoom in on key aspects of these developments and emerging contexts. Table 9.3 summarizes one form of analyses (Collis and Gommer, 2000).

Combining all of these into a final set of two dimensions, the following emerge:

Location: local vs global
Quality control: control with the individual or an expert

The dimension 'Location: local vs global' relates to the term *place and form of transactions*, which is a term commonly used in discussions of the new economy (Kelly, 1998). Similarly, the dimension 'Quality control: control with the individual or an expert' relates to the idea of *individualization of consumer choice* in new-economy discussions. Thus, the dimensions can also be related to the eventual effect that the new economy might have on the educational market (Moonen, 2000a, in press a, in press b). In the next section, we relate these two dimensions to four scenarios for flexible learning that suggest different routes that post-secondary learning may be taking in the future.

Table 9.3 *Summary of major aspects affecting the future evolution of technology for flexible learning in higher education*

	Key Dimensions	Alternatives
Context	Quality control: individual vs expert	a. The Internet as an open system; the user takes responsibility. b. Intranets or controlled WWW sites as closed systems; expert responsibility for quality.
	Local vs global	a. Personal, local transactions, context specific. b. Transactions via the network, context neutral.
Primary processes	Local vs global	a. Based in home institution. b. Can be distributed among many different settings.
	Programme vs self-choice	a. Expert determines programme. b. Learner determines choices.
Support	Quality control: individual vs expert	a. User takes responsibility for choice and consequences. b. Trusted agency or institution provides the services.
	Local vs global	a. Support takes place locally, face to face, and in context. b. Support takes place via the Internet.
Technology	Backlash vs pervasive	a. Become less dependent on technology. b. Become more dependent on technology.
	Vulnerability: local vs distance	a. If technical problems occur, a local help-desk. b. If technical problems occur, remote or non-available support.

Scenarios for flexible learning

Combining the dimensions relating to place and form of transactions (local vs global) and individualization of consumer choice (consumer choice vs quality control by an expert) four scenarios can be derived using the scenario-development approach described by Miles, 2000, as shown in Figure 9.2.

The scenarios have been given names to capture their flavours:

Scenario A *Back to Basics*
Scenario B *The Global Campus*
Scenario C *Stretching the Mould*
Scenario D *The New Economy*

Scenario A *Back to Basics* is the current dominant situation for many traditional post-secondary institutions. In the future, *Back to Basics* may also become a response to a pendulum-swing, away from increased virtuality and commer-

Scenarios of the future in which flexible learning will be part of a setting...

Figure 9.2 *Four scenarios for flexible learning in 2005 and beyond (Collis and Gommer, 2000: 32)*

cialism in education, and back to *what universities are really about*. It is also the case that many universities are starting to experiment with distance participation in their established programmes (see Chapter 2). This can lead to **Scenario B** *The Global Campus*. What if pursuing and serving these off-campus students becomes the dominant mode (as is already happening in several Australian universities) in the institution? **Scenario C** *Stretching the Mould* relates to increased flexibility with or without changing the underlying pedagogical model within the institution (Chapter 5). Many traditional universities are now moving towards some forms of *Stretching the Mould*, by offering more flexibility for participation within their preset programmes (an example of this is the accommodation of part-time students in our own faculty, Chapter 7). **Scenario D** *The New Economy* is the most radical; a systematic example of it does not yet seem to be available in most traditional universities. What if this *learner choice/global and network mediated* scenario becomes the dominant setting in the middle-range future?

Scenario B *The Global Campus* and **Scenario C** *Stretching the Mould* are, in fact, evolving at the same time and in an overlapping way for many universities (Collis, 1999b, 1999f). At the same time as programmes are becoming available to students at a distance, new flexibilities are being integrated into both local and distance courses. The idea of *distance* begins to fade in meaningfulness, as all students make an increasing number of choices about where, when, what and how to study. The course WWW environment is the technology for interaction and communication for much of the learning experience: the core technology (Chapter 4). Whatever other communication and interaction experiences occur are complementary to this core, and thus differing in their value for different students. It may be that **Scenario D** *The New Economy* evolves as an extension of *The Global Campus* and *Stretching the Mould*, and even at the same time an institution may support different blends of the scenarios for different types of learners. Figures 9.3, 9.4 and 9.5 (Collis and Gommer, 2000) show different balances that may all be present at the same institution, for entry-level learners, learners with more capacity for self-guidance and professional-level learners.

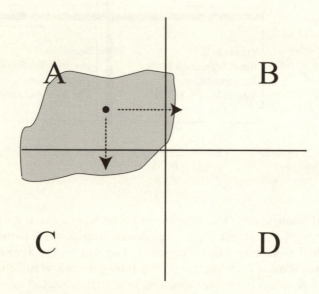

Figure 9.3   *Scenario blend for entry-level learners*

How does this scenario evolution work in practice? We turn back to the four aspects of institution, implementation, pedagogy and technology, as well as the 4-E Model and our lessons learnt to consider the progression.

The scenario evolution in practice

We have started each chapter in this book with a simple figure as a reminder of four integrated and important aspects of any move towards flexible learning in an educational institution. We will use the figure again (see Figure 9.6) to organize our discussion.

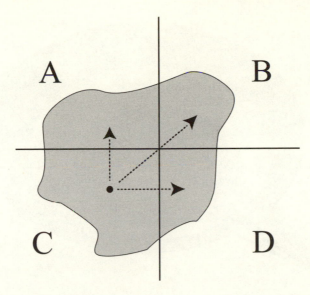

Figure 9.4 *Scenario blend for learner in transition between entry level and professional level*

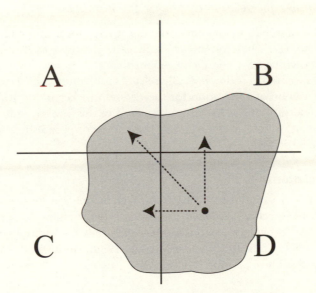

Figure 9.5 *Scenario blend for experienced or professional learners*

For each of the components – institution, implementation, pedagogy and technology – we will relate the future scenarios to the 4 Es and to the lessons learnt, and conclude with some recommendations.

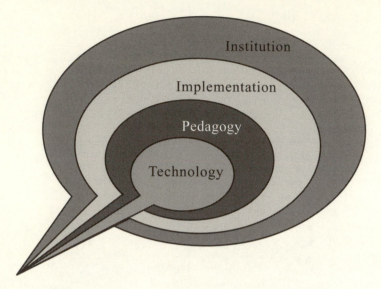

Figure 9.6 *Flexible learning in higher education – the four elements*

Those responsible for decision making in the institution

Which balance of scenarios to choose, moving at what speed and with what partners and technology? There can be no single general answer to this. Every institution has its own context and environment that will profoundly influence the likelihood of success of a technologically related change (the 4 Es, Lesson 5). The lessons learnt can be of application for the decision maker in the institution. In Table 9.4, a selection of the 18 lessons discussed in this book is indicated, along with a statement of how it can relate to the choice of progression for decision makers in the institution.

Recommendations

From Table 9.4, a variety of further recommendations can be formulated that combine various aspects of the lesson implications in the table. The following are some of the final conclusions of an international study on technology in higher education in 1999 (Collis and Van der Wende, 1999; Moonen, 1999) that show this combination. They are related here to the 4 Es.

- *Broaden the mission of the institution and deregulate to enhance responsiveness.* Institutional policy should encourage responsiveness to the chosen scenario(s) by creating an institutional context that is sufficiently deregulated in order to enable the institution to respond to these new approaches. (Environment)
- *Adapt to contextual conditions and provide incentives.* The above implies a strategic use of policy instruments, such as funding and evaluation. In evalu-

Table 9.4 *The lessons learnt and institutional decision makers*

Lesson	Application to Institutional Decision Makers Considering the Progression from A to/through B and/or C perhaps to D *The New Economy*
Lesson 1 *Be specific.*	Be specific about the scenario progression to be given priority in the institution.
Lesson 2 *Move from student to professional.*	In any scenario, stimulate the 'U turn' idea (involving not only more flexibility but also new models of learners as contributors) through incentives and models.
Lesson 3 *You can't not do it.*	Choose the scenario and scenario progression whose 'time has come' for your institution. This will be based on a combination of internal and external aspects.
Lesson 4 *Don't forget the road map.*	Maintain the focus on the long-range plan for progression through scenarios as well as for depth (the 'U turn') within a scenario. Stimulate occasional reflection on major issues, not details of implementation.
Lesson 5 *Watch the 4 Es.*	Test the viability of any scenario against the 4Es; support the pay-off of the scenario for all involved; do what it needs to make ease of use and environmental conditions as positive as possible.
Lesson 6 *Follow the leader.*	Be a participant in some aspect of the scenario chosen, eg (co-)teach a course, contribute learning materials, etc, to be more aware of what is actually involved and to show commitment and engagement.
Lesson 10 *Don't overload.*	Do not expect too much change at the same time, but do keep the change process moving.
Lesson 12 *Watch the speed limit.*	Don't try to move too quickly to Scenario D. A critical mass of experience in C may be necessary first.
Lesson 13 *Process yields product.*	Ensure that policy and support are in place for the reuse of student work as learning materials.
Lesson 16 *Get a new measuring stick.*	Set measurable short-term targets; regularly review long-term targets and state those more concretely.
Lesson 17 *Be aware of the price tag.*	Don't expect that instructors can move to new scenarios with little or no additional compensation for their time and efforts.
Lesson 18 *Play the odds.*	Support ongoing estimates of return on investment, as formative input for the evolution of the scenarios.

ations of institutional performance the use of technology for more flexible learning should be taken into account as a quality issue. (Effectiveness, short-term pay-off; Environment)

● *Develop a strategic and economic rationale, as well as an educational vision.* For technology use to have impact on an institution as a whole, a strategic rationale is necessary and should be expressed in specific and measurable terms. Cost aspects must be included. (Effectiveness, long-term pay-off)

- *Study and respond to hidden costs.* Institutions must come to a sharper realization of the time costs and the opportunity costs for instructors involved in this technology use and take measures to relieve the increasing pressure on faculty for technology-related management tasks. (Effectiveness, short-term pay-off; Environment; see also Chapter 5).
- *Subsidize implementation, not isolated projects.* Funding incentives in the institution should be steered around implementation (including pioneer activity based on extending the institutionalized system), and reward success.

Those responsible for implementation

For those responsible for implementation strategy in an institution, several major issues will need consideration. One issue relates to volunteers versus a planned implementation schedule. To what extent those responsible for implementation should try to stimulate this co-ordination or wait until they are asked will be a challenge. Another issue will be quality management, especially if external partners become involved in courses and modules that will be followed in the local institution. Who takes responsibility for this quality control? At what level of unit size? (Individual resource? Applet? Case resources? Module? Activity? Entire course? Final examination?)

Table 9.5 relates these key issues and other tasks of those responsible for implementation in an institution to a selection of the lessons.

Recommendations

- *Pay more attention to the human aspects of implementations than to the technical.* A careful implementation plan to win instructor engagement is critical. Key to such a plan is flexibility in terms of responsiveness to the individual needs and pedagogical experiences of the instructor. Keep technology as a servant to the situation, not a motivator. (Effectiveness; Engagement)
- *Plan instructor support around a just-in-time model and tools.* General courses for groups of instructors will probably not be useful. Find a combination of contact and tools for personal use that an instructor can call on just in time, as he or she plans for a course or responds to a student asking for some sort of individualized attention. (Effectiveness; Environment)

Those responsible for pedagogy (instructors)

In traditional educational settings it is the individual instructor who is the final determiner of what learning activities occur in a course or module under his or her responsibility. Thus, the success of any scenario will have much to do with the responses of the professionals responsible for teaching and learning. In traditional universities, this is not a team of course authors but the single instructor,

Table 9.5   *The lessons learnt and those responsible for implementation*

Lesson	Application to Those Responsible for Implementation Considering the Progression from A to/through B and/or C perhaps to D *The New Economy*
Lesson 1 *Be specific.*	Relate the steps of the implementation process to specific strategic goals (and the scenarios).
Lesson 4 *Don't forget the road map.*	Keep the goal (the scenario) in mind; avoid becoming overwhelmed with day-to-day aspects.
Lesson 5 *Watch the 4 Es.*	When working with instructors, translate the scenario into elements that matter to them in terms of educational effectiveness. Look for a fit with the instructor's preferred ways of working, at least as a starting-point.
Lesson 6 *Follow the leader.*	The leaders of the implementation process should also have experience themselves in the new scenarios. They should have practised what they now preach.
Lesson 7 *Be just in time.*	Plan support so that it is a balance of stimulating instructors to preparation for change, and at the same time is predominately *just in time*, when they need it and can apply it directly to their courses.
Lesson 10 *Don't overload.*	More is not necessarily better. For a first experience, help instructors add flexibility aspects.
Lesson 12 *Watch the speed limit.*	Do not try to do too much at the same time with instructors.
Lesson 14 *Aim for activity.*	In working with instructors, emphasize ideas for student activities, and how these can be managed.

for whom teaching is not the major part of his or her work. Among the key issues facing instructors are management, time pressures and sustainability. As more and more flexibility is being expected, how can the instructor handle all of the implications of these expectations? Ideally, institutions would hire more instructors, but that is not likely to be the case.

Table 9.6 relates the lessons to the instructor, in the context of an institution's progression to and through the scenarios.

Recommendations

Given the lessons, and the future scenarios, what are the main recommendations for instructors?

● *Fit with conditions.* Instructor fit is critical. Instructors must be able to begin a change process in a way that is comfortable to them. **Scenario C** *Stretching the Mould* is most promising in this respect, **Scenario D** *The New Economy* least promising. (Effectiveness; Engagement)

Table 9.6 *The lessons learnt and those responsible for pedagogy*

Lesson	Application to Instructors, Relating to the Progression from A to/through B and/or C perhaps to D *The New Economy*
Lesson 2 *Move from student to professional.*	Move from a knowledge-transmission model to a contribution-oriented approach or a blend of the two.
Lesson 3 *You can't not do it.*	Go along with the technology that your institution supports.
Lesson 5 *Watch the 4 Es.*	Categorize yourself and your situation in terms of the 4Es: if your situation in terms of the 4 Es is poor, then be realistic in terms of what you can expect of yourself with regard to technology use.
Lesson 9 *After the core, choose more.*	Look for the best medium for each task, and offer alternatives when possible; don't try to use the WWW when a different medium (such as a handout or book) would be better.
Lesson 10 *Don't overload.*	Students don't necessarily appreciate more feedback, more communication, more WWW resources. Keep the level manageable for all.
Lesson 12 *Watch the speed limit.*	Take steps that build on your own way of teaching; do not try to do too many new things at the same time, either with flexibilization or the use of technology.
Lesson 13 *Process yields product.*	Make the U turn: engage your students in the process of the contribution of study materials to the course environments and in the process of (peer) evaluating and discussing these contributions.
Lesson 14 *Aim for activity.*	Select uses of WWW technology that exploit new forms of student activity, rather than only as a distribution channel for the basic study materials in the course. Use the WWW for new flexibility and possibilities in the ways students communicate, in their supplementary readings and for new options in assignments. Don't use the WWW to replace the textbook or lecture but rather to extend these and make them more flexible.
Lesson 15 *Design for activity.*	Move from thinking of a course in terms of content provision towards activity design and management.
Lesson 16 *Get a new measuring stick.*	Define success concretely such as (a) managing different versions of the course for different groups of students, and (b) by students also having responsibility for aspects of the course, such as finding additional cases or external WWW sites and making these available for other students.
Lesson 17 *Be aware of the price tag.*	Watch the costs for yourself, in terms of time and effort and stress. Look for didactic strategies that increase the activity of students so that your own level can be stabilized; reuse instructional resources as much as possible.

- *Change your focus from content provision to activity management.* The students should be busier than the instructor. Plan a course around the idea of active students, as far as relevant contributing examples and resources to the course environment. Use the technology for activity support, not to replace the textbook. (Effectiveness)
- *Be concerned about your own time.* Look continually for strategies to reduce your own time burden relating to increased flexibility for students. The reuse of resources (including student-produced materials as model answers), and different support and feedback methods such as peer feedback or directing the students to model answers can be valuable. Structure assignments and activities so students are clear as to what is expected and do not have to communicate with you for clarification, and so that their submissions are in a form that is relatively quick for you to assess. (Effectiveness, short-term pay-off; Ease of use)

Those responsible for technology

Those responsible for the technology to support the scenarios have a number of burdens. One key issue is the choice of the development of a local solution or the purchase of an external product. A second key issue relates to version control and updates of the technology that has been chosen. There will be a continual push towards new versions, partly in response to user needs and partly as a necessity because of changes in the products as offered by their vendors. Other technology-related issues have to do with access control to resources in a common database, with labelling of those resources for efficient reuse and management, and with ownership aspects and their management in the database.

Table 9.7 relates a selection of the lessons learnt to issues for technology specialists.

Recommendations

- *Support a common WWW-based course-support system for the institution.* From the international trends it is clear that WWW-based course-management systems, integrated with a multimedia database and an administrative database, are a major tool in any institutional attempt to offer more-flexible learning (see Chapter 4). Access to the system by both instructors and students, from home or workplace, at a minimal cost and minimal inconvenience and with responsive and helpful technical-support persons, is a necessary condition. (Ease of use)
- *Move towards the idea of an underlying database and easy-to-use tools to tailor new views for different learners.* Decisions about issues relating to intellectual ownership and multiple use of materials produced by instructors and students and stored in the system database need to be made at the institutional level but the technology must make it easy to handle those decisions in practice. Tools for easily designing new views of an underlying dynamic database, continu-

Table 9.7 *The lessons and the technology specialist*

Lesson	Application to Technology Specialists, Relating to the Progression from A to/through B and/or C perhaps to D *The New Economy*
Lesson 2 *Move from student to professional.*	Choose technology that makes it easy for instructors to use their own professional resources in their courses.
Lesson 5 *Watch the 4 Es.*	Keep ease of use for instructors and students as a top priority.
Lesson 7 *Be just in time.*	Choose a technology system that allows the user to have as little or as much functionality as is useful to him or her at a given time.
Lesson 8 *Get out of the niche.*	Avoid investing time and funds on niche products that will only be used by one or a few instructors.
Lesson 9 *After the core, choose more.*	Use a combination of technologies when appropriate. For reading material suggest to instructors that they use a book rather than a WWW site. Look for complementary resources to use within the WWW-based course environments such as streaming video segments that capture previous moments of good communication.
Lesson 10 *Don't overload.*	More is not necessarily better; an instructor should be able to select as few or as many options as he or she wishes for the course-support environment.
Lesson 11 *Offer something for everyone.*	Choose a technology system that can be used by beginners and experts alike.
Lesson 13 *Process yields product.*	Choose a technology system that optimizes the use and reuse of student contributions as part of the study materials.
Lesson 14 *Aim for activity.*	Choose a technology system with adequate groupware tools, communication tools and tools to support student activities.
Lesson 15 *Design for activity.*	Design templates to support new forms of student activities, rather than tutorial-type electronic study materials.
Lesson 18 *Play the odds.*	Work with the decision makers to identify key variables for estimating return on investment.

ally being enlarged by new contributions from instructors and learners alike, are critical. (Effectiveness, education; Ease of use; Environmental)

- *Select technology based on the 4 Es.* Because instructors will have different ideas about what is educational effectiveness in their own courses, provide a system that is pedagogically neutral or open, but with built-in support tools to help the instructor tailor the use of the system to his or her own needs and situation. Keep the skills needed for use as simple as possible, with no technical training or special clients necessary.

Summing up, and looking forward

How might **Scenario D** *The New Economy* work in the future, particularly in terms of requirements for the technology involved? A critical issue is the filling and maintaining of the underlying database(s) involved. We can picture the steps and requirements shown in Table 9.8.

Table 9.8 *Scenario D The New Economy in operation*

Actions	Technology Requirements
A professional community shares access to a common database or interconnected distributed databases and evolves a procedure for categorizing resources in the database for communal use.	Privileges for distributed users allowing read and write access.
When entering a resource into the shared database, a simple-to-use checklist process allows the addition of metadata tags to the resource. The least number of tags for use in practice is the goal, as instructors will not take the time to make more than a few key indications.	Granularity will be expressed in terms of what can be entered as a single file or linked to from a single-view overview. Tools for users easily to add or adapt metadata tags and add new ones if necessary must be available. Views of the objects in the database selected around any given set of tags or other key categories can be called up in which the associated objects can be listed in terms of frequency of access. Rules can change objects to an archival status after a designated period of non-access.
To create a course-support environment, tools are present in the system leading the instructor through the steps in setting up a course environment, in terms of general organizational features, communication features, a device such as the TeleTOP roster (see Chapters 7 and 8), which presents an integrated overview of study materials and activity instructions and support, groupware features, resource-management features and special features such as quiz tools.	The course-management system should be integrated with an instructor-support tool to lead the instructor through options associated with the organization of his or her course. The tool should directly generate a new database associated with the underlying database.
The instructor should be able to sort and choose from resources from the associated database (the general database and other databases created in relation to this) and copy whatever resources he or she wishes to the new site.	A sort and copy tool relating to all databases to which the user has access is needed to facilitate the copying of resources. Copying allows new privileges to be assigned to the resources, privileges that may be different in different databases.
Learners studying with the new course environment not only see the selected resources provided by the instructor	The system must handle student submissions as ordinary objects, and should provide a tool for the instructor easily to designate

(both from other courses and from non-course related sources) but also enter new resources into the course database. The instructor can indicate with a simple click which of these learner-contributed resources are candidates for reuse and thus transfer to the master database or to a new copy of the course database adapted for a different learner population.

which student submissions should be copied for possible reuse.

Using the copy tool again, the instructor moves the objects from a completed version of the course that he or she wants to reuse in other settings back to the main database. He or she stores these in an appropriate resource-archive area, using categories either already agreed upon by the professional group, or a new category entered by the instructor. The same simple tagging tool allows the quick designation of essential tags.

The system should allow users with write privileges to add new categories for the sorting of resources in various archival areas.

Different views of the database can identify different categories of objects, different patterns and dates of access, and different authors, among other possibilities. Members of the community can also attach comments and rating codes to objects.

The system should allow user-tailored views and the adding of notes or additional codes of objects. Tools such as concept-mapping tools can show different clusters and categories.

The community itself decides on procedures for maintenance of the database, updating categories and assigning read and write privileges.

Tools in the shared workspace can support these activities.

Table 9.8 may seem futurist, but it is a description of the current work going on with the TeleTOP system in our faculty (see Chapter 8). Based on three years of experience with **Scenario C** *Stretching the Mould*, from which **Scenario B** *The Global Campus* has also emerged, we now can begin to move towards **Scenario D** *The New Economy*. But at the moment we are not ready for it in terms of the 4 Es, particularly in terms of organizational procedures. Our best opportunity to gain **Scenario D** *The New Economy* experience will not be within our university for the next few years but rather in corporate-university settings where we are building some collaborative activities.

Thus, in summing up, we believe our lessons learnt can be of benefit to the future as they have been to us in the past. Perhaps there are two meta-lessons that override them all: (a) there will always be new challenges and opportunities relating to flexible learning and technology and (b) the opportunity to learn new lessons will continue. With these thoughts, we close the book but not the learning experience.

References

10 driving principles (2000) 10 driving principles of the New Economy, *Business 2.0*, March, pp 191–284

Alexander, S and McKenzie, J (1998) *An Evaluation of Information Technology Projects for University Learning*, Committee for University Teaching and Staff Development, Canberra, Australia

Anderson, T and Downes, S (2000) *Models and Strategies Towards a Canadian On-line Educational Infrastructure*, Report for Industry Canada, University of Alberta, Faculty of Extension, Edmonton, Alberta

Aronson, E *et al* (1978) *The Jigsaw Classroom*, Sage, Beverly Hills, CA

Bacsich, P *et al* (1999) The costs of networked learning, Internal report, Sheffield Hallam University, Sheffield, UK

Barker, P (in press) Authoring systems, in *Handbook of Information Technologies for Education and Training*, ed H Adelsberger, B Collis and J Pawlowski, Springer Verlag, Berlin

Barron, A E and Rickelman, C (in press) Management systems, in *Handbook of Information Technologies for Education and Training*, ed H Adelsberger, B Collis and J Pawlowski, Springer Verlag, Berlin

Bates, A W (1984) *Selecting and Designing Low-cost Media for Distance Education*, Zentrales Institut für Fernstudienforschung, Hegan, Germany

Bates, A W (1995) *Technology, Open Learning and Distance Education*, Routledge, London

Ben-Jacob, M G, Levin, D S and Ben-Jacob, T K (2000) The learning environment of the 21st century, *International Journal of Educational Telecommunications*, **6** (3), pp 201–11

Bernstein, R (2000) America's 100 most wired colleges, *Yahoo! Internet Life*, May, pp 114–19

Bigelow, J D (1997) Developing a World Wide Web section of a management course: transporting learning premises across media, *International Journal of Educational Telecommunications*, **3** (2/3), pp 131–48

Bloemen, P (ed) (1999) *Evaluation TeleTOP and C@mpus+*, Internal report, Faculty of Educational Science and Technology, University of Twente, Enschede, Netherlands

Bonk, C J (1998) *Pedagogical Activities on the 'Smartweb': Electronically mentoring undergraduate educational psychology students,* http://php.indiana.edu/~cjbonk/paper/smart_paper.html (accessed 31 January 1999)

Brockhaus, M, Emrich, M and Mei-Pochtler, A (2000) *Improving Higher Education through New Technologies: An international comparison of best practice projects,* Report of the Expert Commission, 'Improving Educational Change through New Technologies', The Bertelsmann Foundation, Duisburg, Germany

Brophy, J and Alleman, J (1991) Activities as instructional tools: a framework for analysis and evaluation, *Educational Researcher,* **20** (4), pp 9–24

Brown, B (1999) From the what and why to the how of course support systems: the value of the teachers' perspective, *International Journal of Educational Telecommunications,* **5** (4), pp 361–85

Brynjolfsson, E and Yang, S (1996) Information technology and productivity: a review of the literature, *Advances in Computers,* **43**, pp 179–214, Academic Press, http://ecommerce.mit.edu/erik/itp/index.html

Carleer, G and Collis, B (1998) Extending good teaching with technology, in *Universities in a Digital Age: Transformation, innovation and tradition,* ed A Szucs and A Wagner, pp 368–71, European Distance Education Network, Budapest

Chinowsky, P S and Goodman, R E (1997) The World Wide Web in engineering team projects, *International Journal of Educational Telecommunications,* **3** (2/3), pp 149–62

Clark, R E (1983) Reconsidering research on learning from media, *Review of Educational Research,* **53** (4), pp 445–59

Clark, R E (1999) Yin and yang cognitive motivational processes operating in multimedia learning environments, in *Cognition and multimedia design,* pp 73–107, Open University of The Netherlands, Heerlen

Collis, B (1982) Simulation and the microcomputer: an approach to teaching probability, *The Mathematics Teacher,* **75** (7), pp 584–87

Collis, B (1988) *Computers, curriculum, and whole-class instruction,* Wadsworth, Belmont, CA

Collis, B (1992a) Supporting educational uses of telecommunications in the secondary school, part I, An overview of experiences, *International Journal of Instructional Media,* **19** (10), pp 23–44

Collis, B (1992b) Supporting educational uses of telecommunications in the secondary school, part II, Strategies for improved implementation, *International Journal of Instructional Media,* **19** (12), pp 97–109

Collis, B (1996a) Does more technology mean more flexibility for the learner? Experiences from the TeleScopia Project, *European Vocational Training Journal,* **7** (1), pp 13–21

Collis, B (1996b) The evolution of educational software portability, in *Media and Technology Yearbook 1995/96,* ed D Ely and B B Minor, pp 76–97, Libraries Unlimited, Englewood, CO

Collis, B (1996c) The Internet as an educational innovation: lessons from experience with computer implementation, *Educational Technology,* **36** (7), pp 21–30

Collis, B (1996d) *Tele-learning in a Digital World: The future of distance education*, International Thomson Publications, London

Collis, B (1997a) Implementing ICT in the faculty: letting 1000 flowers bloom or managing change?, in *De Digitale Leeromgeving* [The Digital Learning Environment], ed M Mirande, J Riemersma and W Veen, pp 121–36, Wolters-Noordhoff Hoger Onderwijs Reeks, Wolters-Noordhoff, Groningen, Netherlands

Collis, B (1997b) Pedagogical re-engineering: a new approach to course enrichment and re-design with the WWW, *Educational Technology Review*, **8**, pp 11–15

Collis, B (1997c) Supporting project-based collaborative learning via a WWW environment, in *Web-based Instruction*, ed B Khan, pp 213–20, Educational Technology Publications, Englewood Cliffs, NJ

Collis, B (1998a) Expanding boundaries in the university: the WWW as a tool, in *Virtual Mobility: New technology and the internationalisation of higher education*, ed M van der Wende, pp 65–78, Nuffic, The Hague

Collis, B (1998b) New didactics in university instruction: why and how, *Computers & Education*, **31** (4), pp 373–95

Collis, B (1998c) *TeleTOP Year 1 report*, Faculty of Educational Science and Technology, University of Twente, Enschede, Netherlands

Collis, B (1998d) WWW-based environments for collaborative group work, *Educational and Information Technology*, **3** (3/4), pp 223–37

Collis, B (1999a) Design, development, and implementation of a WWW-based course-support system, in *Advanced Research in Computers and Communications in Education*, ed G Cumming, T Okamoto and L Gomez, pp 11–20, IOS Press, Amsterdam

Collis, B (1999b) Pedagogical perspectives on ICT use in higher education, in *The Use of Information and Communication Technology in Higher Education: An international orientation on trends and issues*, ed B Collis and M van der Wende, Study commissioned by the Dutch Ministry of Education, Culture, and Science, pp 51-86, Centre for Higher Education Policy Studies (CHEPS), Enschede, Netherlands

Collis, B (1999c) *A Perspective on the Usability of Evaluation Frameworks for WWW-based Course-support Systems*, Report in contract to SURF-Educatief, DINKEL Institute, University of Twente, Enschede, Netherlands, http://www.oc.utwente.nl/w3ls/english/index.htm

Collis, B (1999d) Summary of study leave, and implications for the faculty and university, Internal report, Faculty of Educational Science and Technology, University of Twente, Enschede, Netherlands

Collis, B (ed) (1999e) Systems for WWW-based course support: technical, pedagogical, and organizational perspectives, Special issue of *International Journal for Educational Telecommunications*, **5** (4), pp 267–453

Collis, B (1999f) Telematics supported education for traditional universities in Europe, *Performance Improvement Quarterly*, **12** (2), pp 36–65

Collis, B (in press a) Leading and managing change via a WWW-based course-management system, in *Leadership and Management in Open and Flexible Learning*, ed D Hanna and C Latchem, Kogan Page, London

Collis, B (in press b) An overview of information technologies for education and training, in *Handbook of Information Technologies for Education and Training*, ed H Adelsberger, B Collis and J Pawlowski, Springer Verlag, Berlin

Collis, B, Andernach, T and Van Diepen, N (1997) Web environments for group-based project work in higher education, *International Journal of Educational Telecommunications*, **3** (2/3), pp 109–30

Collis, B A and Breman, J (1997) Information technology education in a cooperative environment: design and evaluation, in *Selected and Development Presentations at the 1997 National Convention for Educational Communications and Technology*, ed M R Simonson, pp 5–20, Iowa State University, Technology Research and Evaluation Group, Ames, IA

Collis, B and De Boer, W F (1998) Rapid prototyping as a faculty-wide activity: an innovative approach to the redesign of courses and instructional methods at the University of Twente, *Educational Media International*, **35** (2), pp 117–21

Collis, B and De Boer, W (1999a) Scaling up from the pioneers: the TeleTOP Method at the University of Twente, *Interactive Learning Environments*, **7** (2/3), pp 93–112

Collis, B and De Boer, W (1999b) The TeleTOP Decision Support Tool (DST), in *Design Approaches and Tools in Education and Training*, ed J van den Akker *et al*, pp 235–48, Kluwer Academic Publishers, Dordrecht, Netherlands

Collis, B, De Boer, W F and Slotman, K (in press) Feedback for Web-based assignments, *Journal of Computer-assisted Learning*

Collis, B and De Diana, I (1990) The portability of computer-related educational resources: an overview of issues and directions, *Journal of Research on Computing in Education*, **23** (2), pp 147–59

Collis, B and De Vries, P (1991) *Vooronderzoek: Telematica in het onderwijs* [Preliminary Research: Telematics in education], Report for the Ministry of Education, Culture, and Science, PRINT-VO, Hoevelaken, Netherlands

Collis, B and De Vries, P (1993) *The Emerging Trans-European Network for Education and Training: Guidelines for decision makers*, Report commissioned by the Task Force Human Resources, Education, Training and Youth, no 92–001–NIT–109/NL, Commission of the European Community, Brussels

Collis, B and Gervedink Nijhuis, G (2001) The instructor as manager: time and task, *The Internet in Higher Education*, **3** (1/2), pp 25–40

Collis, B and Gommer, L (2000) *C@mpus+ 2005: Scenarios for future learning environments involving the University of Twente*, DINKEL Institute, University of Twente, Enschede, Netherlands

Collis, B and Meeuwsen, E (1999) Learning to learn in a WWW-based environment, in *Internet Based Learning: Higher education and industry*, ed D French *et al*, pp 25–46, Stylus Publishing, Sterling, VA

Collis, B and Messing, J (in press) Usage, attitudes and workload implications for a Web-based learning environment, *Journal of Advanced Learning Technologies (ALT–J)*

Collis, B and Moonen, B H (1995) Teacher networking: a nationwide approach to supporting the instructional use of computers in The Netherlands, *Australian Educational Computing Journal*, **10** (2), pp 4–9

Collis, B and Moonen, J (1994) Leadership for transition: moving from the special project to systemwide integration in education, in *Educational Technology: Leadership perspectives*, ed G Kearsley and W Lynch, pp 113–36, Educational Technology Press, Englewood Cliffs, NJ

Collis, B and Oliver, R (1999) Preface, *Proceedings of ED-MEDIA '99*, vols 1 and 2, pp i-iii, AACE, Charlottesville, VA

Collis, B and Pals, N (1999) A model for predicting an individual's use of a telematics application for a learning-related purpose, *International Journal of Educational Communications*, **6** (1), pp 63–103

Collis, B and Peters, O (1999) At the frontier: asynchronous video and the WWW for new forms of learning, in *Distance Learning at the Dawn of the Third Millennium*, ed G Weidenfeld and D Keegan, pp 269–88, CNED, Futuroscope Cedex

Collis, B and Peters, O (2000) Educational applications of WWW–based asynchronous video, in *Multimedia '99*, ed N Corrie, T Chambel and G Davenport, pp 177–86, Springer-Verlag, Vienna

Collis, B, Peters, O and Pals, N (2000) Influences on the educational use of the WWW, e-mail and videoconferencing, *Innovations in Education and Training International*, **37** (2), pp 108–19

Collis, B, Peters, O and Pals, N (in press) A model for predicting the educational use of information and communication technologies, *Instructional Science*

Collis, B and Ring, J (eds) (1999) Scaling up: faculty change and the WWW, Special double issue of *Interactive Learning Environments*, **7** (2/3), pp 87–315

Collis, B and Van der Wende, M (eds) (1999) *The Use of Information and Communication Technology in Higher Education: An international orientation on trends and issues*, Study commissioned by the Dutch Ministry of Education, Culture, and Science, Centre for Higher Education Policy Studies (CHEPS), Enschede, Netherlands

Collis, B, Veen, W and De Vries, P (1994) *The CISO Project: Recommendations for an on-line service for Dutch education*, PTT Telecom, The Hague

Collis, B, Vingerhoets, J and Moonen, J (1997) Flexibility as a key construct in European training: experiences from the TeleScopia Project, *British Journal of Educational Technology*, **28** (3), pp 199–218

Collis, B, Winnips, K and Moonen, J (2000) Structured support vs learner choice via the WWW: where is the payoff?, *Interactive Learning Research*, **11** (2), pp 163–96

Collis, B *et al* (1996) *Building on Experience: ISM-1, 1996-97: Comments on the evolution of the course ISM-1*, Internal report, University of Twente, Enschede, Netherlands, http://www.to.utwente.nl/ism/ism1-97/papers/ismdec96.htm

CRE (1998) *Restructuring the Universities: New technologies and teaching and learning*, CRE Guide no 1, CRE, Geneva

Cuban, L (1985) *Teachers and Machines: The classroom use of technology since 1920*, Teachers College Press, New York

Cunningham, S *et al* (2000) *The Business of Borderless Education*, Report prepared for the Evaluations and Investigations Programme, Higher Education Division, Department of Education, Training and Youth Affairs, Canberra, Australia

Daniel, J S (1996) *Mega-universities and Knowledge Media: Technology strategies for higher education*, Kogan Page, London

Darling-Hammond, L (1996) The right to learn and the advancement of teaching: research, policy, and practices for democratic education, *Educational Researcher*, **25** (6), pp 5–16

De Boer, W F (2000) Design and development: TeleTOP V3, Internal document, Faculty of Educational Science and Technology, University of Twente, Enschede, Netherlands

De Boer, W F and Collis, B (2000) The adaptation and use of a WWW-based course management system within two different types of faculties at the University of Twente, in *Proceedings of ED-MEDIA 2000*, ed J Bourdeau and R Heller, pp 237–42, AACE, Charlottesville, VA

De Boer, W F and Collis, B (in press) The TeleTOP Implementation Model: establishing the use of a WWW-based course-management system in a university, *Interactive Learning Environments*

De Boer, W F and Peters, O (2000) New didactics for WWW-based learning environments: examples of good practice at the University of Twente, Paper presented at the Campus 2000: Lernen in neuen Organisationsformen Conference, September, Innsbruck, Austria

Dijkstra, S, Collis, B and Eseryl, D (1999) Instructional design for tele-learning, *Computers in Higher Education*, **10** (2), pp 3–28

Dopper, S and Dijkman, B (1997) Action learning geschikt voor deeltijdonderwijs [Action learning appropriate for part-time students], *Onderzoek van Onderwijs* [Research in Education], **23**, pp 57–59

Draper, S W (1998) Niche-based success in CAL, *Computers & Education*, **30** (1/2), pp 5–8

Duchastel, P (1997) A web-based model for university instruction, *Journal of Educational Technology Systems*, **25** (3), pp 221–28

Dunkin, M J (1987) Introduction to Section 4: classroom practices, in *The International Encyclopedia of Teaching and Teacher Education*, ed M J Dunkin, pp 313–26, Pergamon Press, Oxford

Encarnaçāo, J L, Leidhold, W and Reuter, A (2000) *Scenario: University in the year 2005*, Report of the Expert Commission, 'Improving Higher Education through New Technologies', funded by the Bertelsmann Foundation and the Heinz Nixdorf Foundation, Germany

European Association of Distance Teaching Universities (EADTU) (1998) *Survey of Telematics for Education and Training: United States, Canada & Australia*, http://www.ethoseurope.org/ethos/survey/default.htm

Financial Times (2000) Business education, 3 April

Fisser, P (2000) Using ICT in education: a process of change, Internal report, Faculty of Educational Science and Technology, University of Twente, Enschede, Netherlands

Fisser, P, Van der Kamp, I and Slot, C (1999) TeleTOP at the Telematics Faculty, Internal report, DINKEL Institute, University of Twente, Enschede, Netherlands

Fisser, P *et al* (1998) Implementing tele-learning: decision support for instructors, the TeleTOP project, in *Networked Lifelong Learning: Innovative approaches to education and training through the Internet*, ed S Banks, C Graebner and D McConnell, pp 210-14, The University of Sheffield Centre for the Study of Networked Learning, Sheffield, UK

Fleming, D (1993) A gradualist model for the development of a flexible learning framework, *Education and Training International*, **30** (4), pp 319–24

Friedlob, G T and Plewa, F J (2000) *Understanding Return on Investment*, John Wiley & Sons, New York

Fullan, M (1991) *The Meaning of Educational Change*, Teachers College Press, New York

Gazzard, S and Dalziel, J R (1998) Comdesign principles for 'next wave' educational tools: the development of the WebMCQ assessment system, in *Proceedings of ASCILITE '98*, ed R Corderoy, pp 289-96, University of Wollongong, Wollongong, Australia

Gibbs, W W (1997) Taking computers to task, *Scientific American*, **278** (9), pp 82–89

Gustafson, K and Watkins, K (eds) (1998) Return on investment (ROI): an idea whose time has come – again?, *Educational Technology*, **38** (4), pp 5–6

Hall, G E, George, A and Rutherford, W L (1979) *Measuring Stages of Concern about the Innovation: A manual for the use of the SoC questionnaire*, ERIC Document Reproduction Series no ED 147 342, US Government Printing Office, Washington, DC

Hammond, R and Karran, T (1998) Implementing a computer mediated learning environment: people, problems and practicalities, in *Universities in a Digital Age: Transformation, innovation, and tradition*, ed A Szucs and A Wagner, pp 230-34, European Distance Education Network, Budapest

Hawkridge, D (1991) Machine-mediated learning in third-world schools?, *Machine-mediated Learning*, **3**, pp 319–28

Hazari, S I (1998) *Evaluation and Selection of Web Course Management Tools*, http://sunil.umd.edu/webct/

Heeren, E (1996) *Technology Support for Collaborative Distance Learning*, Doctoral dissertation, CTIT PhD thesis series no 96-08, Centre for Telematics and Information Technology, University of Twente, Enschede, Netherlands

Heeren, E, Verwijs, C and Moonen, J (1998) Guidelines for media selection, Paper presented at ED-MEDIA '98, 28 June, Freiburg, Germany

Hietala, P (1998) Procedural facilitation in Web discussions, in *Tele-teaching '98: Distance learning, training and education*, ed G Davies, part I, pp 445–54, Austrian Computer Society, Vienna

Holtham, C and Tiwari, A (1998) Physical universities can apply virtual technologies: the use of networked technologies to support collaborative learning, in *Networked Lifelong Learning: Innovative approaches to education and training through the Internet*, ed S Banks, C Graebner and D McConnell, pp 2.26–2.32, The University of Sheffield Centre for the Study of Networked Learning, Sheffield, UK

Horngren, C T, Foster, G and Datar, S M (1997) *Cost Accounting: A managerial emphasis*, 9th edn, Prentice Hall, Upper Saddle River, NJ

Inge, C (1998) *Staff Development and Training Policy: Directions for the new millennium*, Project report, US WEST Foundation, Denver, CO, http://www.uswest.com

Jonassen, D H, Peck, K L and Wilson, B G (1999) *Learning with Technology: A constructivist perspective*, Prentice Hall, Upper Saddle River, NJ

Karmel, T (1998) Distance education and flexible delivery in the Australian higher education context: is distance education becoming an anachronism?, in *Universities in a Digital Age: Transformation, innovation, and tradition*, ed A Szucs and A Wagner, pp 614–17, European Distance Education Network, Budapest

Kauppi, A and Vainio, L (1998) The state of the art of learning technology in universities and polytechnics: findings of the assessment project of the Finnish National Fund for Research & Development (SITRA), Paper presented at the conference 'Networks of Skills & Competencies', 23 September, Joensuu, Finland

Kearsley, G and Shneiderman, G (1998) Engagement Theory: a framework for technology-based teaching and learning, *Educational Technology*, **38** (5), pp 20–24

Kelly, K (1998) *New Rules for the New Economy: 10 radical strategies for a connected world*, Penguin, New York

Krempl, S (1997) The virtual university: education in the cross light between economy, politics, and society, in *Proceedings of Rufis '97: Role of the university in the future information society*, ed J Hlavicka and K Kveton, pp 99-102, UNESCO International Centre for Scientific Computing, Prague

Lan, J and Gemmill, J (2000) The networking revolution for the new millennium: Internet2 and its educational implications, *International Journal of Educational Telecommunications*, **6** (2), pp 179–98

Landon, B (2000) *Online Educational Delivery Applications: A Web tool for comparative analysis*, http://www.c2c2.ca/landonline

Langlois, C (1997) Information technologies and university teaching, learning and research, in *Proceedings of Rufis '97: Role of the university in the future information society*, ed J Hlavicka and K Kveton, pp 183–87, UNESCO International Centre for Scientific Computing, Prague

Latchem, C (1998) A global perspective on flexible delivery, in *Virtual Mobility: New technologies and internationalisation of higher education*, ed M C van der Wende, pp 25-45, Nuffic Paperback no 10, Nuffic, The Hague

Laurillard, D (1993) *Rethinking University Teaching: A framework for the effective use of educational technology*, Routledge, London

Lockyer, L, Patterson, J and Harper, B (1998) Delivering health education via the Web: design and formative evaluation of a discourse-based learning environment, in *Proceedings of ASCILITE '98*, ed R Corderoy, pp 465–75, University of Wollongong, Wollongong, Australia

Maslowski, R *et al* (2000) The formative evaluation of a Web-based course-management system within a university setting, *Educational Technology*, **40** (3), pp 5–19

Meisalo, V *et al* (1998) Combining algorithmic and creative problem solving on the Web, in *Tele-teaching '98: Distance learning, training and education*, ed G Davies, part II, pp 715-24, Austrian Computer Society, Vienna

Messing, J (2000) Report on TeleTOP survey, May 2000, Internal report, Faculty of Educational Science and Technology and the DINKEL Institute, University of Twente, Enschede, Netherlands

Miles, I (2000) *TAP-Assess: A scenario analysis*, Final report, vol IV, PREST, University of Manchester, http://www.databank.it/dbc/tap-ass/4.htm

Mombarg, J (2000) Kosteneffectiviteit van TeleTOP voor het vak 'Inleiding in Telematica' [Cost-effectiveness of TeleTOP in the course 'Introduction to Telematics'], Internal report, Faculty of Educational Science and Technology, University of Twente, Enschede, Netherlands

Moonen, J (1989a) Courseware development at the crossroads?, *Education & Computing*, **5**, pp 103–09

Moonen, J (1989b) Involvement and information: 15 challenges for computers in education, *Educational Technology*, **29** (12), pp 7–12

Moonen, J (1994) How to do more with less?, in *Interactive Multimedia in University Education: Designing for change in teaching and learning*, ed S Wills and C McNaught, pp 155–64, Elsevier, Amsterdam

Moonen, J (1997) The efficiency of telelearning, *Journal of Asynchronous Learning Networks*, 1 (2), http://www.aln.org/alnweb/journal/issue2/moonen.htm

Moonen, J (1998) *Potential of MESH Technology for High-quality and Flexible Tele-collaboration*, MESH project, Faculty of Educational Science and Technology, University of Twente, Enschede, Netherlands

Moonen, J (1999) Costs and effectiveness of ICT in higher education, in *The Use of Information and Communication Technology in Higher Education: An international orientation on trends and issues*, ed B Collis and M van der Wende, pp 87–106, Study commissioned by the Dutch Ministry of Education, Culture, and Science, Centre for Higher Education Policy Studies (CHEPS), Enschede, Netherlands

Moonen, J (2000a) Institutional perspectives for on-line learning: return on investment, Internal report, Faculty of Educational Science and Technology, University of Twente, Enschede, Netherlands

Moonen, J (2000b) Is there a new economy in education? What will it mean for you?, Presentation at Educador 2000, 27 May, Sao Paulo, Brazil

Moonen, J (2000c) A new economy in education?, Presentation at the IDYLLE Conference 'From Illusion to Implementation', 29 January, University of Twente, Enschede, Netherlands

Moonen, J (2000d) Report, educational leave, Internal report, Faculty of Educational Science and Technology, University of Twente, Enschede, Netherlands, http://users.edte.utwente.nl/collis/StudyTrip/WWWJournal/triphome.htm

Moonen, J (2000e) A three-space design strategy for digital learning material, *Educational Technology*, **40** (2), pp 26–32

Moonen, J (in press a) Cost effectiveness and the new economy in education, in *The Bookmark of the School of the Future* (in press), ed H Taylor and P Hogenbirk, Chapman Hall, London

Moonen, J (in press b) Design methodologies, in *Handbook of Information Technologies for Education and Training*, ed H Adelsberger, B Collis and J Pawlowski, Springer Verlag, Berlin

Moonen, J and Beishuizen, J J (1992) *Technology-enriched schools in The Netherlands*, in *Technology-enriched Schools: Nine case studies with reflections*, ed B Collis and G Carleer, pp 86–117, ISTE, Eugene, OR

Moonen, J and Gastkemper, F (1983) *Computer-gestuurd Onderwijs* [Computer-based Education], Aula, Utrecht, Netherlands

Moonen, J and Kommers, P (1995) *Implementation of Communication and Information Technologies in Education*, Report to the Advice Committee for Educational Research, Dutch Organisation for Scientific Research, Netherlands

Moonen, J and Schoenmaker, J (1992) Evolution of courseware development methodology, *International Journal of Educational Research*, **17** (1), pp 109–21

Moonen, J and Wuite-Harmsma, H E (eds) (1984) *Computers and Education: Policy and experiences*, North-Holland, Amsterdam

National Committee of Inquiry into Higher Education (1997) *Higher Education in the Learning Society*, HMSO, Norwich, UK

NCHEMS (2000) *Technology Costing Methodology*, http://www.wiche.edu/telecom/projects/tcm/index.htm

Nicaise, M and Crane, M (1999) Knowledge constructing through hypermedia authoring, *Educational Technology Research & Development*, **47** (1), pp 29–50

Northrup, P T (1997) Faculty perceptions of distance education: factors influencing utilization, *International Journal of Educational Telecommunications*, **3** (4), pp 323–58

Oliver, R, Omari, A and Herrington, J (1998) Developing converged learning environments for on and off-campus students using the WWW, in *Proceedings of ASCILITE '98*, ed R Corderoy, pp 529–38, University of Wollongong, Wollongong, Australia

Oliver, W C and Nelson, T (1997) Un meurtre à Cinet: a Web and email unit to develop writing competence in intermediate language classes, *International Journal of Educational Telecommunications*, **3** (2/3), pp 205–18

Philips, J (1997) *Return on Investment,* Gulf Publishing Company, Houston

Plomp, Tj (1992) *Ontwerpen van Onderwijs en Training* [Design of Education and Training], Lemma, Utrecht, Netherlands

Plomp, Tj, Van Deursen, K and Moonen, J (eds) (1987) *CAL for Europe*, North-Holland, Amsterdam

Pohjonen, J (1994) *On Media Selection*, Continuing Education Centre, Centre for Educational Technology, University of Oulu, Oulu, Finland

Rada, R (1998) Efficiency and effectiveness in computer-supported peer-peer learning, *Computers & Education*, **30** (3/4), pp 137–46

Ratcliff, M and Davies, T P (1998) Supporting distance education, in *Universities in a Digital Age: Transformation, innovation, and tradition*, ed A Szucs and A Wagner, pp 433–38, European Distance Education Network, Budapest

Reigeluth, C M (1996) Instructional design theories, in *International Encyclopedia of Educational Technology*, ed Tj Plomp and D Ely, 2nd edn, pp 163–69, Elsevier, London

Reisner, R and Gagné, R M (1982) The *Selection of Media for Instruction*, Educational Technology Publications, Englewood Cliffs, NJ

Remmers, E and Collis, B (2000) Didactical activities and strategies in the use of WWW-based course-support environments: design guidelines for instructors, in *Proceedings of ED-MEDIA 2000*, ed J Bourdeau and R Heller, pp 898–903, AACE, Charlottesville, VA

Riel, M and Levine, J A (1990) Building electronic communities: success and failure in computer networking, *Instructional Science*, **19** (2), pp 145–69

Robson, R (1999) Course support systems: the first generation, *International Journal of Educational Telecommunications*, **5** (4), pp 271–82

Rogers, E M (1983) *Diffusion of Innovations*, 1st edn, Free Press, New York

Rogers, E M (1995) *Diffusion of Innovations*, 3rd edn, Free Press, New York

Romiszowski, A (1993) *Telecommunications and Distance Education*, ERIC Digest EDO-IR-93-2, ERIC Clearinghouse on Information Resources, Syracuse University, Syracuse, NY

Russell, T (2000) *The No Significant Difference Phenomenon*, Office of Instructional Communications, North Carolina State University, Durham, NC

Saga, H (1993) Students' perceptions of media and teachers as related to the depth of their learning, *Educational Media International*, **30** (3), pp 158–67

Salomon, G (1984) Television is 'easy' and print is 'tough': the differential investment of mental effort in learning as a function of perceptions and attributions, *Journal of Educational Psychology*, **76**, pp 647–58

Salomon, G (1995) *What Does the Design of Effective CSCL Require and How Do We Study its Effects?*, http://www.cica.indiana.edu/cscl95/outlook/62_Salomon.html

Salomon, G, Perkins, D N and Globerson, T (1991) Partners in cognition: extending human intelligence with intelligent technologies, *Educational Researcher*, **20** (3), pp 2–10

Sfard, A (1998) On two metaphors for learning and the dangers of choosing just one, *Educational Researcher*, **27** (2), pp 4–13

Shepherd, C (1999) *Three Roads to Cost-effectiveness, Or... how to have your cake and eat it*, http://www.fastrak-consulting.co.uk/tactix/Features/roads/roads.htm

Siegel, M E (1998) *Instructional Infrastructure Planning: Innovation theory, systems theories, and computer modelling*, http://horizon.unc.edu/projects/monograph/CD/Change-Innovations/Siegel.asp

Simons, P R J (1999) Three ways to learn in a new balance, *Lifelong Learning in Europe*, **IV** (1), pp 14–23

Smith, M and Birchall, D (1998) From delivery to development: moving distance education from content dissemination to personal development through the use of groupware, in *Proceedings of EDEN '98*, ed A Szucs and A Wagner, pp 363–67, EDEN, Bologna, Italy

Sorenson, B H (1991) An assessment of training and educational media selection models, in *Strategies for Using Technologies: Proceedings of the Ninth Annual Conference on Technology and Innovations in Training*, ed E Schufletowski, pp 146–66, TITE, Los Angeles

Stern, E (1997) The evaluation of the Teaching and Learning Technology Programme of the UK Higher Education Funding Council, *European Journal in Open and Distance Learning*, http://kurs.nks.no/eurodl/eurodlen/index.html

Strijker, A (2000) Re-use and metadata, Presentation at the seminar 'Qualities in Using Internet in Schools', November, Stockholm

Sweeney, M, Maguire, M and Shackel, B (1993) Evaluating user–computer interaction: a framework, *International Journal of Man-Machine Studies*, **38**, pp 689–711

Tielemans, G and Collis, B (1999) Strategic requirements for a system to generate and support Web-based environments in a faculty, in *Proceedings, ED-MEDIA 1999*, ed B Collis and R Oliver, vol 1, pp 346–51, AACE, Charlottesville, VA

Toynton, R (1998) The interactive website as a medium for teaching and learning: a case study in presenting introductory science, in *Networked Lifelong Learning: Innovative approaches to education and training through the Internet*, ed S Banks, C Graebner and D McConnell, pp 1.33–1.41, The University of Sheffield Centre for the Study of Networked Learning, Sheffield, UK

Twigg, C A (2000) *Improving Learning and Reducing Costs: Redesigning large-enrollment courses*, The Pew Learning and Technology Program, http://www.center.rpi.edu/PweNews1.html

Van den Brande, L (1993) *Flexible and Distance Learning*, John Wiley, Chichester, UK

Van der Perre, G (1998) Levenslang leren aan de virtuele universiteit(en) van Leuven, Vlaanderen en Europa? [Life-long learning for the virtual universities of Leuven, Flanders and Europe?], Presentation to the Ministry of Education, Culture, and Science, 3 December, The Hague

Van der Veen, J (2000) Telematics support for group learning, Doctoral dissertation, CTIT, University of Twente, Enschede, Netherlands

Van der Veen, J and De Boer, W (1999) *World Wide Web Learning Support: Evaluation framework for World Wide Web learning environments*, Report in contract to SURF-Educatief, DINKEL Institute, University of Twente, Enschede, Netherlands, http://www.oc.utwente.nl/w3ls/english/index.htm

Van der Veen, J, De Boer, W F and Collis, B (2000) *Didactics for Web Learning Environments: Active learning*, Report for the SURF-TeleTOP Alpha-Beta Project, DINKEL Institute, University of Twente, Enschede, Netherlands

Van der Wende, M and Beerkens, E (1999) Policies and strategies on ICT in higher education, in *The Use of Information and Communication Technology in Higher Education: An international orientation on trends and issues*, ed B Collis and M van der Wende, pp 21–50, Study commissioned by the Dutch Ministry of Education, Culture, and Science, Centre for Higher Education Policy Studies (CHEPS), Enschede, Netherlands

Van Enckevort, G *et al* (eds) (1986) *Distance Higher Education and the Adult Learner*, The Open University, Heerlen, Netherlands

Van Rennes, L (1998) WWW-based support environment for part-time students studying at a distance: social and technical issues and guidelines, Master's thesis, Faculty of Educational Science and Technology, University of Twente, Enschede, Netherlands

Van Rennes, L and Collis, B A (1998) User interface design for WWW-based courses, in *Proceedings of ED-MEDIA '98*, ed T Ottmann and I Tomac, vol 1, pp 1452–57, AACE, Charlottesville, VA

Verwijs, C (1998) A mix of core and complementary media: new perspectives in media-decision making, PhD dissertation, Faculty of Educational Science and Technology, University of Twente, Enschede, Netherlands

Wells, J G and Anderson, D K (1997) Learners in a telecommunications course: adoption, diffusion, and stages of concern, *Journal of Research on Computing in Education*, **30** (1), pp 83–105

Whittington, D (1998) Web-based assessment, Presentation at the conference 'The Web for Teaching and Learning', organized jointly by CTI Computing and the Learning Development Group of the Conference of Professors and Heads of Computing (CPHC-LDG), 25 November, Keele University, UK

Winnips, K (2000) Scaffolding by design: a model for Web-based learning support, Doctoral dissertation, Faculty of Educational Science and Technology, University of Twente, Enschede, Netherlands

Yetton, P (1997) *Managing the Introduction of Technology in the Delivery and Administration of Higher Education*, Evaluations and Investigations Programme, Department of Employment, Education, Training and Youth Affairs, Canberra, Australia, http://www.deetya.gov.au/highered/eippubs/

Subject index

Author index

Open and Distance Learning Series

Series Editor: Fred Lockwood